Winning the War on Poverty

Winning the War on Poverty

Applying the Lessons of History to the Present

Brian L. Fife

 PRAEGER™

An Imprint of ABC-CLIO, LLC

Santa Barbara, California • Denver, Colorado

Library of Congress Cataloging-in-Publication Data

Names: Fife, Brian L., author.
Title: Winning the war on poverty : applying the lessons of history to the
   present / Brian L. Fife.
Description: Santa Barbara, California : Praeger, [2018] | Includes bibliographical
   references and index.
Identifiers: LCCN 2018006492 (print) | LCCN 2018006735 (ebook) |
   ISBN 9781440832826 (ebook) | ISBN 9781440832819 (set : alk. paper)
Subjects: LCSH: Poverty—United States—History. | Income
   distribution—United States—History. | Public welfare—United
   States—History. | United States—Economic policy. | United States—
   Social policy.
Classification: LCC HC110.P6 (ebook) | LCC HC110.P6 F54 2018 (print) |
   DDC 339.4/60973—dc23
LC record available at https://lccn.loc.gov/2018006492

ISBN: 978-1-4408-3281-9 (print)
      978-1-4408-3282-6 (ebook)

22 21 20 19 18   1 2 3 4 5

This book is also available as an eBook.

Praeger
An Imprint of ABC-CLIO, LLC

ABC-CLIO, LLC
130 Cremona Drive, P.O. Box 1911
Santa Barbara, California 93116-1911
www.abc-clio.com

This book is printed on acid-free paper ∞

Manufactured in the United States of America

To Jill,
my effervescent, fun-loving sister with a great sense of humor.

Contents

Acknowledgments

I would like to thank the editor at Praeger, Jessica Gribble, for her insightful comments throughout the drafting phase of this book. Further gratitude is extended to Beth Ptalis, who endorsed the premise of the book a few years ago. Additionally, I am grateful for the assistance of a multitude of librarians at Helmke Library at Indiana University–Purdue University Fort Wayne (soon to be known as Purdue University Fort Wayne) as well as the downtown Fort Wayne branch of the Allen County Public Library.

What Is Poverty, and How Is It Measured?

For researchers and citizens alike, "poverty" generally has two different meanings. Absolute poverty is an established standard that is uniform across all countries and does not change over time. An income-related example of absolute poverty would be living on less than X dollars a day. According to the United Nations Educational, Scientific and Cultural Organization, the current standard for absolute poverty is set to an income of less than US$1 a day.[1] Relative poverty is what most people envision when they discuss and debate poverty in the United States today. Relative poverty is defined in terms of the society in which an individual lives. Relative poverty definitions vary, as a result, between and among countries and over time. Federal officials in the United States measure poverty in relation to other citizens in the country in a given year. The official poverty measure in the United States, therefore, is an indicator of relative poverty.[2]

Any discussion of relative poverty and how to measure it in the United States, at least from a governmental perspective, has to begin with Mollie Orshansky. Those interested in defining and measuring poverty should carefully consider Orshansky's premise from the late 1960s:

> Counting the poor is an exercise in the art of the possible. For deciding who is poor, prayers are more relevant than calculation because poverty, like beauty, lies in the eye of the beholder. Poverty is a value judgment; it is not something one can verify or demonstrate, except by inference and suggestion, even with a measure of error. To say who is poor is to use all sorts of value judgments. The concept has to be limited by the purpose which is to be served by the definition. There is no particular reason to

count the poor unless you are going to do something about them. Whatever the possibilities for socioeconomic research in general, when it comes to defining poverty, you can only be more subjective or less so. You cannot be nonsubjective.[3]

Researchers make a value judgment, quantitative or qualitative, when analyzing poverty, and they operate on the theoretical premise that it is important for society to address, through targeted public policy initiatives, the vicissitudes of poverty. This theoretical foundation pervades many federal and state programs that were established by law to reduce the vestiges of poverty in the United States.

Mollie Orshansky (1915–2006)

Mollie Orshansky was born in New York City in 1915. Her parents were immigrants from what is now Ukraine. Her family was poor, and she was accustomed to standing in relief lines with her mother to get surplus food. Her direct experience with poverty provided her with a keen awareness of it. She understood that a person could work full time and still be poor.[4]

Orshansky was the first person in her family to graduate from high school and college. In 1935, she received an AB in mathematics and statistics from Hunter College. She later took graduate courses in economics and statistics after starting work as a federal employee in Washington, DC, at both the Department of Agriculture Graduate School and at American University.[5] She started her first job in 1935 in New York City as a statistical clerk for the New York Department of Health. She had jobs in the federal government for the rest of her career, except for one position. In 1936, she moved to Washington, DC, and began work as a junior statistical clerk with the U.S. Children's Bureau. Subsequently, she was promoted to research clerk in 1939. She later held more advanced-level statistical jobs at the New York City Department of Health, the U.S. National War Labor Board, and the U.S. Wage Stabilization Board. She also worked as a family economist and later as a food economist at the U.S. Department of Agriculture (USDA). It was at the USDA that Orshansky became familiar with the food plans and the food survey she would later use to develop poverty thresholds in the United States.[6]

Orshansky was a family economist from 1945 to 1951, during which time she conducted research in family consumption patterns and levels of living. She worked with the USDA's food plans for 15 years before she used them to develop her poverty thresholds when, in 1948, she and a colleague were responsible for responding to citizen inquiries regarding how people could survive on their existing income when they were confronted with inflation in the post–World War II era. As a food economist from 1953 to 1958, she directed the collection and analysis of data on food consumption and expenditures in U.S. households.[7]

In 1958, Orshansky became a social science research analyst in the Division of Program Research (it later became the Division of Research and Statistics) at the Social Security Administration (SSA). Her first assignment at the SSA was to prepare an article on estimating necessary family living costs, or standard budgets, for families in 21 large cities. Later, in 1960, a senator asked Arthur Flemming, secretary of health, education, and welfare (HEW), in a congressional hearing if he had data on how much it costs a retired couple to live. Flemming responded by saying that HEW would provide the information in writing. Mollie Orshansky anonymously did so, but this report remained unknown to people outside her office. In her budgetary estimates, she devised two measures of income inadequacy for an elderly couple using the USDA's 1955 Household Food Consumption Survey and the cheapest of USDA's three food plans. Orshansky again used the cheapest food plan in 1963, when she devised the first federal poverty measure.[8]

In 1963, Orshansky was commissioned to do an in-house research project entitled "Poverty as It Affects Children."[9] This was one year before President Lyndon Johnson announced his War on Poverty.[10] Johnson articulated his vision in early 1964:

> Unfortunately, many Americans live on the outskirts of hope—some because of their poverty, and some because of their color, and all too many because of both. Our task is to help replace their despair with opportunity.
>
> This administration today, here and now, declares unconditional war on poverty in America. I urge this Congress and all Americans to join with me in that effort.
>
> It will not be a short or easy struggle, no single weapon or strategy will suffice, but we shall not rest until that war is won. The richest Nation on earth can afford to win it. We cannot afford to lose it. One thousand dollars invested in salvaging an unemployable youth today can return $40,000 or more in his lifetime.
>
> Poverty is a national problem, requiring improved national organization and support. But this attack, to be effective, must also be organized at the State and local level and must be supported and directed by State and local efforts.
>
> For the war against poverty will not be won here in Washington. It must be won in the field, in every private home, in every public office, from the courthouse to the White House.
>
> The program I shall propose will emphasize this cooperative approach to help that one-fifth of all American families with incomes too small to even meet their basic needs.
>
> Our chief weapons in a more pinpointed attack will be better schools, and better health, and better homes, and better training, and better job

opportunities to help more Americans, especially young Americans, escape from squalor and misery and unemployment rolls where other citizens help to carry them.

Very often a lack of jobs and money is not the cause of poverty, but the symptom. The cause may lie deeper in our failure to give our fellow citizens a fair chance to develop their own capacities, in a lack of education and training, in a lack of medical care and housing, in a lack of decent communities in which to live and bring up their children.

But whatever the cause, our joint Federal-local effort must pursue poverty, pursue it wherever it exists—in city slums and small towns, in sharecropper shacks or in migrant worker camps, on Indian Reservations, among whites as well as Negroes, among the young as well as the aged, in the boom towns and in the depressed areas.

Our aim is not only to relieve the symptom of poverty, but to cure it and, above all, to prevent it. No single piece of legislation, however, is going to suffice.

We will launch a special effort in the chronically distressed areas of Appalachia.

We must expand our small but our successful area redevelopment program.

We must enact youth employment legislation to put jobless, aimless, hopeless youngsters to work on useful projects.

We must distribute more food to the needy through a broader food stamp program.

We must create a National Service Corps to help the economically handicapped of our own country as the Peace Corps now helps those abroad.

We must modernize our unemployment insurance and establish a high-level commission on automation. If we have the brain power to invent these machines, we have the brain power to make certain that they are a boon and not a bane to humanity.

We must extend the coverage of our minimum wage laws to more than 2 million workers now lacking this basic protection of purchasing power.

We must, by including special school aid funds as part of our education program, improve the quality of teaching, training, and counseling in our hardest hit areas.

We must build more libraries in every area and more hospitals and nursing homes under the Hill-Burton Act, and train more nurses to staff them.

We must provide hospital insurance for our older citizens financed by every worker and his employer under Social Security, contributing no more than $1 a month during the employee's working career to protect him in his old age in a dignified manner without cost to the Treasury, against the devastating hardship of prolonged or repeated illness.

We must, as a part of a revised housing and urban renewal program, give more help to those displaced by slum clearance, provide more housing for our poor and our elderly, and seek as our ultimate goal in our free enterprise system a decent home for every American family.

We must help obtain more modern mass transit within our communities as well as low-cost transportation between them.

Above all, we must release $11 billion of tax reduction into the private spending stream to create new jobs and new markets in every area of this land.[11]

A few months later, Johnson articulated his vision for a Great Society. In a speech delivered at the University of Michigan, the new president, who began his tenure when John F. Kennedy was assassinated on November 22, 1963, offered the following scenario in the aftermath of declaring war on poverty:

The purpose of protecting the life of our Nation and preserving the liberty of our citizens is to pursue the happiness of our people. Our success in that pursuit is the test of our success as a Nation.

For a century we labored to settle and to subdue a continent. For half a century we called upon unbounded invention and untiring industry to create an order of plenty for all of our people.

The challenge of the next half century is whether we have the wisdom to use that wealth to enrich and elevate our national life, and to advance the quality of our American civilization.

Your imagination, your initiative, and your indignation will determine whether we build a society where progress is the servant of our needs, or a society where old values and new visions are buried under unbridled growth. For in your time we have the opportunity to move not only toward the rich society and the powerful society, but upward to the Great Society.

The Great Society rests on abundance and liberty for all. It demands an end to poverty and racial injustice, to which we are totally committed in our time. But that is just the beginning.

The Great Society is a place where every child can find knowledge to enrich his mind and to enlarge his talents. It is a place where leisure is a welcome chance to build and reflect, not a feared cause of boredom and restlessness. It is a place where the city of man serves not only the needs of the body and the demands of commerce but the desire for beauty and the hunger for community.

It is a place where man can renew contact with nature. It is a place which honors creation for its own sake and for what it adds to the understanding of the race. It is a place where men are more concerned with the quality of their goals than the quantity of their goods.

But most of all, the Great Society is not a safe harbor, a resting place, a final objective, a finished work. It is a challenge constantly renewed, beckoning us toward a destiny where the meaning of our lives matches the marvelous products of our labor.

So I want to talk to you today about three places where we begin to build the Great Society—in our cities, in our countryside, and in our classrooms.

Many of you will live to see the day, perhaps 50 years from now, when there will be 400 million Americans four-fifths of them in urban areas. In the remainder of this century urban population will double, city land will double, and we will have to build homes, highways, and facilities equal to all those built since this country was first settled. So in the next 40 years we must rebuild the entire urban United States.

Aristotle said: "Men come together in cities in order to live, but they remain together in order to live the good life." It is harder and harder to live the good life in American cities today.

The catalog of ills is long: there is the decay of the centers and the despoiling of the suburbs. There is not enough housing for our people or transportation for our traffic. Open land is vanishing and old landmarks are violated.

Worst of all expansion is eroding the precious and time honored values of community with neighbors and communion with nature. The loss of these values breeds loneliness and boredom and indifference.

Our society will never be great until our cities are great. Today the frontier of imagination and innovation is inside those cities and not beyond their borders.

New experiments are already going on. It will be the task of your generation to make the American city a place where future generations will come, not only to live but to live the good life.

I understand that if I stayed here tonight I would see that Michigan students are really doing their best to live the good life.

This is the place where the Peace Corps was started. It is inspiring to see how all of you, while you are in this country, are trying so hard to live at the level of the people.

A second place where we begin to build the Great Society is in our countryside. We have always prided ourselves on being not only America the strong and America the free, but America the beautiful. Today that beauty is in danger. The water we drink, the food we eat, the very air that we breathe, are threatened with pollution. Our parks are overcrowded, our seashores overburdened. Green fields and dense forests are disappearing.

A few years ago we were greatly concerned about the "Ugly American." Today we must act to prevent an ugly America.

For once the battle is lost, once our natural splendor is destroyed, it can never be recaptured. And once man can no longer walk with beauty or wonder at nature his spirit will wither and his sustenance be wasted.

A third place to build the Great Society is in the classrooms of America. There your children's lives will be shaped. Our society will not be great until every young mind is set free to scan the farthest reaches of thought and imagination. We are still far from that goal.[12]

In the context of the 1960s, and stemming from a desire to not only document the extent of poverty in the United States but also to attempt to do something proactive about it, Kennedy, and later Johnson, used the bully pulpit in order to promote their policy agenda. This provided technical expert Orshansky the substantive opportunity to operationalize her conception of measuring poverty.[13]

The Orshansky Poverty Thresholds

Mollie Orshansky developed her poverty thresholds based on the "economy food plan," which was the cheapest of the food plans developed by analysts for the USDA. She made a key assumption based on the USDA's 1955 Household Food Consumption Survey: that families of three or more persons allocated approximately one-third of their after-tax revenue to food.[14] As Gordon Fisher noted:

> Mollie assumed that expenditures for food and non-food would be cut back at the same rate, so the family would continue to spend a third of its income for food. When the food expenditures of the hypothetical family reached the cost of the economy food plan, she assumed that the amount the family would then be spending on non-food items would also be minimal but adequate. (Her procedure did not assume specific dollar amounts for any budget category besides food.) Following this logic, she calculated poverty thresholds for families of various sizes by taking the dollar costs of the economy food plan for families of those sizes and multiplying the costs by a factor of 3. (She followed somewhat different procedures to develop thresholds for two-person and one-person units.) She differentiated her thresholds not only by family size but also by farm/nonfarm status, by the gender of the family head, by the number of family members who were children, and (for one- and two-person units only) by aged/non-aged status. The result was a detailed matrix of 124 poverty thresholds (later reduced to 48). Instead of citing all 124 or 48 detailed thresholds, people commonly cite weighted average thresholds, one for each family size.[15]

Fisher further notes:

> To avoid confusion, the preceding explanation has been phrased in terms of the economy food plan. However, Mollie actually developed and discussed two sets of poverty thresholds, one derived from the economy food plan and one derived from the somewhat less stringent low-cost food plan.

(The latter set was the one she preferred.) It was the lower of the two sets of poverty thresholds—the set derived from the economy food plan—that the Office of Economic Opportunity adopted as a working definition of poverty in May 1965. One probable reason for the adoption of the lower set of thresholds was that the lower set yielded approximately the same number of persons in poverty as the Council of Economic Advisers' rough measure of poverty.[16]

It is important to note that Mollie Orshansky's measure of poverty was based on data from the mid-1950s and that she preferred the low-cost food plan over the more stringent economy food plan. This means that the data and assumptions that factored into the creation of the measure are now over 60 years old. This in no way denigrates Orshansky's great contributions to the poverty debate in the United States. She is a true pioneer in every sense of the term; she created a measure so that policy makers could have a better idea of the magnitude of the challenges of poverty in the United States. Her work was based on a fundamental value system premised on the notion that poverty was a systemic reality in the United States and that proactive measures to alleviate the ravages of poverty were necessary. For that, we are all indebted to her for her work and dedication. Fisher provided a fitting tribute to the legendary Mollie Orshansky:

> In 1982, Mollie Orshansky retired from SSA after a government career that had lasted for more than 40 years. She died at age 91 in December 2006. Her development of the poverty thresholds was a major contribution to American public policy, providing a means of identifying the groups in our society with the least resources. As a result, the question "How does it affect the poor?" has become a test for proposed public policies and programs. Mollie's thoughtful analyses of the poverty population began a tradition, providing information on the hardships faced by families with children, the elderly, and other vulnerable groups; numerous researchers have followed her example by conducting similar analyses and drawing policy implications from them. She received a Commissioner's Citation from the Social Security Administration in 1965 for her creative research and analytical work, and in 1976 she received the Distinguished Service Award from the U.S. Department of Health, Education, and Welfare (of which SSA was then a part) for her "leadership in creating the first nationally accepted measures of income inadequacy and applying them diligently and skillfully to public policy." Today Mollie's poverty thresholds remain a major feature of the architecture of American social policy.[17]

Indeed, every year, government officials promulgate new poverty thresholds based on Orshansky's work from over half a century ago. Figures from 1959 to the present are shown in tables 1.1 and 1.2. From 1959 to 1979, poverty thresholds were reported by gender of the head of the household as well as

Table 1.1　Poverty Thresholds by Gender of Head and Farm-Nonfarm Residence, 1959–1979

	(Family of Four)			
Year	Male Head (Nonfarm)	Female Head (Nonfarm)	Male Head (Farm)	Female Head (Farm)
1959	3,016	2,896	–	–
1960	3,062	2,941	–	–
1961	3,094	2,971	–	–
1962	3,098	2,976	–	–
1963	3,166	3,041	–	–
1964	3,207	3,080	–	–
1965	3,265	3,136	–	–
1966	3,374	3,240	–	–
1967	3,455	3,318	–	–
1968	3,597	3,455	3,057	2,937
1969	3,790	3,641	3,222	3,095
1970	3,970	3,948	3,387	3,345
1971	4,139	4,116	3,528	3,513
1972	4,277	4,254	3,644	3,598
1973	4,598	4,415	3,909	3,754
1974	5,103	4,900	4,338	4,165
1975	5,569	5,347	4,734	4,547
1976	5,890	5,655	5,007	4,809
1977	6,270	6,020	5,330	5,119
1978	6,747	6,478	5,736	5,508
1979	7,506	7,208	6,382	6,129

Source: U.S. Census Bureau. 2017. Poverty Thresholds. Accessed April 8, 2017, from https://www.census.gov/data/tables/time-series/demo/income-poverty/historical-poverty-thresholds.html.

farm versus nonfarm residence. Since 1980, poverty thresholds have been presented by family size only.

There is typically not much media attention given to the annual updates of the poverty thresholds. Instead, much more press coverage is allocated to the annual adjustments in the poverty level. These data are revised annually and promulgated by officials in the Department of Health and Human Services (HHS). According to researchers in the Office of the Assistant Secretary for Planning and Evaluation in HHS, poverty thresholds are used to calculate all

Table 1.2   Poverty Thresholds by Family Size, 1980–2016

(Family of Four)			
Year	Family of Four	Year	Family of Four
1980	8,414	1998	16,660
1981	9,287	1999	17,029
1982	9,862	2000	17,603
1983	10,178	2001	18,104
1984	10,609	2002	18,392
1985	10,989	2003	18,810
1986	11,203	2004	19,307
1987	11,611	2005	19,971
1988	12,092	2006	20,614
1989	12,674	2007	21,203
1990	13,359	2008	22,025
1991	13,924	2009	21,954*
1992	14,335	2010	22,315
1993	14,763	2011	23,021
1994	15,141	2012	23,492
1995	15,569	2013	23,834
1996	16,036	2014	24,418
1997	16,400	2015	24,447
		2016	24,755

* The poverty thresholds are updated each year using the change in the average annual Consumer Price Index for All Urban Consumers (CPI-U). Since the average annual CPI-U for 2009 was lower than the average annual CPI-U for 2008, poverty thresholds for 2009 are slightly lower than the corresponding thresholds for 2008.

Source: U.S. Census Bureau. 2017. Poverty Thresholds. Accessed April 8, 2017, from https://www.census.gov/data/tables/time-series/demo/income-poverty/historical -poverty-thresholds.html.

official poverty population statistics in the country, such as figures on the number of Americans in poverty each year. The poverty guidelines are a simplified version of the federal poverty thresholds used for administrative purposes, especially for determining financial eligibility for certain federal programs. They are issued each year in the Federal Register by HHS officials.[18] The key differences between the poverty thresholds and poverty-level guidelines are presented in table 1.3. HHS poverty guidelines since 1982 are presented in table 1.4.

In the United States, poverty thresholds are used for calculating all official poverty population statistics, so Mollie Orshansky's fundamental conception

Table 1.3 Differences between Poverty Thresholds and Poverty Guidelines

	U.S. Census Bureau	Department of Health and Human Services
Purpose/Use	Statistical: calculating the number of people living in poverty.	Administrative: determining financial eligibility for certain social programs.
Characteristics by Which They Vary	Detailed matrix of thresholds which vary by family size, number of children. There is no geographic variation; the same figures are used for all 50 states and for D.C.	Guidelines vary by family size. In addition, there is one set of figures for the 48 contiguous states and D.C. Alaska and Hawaii have their own guidelines.
Timing of Annual Update	Preliminary poverty thresholds are announced in January, and final poverty thresholds are announced in September of the year after the year for which poverty is measured (e.g., poverty thresholds in calendar year 2013 were issued in 2014 [preliminary figures in January and final figures in September]).	Poverty guidelines are issued in late January of each year (e.g., the 2014 poverty guidelines were issued in January 2014, calculated from the 2012 thresholds in September 2013, updated to reflect the price level of calendar year 2013. The 2014 poverty guidelines are approximately equal to the poverty thresholds for 2014).
How Updated or Calculated	The detail matrix is updated each year from the 1978 threshold matrix using the CPI-U. The preliminary weighted average thresholds are updated from the previous year's final weighted average thresholds using the CPI-U. The final weighted average thresholds are calculated from the current year's matrix using family weighting figures from the Current Population Survey's Annual Social and Economic Supplement.	Guidelines are updated from the latest published (final) weighted average poverty thresholds using the CPI-U. Figures are rounded, and differences between adjacent family size figures are equalized.
Rounding	Rounded to the nearest dollar.	Rounded to various multiples of $10. The numbers must end in zero.

Source: U.S. Department of Health and Human Services, Office of the Assistant Secretary for Planning and Evaluation. 2015. Frequently Asked Questions Related to the Poverty Guidelines and Poverty. Accessed February 16, 2015, from http://aspe.hhs.gov/poverty/faq.cfm.

Table 1.4   Department of Health and Human Services Poverty Guidelines, 1982–2017

(Family of Four)			
Year	Family of Four	Year	Family of Four
1982	9,300	2000	17,050
1983	9,900	2001	17,650
1984	10,200	2002	18,100
1985	10,650	2003	18,400
1986	11,000	2004	18,850
1987	11,200	2005	19,350
1988	11,650	2006	20,000
1989	12,100	2007	20,650
1990	12,700	2008	21,200
1991	13,400	2009	22,050
1992	13,950	2010	22,050
1993	14,350	2011	22,350
1994	14,800	2012	23,050
1995	15,150	2013	23,550
1996	15,600	2014	23,850
1997	16,050	2015	24,250
1998	16,450	2016	24,300
1999	16,700	2017	24,600

Source: U.S. Department of Health and Human Services. 2017. Poverty Guidelines. Accessed April 8, 2017, from https://aspe.hhs.gov/poverty-guidelines.

of poverty is still very much intact in the early 21st century.[19] At the beginning of each calendar year, officials from HHS promulgate the new poverty guidelines. For a family of four living in the 48 contiguous states, the figure is $24,600 for 2017. This means that if the total gross income of a family of four exceeds $24,600, then those four individuals are not living in poverty under federal guidelines. This translates to an income of $473.08 per week for four people over the course of a year, factoring in no vacation weeks. Bear in mind that this figure is for gross annual income; obviously local, state, and federal taxes reduce this figure accordingly. Whether or not the poverty guidelines are reasonable will be discussed later.

The number and percentage of Americans living in poverty since 1959 are presented in table 1.5. In 1959, toward the end of Dwight Eisenhower's

Table 1.5   Poverty in the United States, 1959–2015

Year	Total Population	Number Below Poverty	Percentage Below Poverty
1959	176,557,000	39,490,000	22.4
1960	179,503,000	39,851,000	22.2
1969	199,517,000	24,147,000	12.1
1970	202,183,000	25,420,000	12.6
1971	204,554,000	25,559,000	12.5
1972	206,004,000	24,460,000	11.9
1973	207,621,000	22,973,000	11.1
1974	209,362,000	23,370,000	11.2
1975	210,864,000	25,877,000	12.3
1976	212,303,000	24,975,000	11.8
1977	213,867,000	24,720,000	11.6
1978	215,656,000	24,497,000	11.4
1979	222,903,000	26,072,000	11.7
1980	225,027,000	29,272,000	13.0
1981	227,157,000	31,822,000	14.0
1982	229,412,000	34,398,000	15.0
1983	231,700,000	35,303,000	15.2
1984	233,816,000	33,700,000	14.4
1985	236,594,000	33,064,000	14.0
1986	238,554,000	32,370,000	13.6
1987	240,982,000	32,221,000	13.4
1988	243,530,000	31,745,000	13.0
1989	245,992,000	31,528,000	12.8
1990	248,644,000	33,585,000	13.5
1991	251,192,000	35,708,000	14.2
1992	256,549,000	38,014,000	14.8
1993	259,278,000	39,265,000	15.1
1994	261,616,000	38,059,000	14.5
1995	263,733,000	36,425,000	13.8
1996	266,218,000	36,529,000	13.7
1997	268,480,000	35,574,000	13.3
1998	271,059,000	34,476,000	12.7

(Continued)

Table 1.5   *(Continued)*

Year	Total Population	Number Below Poverty	Percentage Below Poverty
1999	276,208,000	32,791,000	11.9
2000	278,944,000	31,581,000	11.3
2001	281,475,000	32,907,000	11.7
2002	285,317,000	34,570,000	12.1
2003	287,699,000	35,861,000	12.5
2004	290,617,000	37,040,000	12.7
2005	293,135,000	36,950,000	12.6
2006	296,450,000	36,460,000	12.3
2007	298,699,000	37,276,000	12.5
2008	301,041,000	39,829,000	13.2
2009	303,820,000	43,569,000	14.3
2010	306,130,000	46,343,000	15.1
2011	308,456,000	46,247,000	15.0
2012	310,648,000	46,496,000	15.0
2013	313,096,000	46,269,000	14.8
2014	315,804,000	46,657,000	14.8
2015	318,454,000	43,123,000	13.5

Source: U.S. Census Bureau. 2017. Historical Poverty Tables-People. Accessed April 8, 2017, from https://www.census.gov/data/tables/time-series/demo/income-poverty/historical-poverty-people.html.

tenure as president, over 22 percent of Americans lived in poverty (almost 40 million people out of a total population of over 176 million). By 1969 (the end of the Lyndon Johnson era and beginning of Richard Nixon's presidency), poverty had declined to about 12 percent (over 24 million out of almost 200 million citizens). Between 1970 and 2007, poverty ranged between a low of 11.1 percent (1973) and a high of 15.2 percent (1983). Since the recession of 2007–2008, about 15 percent of Americans have been living in poverty. In 2015, this translated to over 43 million of over 318 million Americans living in poverty.

The Context of Poverty in the United States

When attempting to ascertain how the United States compares with other nations of the world in terms of poverty, it is important to understand the

Table 1.6   Gross Domestic Product, 2015 ($1 trillion or higher)

Ranking in World	Country	Total Gross Domestic Product (in millions of U.S. dollars)
1	United States	18,036,648
2	China	11,007,721
3	Japan	4,383,076
4	Germany	3,363,447
5	United Kingdom	2,858,003
6	France	2,418,836
7	India	2,095,398
8	Italy	1,821,497
9	Brazil	1,774,725
10	Canada	1,550,537
11	South Korea	1,377,873
12	Australia	1,339,141
13	Russian Federation	1,331,208
14	Spain	1,199,057
15	Mexico	1,143,793

Source: World Bank. 2017. World Development Indicators Database. Accessed April 8, 2017, from http://databank.worldbank.org/data/download/GDP.pdf.

reality that domestic economies vary considerably across the globe. A common measure of the health of national economies is gross domestic product (GDP). GDP consists of all the goods and services produced in a given country and also includes some nonmarket production, such as spending on defense and education services provided by the government. GDP does not take into account depreciation of capital stock, such as wear and tear on buildings and machinery that are used in producing the output in question.[20] The 15 countries that had a GDP in excess of US$1 trillion in 2015 are presented in table 1.6.[21] The United States had the highest GDP by a significant margin over the People's Republic of China ($18 trillion compared to $11 trillion). Japan was a distant third at $4.4 trillion, and Germany was fourth at $3.4 trillion. The remaining 11 countries had a GDP in the $1 trillion to $3 trillion range. By this measure, the United States is the richest country on earth by a substantial margin.

Another indicator of relative wealth can be found in an annual compendium of military expenditures. Since the Cold War era, superpower status has typically been measured by economic and military might. Included in

Table 1.7   World Military Expenditures (2014)

Ranking in World	Country	Total Military Spending (in billions of U.S. dollars)
1	United States	610
2	China	216
3	Russia	84.5
4	Saudi Arabia	80.8
5	France	62.3
6	United Kingdom	60.5
7	India	50
8	Germany	46.5
9	Japan	45.8
10	South Korea	36.7
11	Brazil	31.7
12	Italy	30.9
13	Australia	25.4
14	United Arab Emirates	22.8
15	Turkey	22.6

Source: Stockholm International Peace Research Institute. 2016. Trends in World Military Expenditure, 2014. Accessed February 25, 2016, from http://books.sipri.org /files/FS/SIPRIFS1504.pdf.

table 1.7 are the top 15 countries in the world in terms of military spending in 2014, according to the Stockholm International Peace Research Institute.[22] Once again, the United States is ranked first in the world in military spending ($610 billion). China is a distant second at $216 billion. Rounding out the top 15 are Russia ($84.5 billion), Saudi Arabia ($80.8 billion), France ($62.3 billion), United Kingdom ($60.5 billion), India ($50 billion), Germany ($46.5 billion), Japan ($45.8 billion), South Korea ($36.7 billion), Brazil ($31.7 billion), Italy ($30.9 billion), Australia ($25.4 billion), United Arab Emirates ($22.8 billion), and Turkey ($22.6 billion). Between 2005 and 2014, military spending in the United States actually declined by 0.4 percent. During the same period, it increased by over 100 percent in three countries: China (167 percent), Saudi Arabia (112 percent), and the United Arab Emirates (135 percent). In Russia, over the same decade, military spending increased by 97 percent.[23] Nevertheless, military spending is almost three times higher in the United States than in China, a considerable difference.

The level of wealth in a country may, in part, be a function of its population. Included in table 1.8 are the top 15 most populated nations as of July

Table 1.8 Populations of the World (July 2016 Estimates)

Ranking in World	Country	Total Population
1	China	1,373,541,278
2	India	1,266,883,598
3	European Union	513,949,445
4	United States	323,995,528
5	Indonesia	258,316,051
6	Brazil	205,823,665
7	Pakistan	201,995,540
8	Nigeria	186,053,386
9	Bangladesh	156,186,882
10	Russia	142,355,415
11	Japan	126,702,133
12	Mexico	123,166,749
13	Philippines	102,624,209
14	Ethiopia	102,374,044
15	Vietnam	95,261,021

Source: Central Intelligence Agency. 2017. The World Factbook. Accessed April 8, 2017, from https://www.cia.gov/library/publications/the-world-factbook/rankorder/2119rank .html.

2015.[24] China and India are by far the most populated nations on earth at over 1 billion citizens each. The United States, which has the largest economy and the highest military expenditure, is the fourth most populated nation at almost 200 million fewer citizens than the European Union. Indonesia and Brazil have over 200 million residents, and Pakistan, Nigeria, Bangladesh, Russia, Japan, Mexico, and the Philippines have over 100 million people. Ethiopia and Vietnam are currently just under this threshold. From a comparative perspective, the wealth in the United States cannot be matched by any other country. This does not mean, however, that the relative affluence in the United States is equitably distributed among the people.

A quantitative measure of economic inequality has existed since 1912.[25] The most widely used indicator of economic inequality is the Gini index, named after its creator, Corrado Gini.[26] Gini (1884–1965) published his book *Variability and Mutability* in 1912 in Italian; although it was never translated into English, the Gini index was extracted from it shortly after Gini engaged in a brief exchange with Hugh Dalton in *The Economic Journal* in 1921.[27] The Gini index is a measure of dispersion that was later modified to measure segregation.[28] There are many mathematical expressions for the Gini index.[29] One such manifestation is as follows:

$$G = \sum_i \sum_j t_i t_j |p_i - p_j| / 2T^2 P(1-P)^{30}$$

Where

$|.|$ = absolute value

T and P = total population size and proportion of one of the component groups

t_i and p_i = analogous values for one of the component groups

The Gini coefficient ranges from 0, which reflects complete equality, to 1, which is indicative of perfect inequality, meaning that one person has all the income in society and others have nothing.

All nations that are defined as "free" in the annual compendium of the Freedom House were used in order to compare income inequality ($N = 89$).[31] Gini coefficients were compiled by researchers at the World Bank for selected countries.[32] Of the 89 countries included in the Freedom House survey, Gini coefficients were provided in selected years for 69 countries. The United States garnered a Gini index of 41.1. Of the remaining 68 nations, 44 had Gini scores lower than the United States', and 24 countries had higher Gini scores. The results are presented in table 1.9. The mean for all 69 nations is 38.4, and the standard deviation is 9.6. The range is from a low of 25.6 (Slovenia) to a high

Table 1.9 Gini Index for Free Countries of the World (2014)

Country	Gini Index	Reference Year
Andorra	–	–
Antigua and Barbuda	–	–
Argentina	43.6	2011
Australia	34.0	2003
Austria	30.0	2004
Bahamas	–	–
Barbados	–	–
Belgium	33.1	2000
Belize	53.1	1999
Benin	43.5	2011
Botswana	60.5	2009
Brazil	52.7	2012

Table 1.9 (*Continued*)

Country	Gini Index	Reference Year
Bulgaria	34.3	2011
Canada	33.7	2010
Cape Verde	43.8	2007
Chile	50.8	2011
Costa Rica	48.6	2012
Croatia	33.6	2008
Cyprus	–	–
Czech Republic	26.4	2011
Denmark	26.9	2010
Dominica	–	–
Dominican Republic	45.7	2012
El Salvador	41.8	2012
Estonia	32.7	2011
Finland	27.8	2010
France	31.7	2005
Germany	30.6	2010
Ghana	42.8	2005
Greece	34.7	2010
Grenada	–	–
Guyana	44.5	1998
Hungary	28.9	2011
Iceland	26.3	2010
India	33.6	2011
Ireland	32.1	2010
Israel	42.8	2010
Italy	35.5	2010
Jamaica	45.5	2004
Japan	32.1	2008
Kiribati	–	–
Latvia	36.0	2011
Lesotho	54.2	2010
Liechtenstein	–	–
Lithuania	32.6	2011

(Continued)

Table 1.9   *(Continued)*

Country	Gini Index	Reference Year
Luxembourg	—	—
Malta	—	—
Marshall Islands	—	—
Mauritius	35.9	2012
Micronesia	61.1	2000
Monaco	—	—
Mongolia	36.5	2007
Montenegro	40.9	2011
Namibia	61.3	2009
Nauru	—	—
Netherlands	28.9	2010
New Zealand	—	—
Norway	26.8	2010
Palau	—	—
Panama	51.9	2012
Peru	45.3	2012
Poland	32.8	2011
Portugal	—	—
Romania	27.3	2012
Saint Kitts and Nevis	—	—
Saint Lucia	42.6	1995
Saint Vincent and Grenadines	—	—
Samoa	—	—
San Marino	—	—
São Tomé and Príncipe	33.9	2010
Senegal	40.3	2011
Serbia	29.7	2010
Slovakia	26.6	2011
Slovenia	24.9	2011
South Africa	65.0	2011
South Korea	—	—
Spain	35.8	2010

Table 1.9 (*Continued*)

Country	Gini Index	Reference Year
Suriname	52.9	1999
Sweden	26.1	2005
Switzerland	32.4	2004
Taiwan	–	–
Tonga	–	–
Trinidad and Tobago	–	–
Tunisia	35.8	2010
Tuvalu	–	–
United Kingdom	38.0	2010
United States	41.1	2010
Uruguay	41.3	2012
Vanuatu	–	–

Mean=38.6; standard deviation=9.9. 62 values and 27 missing values. Range 24.9 (Slovenia) to 65 (S. Africa)

Gini Index Source: World Bank. 2016. World Development Indicators: Distribution of Income or Consumption. Accessed March 1, 2016, from http://wdi.worldbank.org/table /2.9?tableNo=2.9.

Free Countries Source: Freedom House. 2016. Freedom in the World 2015. Accessed March 1, 2016, from https://freedomhouse.org/sites/default/files/01152015_FIW_2015 _final.pdf.

of 63.4 (South Africa). Simply put, income inequality is a bit higher in the United States than in the rest of the free world.[33]

Child poverty is also considerably higher in the United States than in other industrialized nations. In 2012, researchers at the United Nations Children's Fund conducted a comparative study of 35 economically advanced countries (Australia, Austria, Belgium, Bulgaria, Canada, Cyprus, Czech Republic, Denmark, Estonia, Finland, France, Germany, Greece, Hungary, Iceland, Ireland, Italy, Japan, Latvia, Lithuania, Luxembourg, Malta, the Netherlands, New Zealand, Norway, Poland, Portugal, Romania, Slovakia, Slovenia, Spain, Sweden, Switzerland, United Kingdom, and the United States).[34] The evaluators wanted to determine the percentage of all children (aged 0 to 17) who were living in relative poverty, defined as those living in a household in which disposable income, when adjusted for family size and composition, was less than 50 percent of the national median income.[35] The results of the study are presented in table 1.10.

Table 1.10   Children's Poverty in Economically Advanced Nations, 2009

Nation	Percentage of Children Living in Relative Poverty
Iceland	4.7
Finland	5.3
Cyprus	6.1
Netherlands	6.1
Norway	6.1
Slovenia	6.3
Denmark	6.5
Sweden	7.3
Austria	7.3
Czech Republic	7.4
Switzerland	8.1
Ireland	8.4
Germany	8.5
France	8.8
Malta	8.9
Belgium	10.2
Hungary	10.3
Australia	10.9
Slovakia	11.2
New Zealand	11.7
Estonia	11.9
United Kingdom	12.1
Luxembourg	12.3
Canada	13.3
Poland	14.5
Portugal	14.7
Japan	14.9
Lithuania	15.4
Italy	15.9
Greece	16.0
Spain	17.1
Bulgaria	17.8

Table 1.10 (*Continued*)

Nation	Percentage of Children Living in Relative Poverty
Latvia	18.8
United States	23.1
Romania	25.5

Source: Adapted from United Nations Children's Fund. May 2012. Measuring Child Poverty: New League Tables of Child Poverty in the World's Rich Countries. Accessed April 8, 2017, from https://www.unicef-irc.org/publications/660/.

Mean=11.5; standard deviation=5.1. Range 4.7 (Iceland) to 25.5 (Romania).

The child poverty level in the United States was the highest among the economically advanced countries of the world with one exception, Romania, a former communist dictatorship. The average poverty level for children in this sample was 11.5 percent, while the child poverty rate in the United States was 23.1 percent. Almost one-fourth of all children in the world's wealthiest nation are living in relative poverty, a rate that is much higher than in most advanced industrialized democracies. To the comparative policy analyst, this is not a new revelation; in fact, income inequality in the United States has been increasing since the 1970s, with a significant increase in the income of the very affluent in particular.[36] There are undoubtedly a multitude of reasons why this is happening, and two researchers focusing on state policies, Megan E. Hatch and Elizabeth Rigby, offer some insight:

> The causes of rising inequality in the United States are likely numerous and interactive. However, our study suggests that even if state policymakers cannot reverse the trend of increasing market income inequality, they can slow the increase through comprehensive redistributive policies. Further research is needed to determine the mechanisms through which policies alter income distribution. Our findings hint that the incentive effects of various redistributive policies play a key role, one that needs to be teased apart in order for policymakers to design effective redistributive policies aimed at reducing or at least slowing the growth of inequality in their states. The results of the inequality simulations indicate that redistributive policies have the potential to make large changes in inequality over time. Therefore, it is important for policymakers to understand that there is not one redistributive policy that has a uniform effect on inequality; rather, the basket of redistributive policies shape income and wealth distributions in the state.[37]

Indeed, the challenges regarding income inequality are vexing for the practitioner, elected official, and citizen alike. Finding ways to overcome the ravages of poverty have proven elusive, especially in the United States.

Rising inequality in the United States prompted political scientists in the American Political Science Association (APSA) to create the Task Force on Inequality and American Democracy.[38] The task force members issued a report in 2004.[39] By way of introduction, the experts declared:

> Equal political voice and democratically responsive government are widely cherished American ideals. Indeed, the United States is vigorously promoting democracy abroad. Yet, what is happening to democracy at home? Our country's ideals of equal citizenship and responsive government may be under growing threat in an era of persistent and rising inequalities. Disparities of income, wealth, and access to opportunity are growing more sharply in the United States than in many other nations, and gaps between races and ethnic groups persist. Progress toward realizing American ideals of democracy may have stalled, and in some arenas reversed.[40]

Though many Americans have worked diligently to promote more equality and fairness, there are numerous disconcerting realities that thwart equality and therefore democracy in the United States today, where the concentration of wealth is shrinking to a privileged few, and citizens are growing increasingly frustrated with government. Many Americans perceive that federal officials are attentive to the rich and powerful in making public policy decisions but are relatively indifferent to the plight of average citizens. This is certainly indicated when citizens issue their approval ratings of the U.S. Congress in public opinion polls: in recent years, typically fewer than one in five adults approve of the way that members of Congress represent the people.[41] Since the case of *Citizens United v. Federal Election Commission*, it has been clear that the rich dominate the funding of federal political campaigns, and it is no wonder that most Americans believe that federal elected officials only respond to the interests of an elite as opposed to the needs of middle- and lower-income people.[42]

Embracing an expansive conception of the term "public policy" is essential in order to address issues related to poverty, or other substantive policy issues for that matter. The members of the APSA task force highlight this reality by way of conclusion in their report:

> What government does not do is just as important as what it does. What our government does these days is especially responsive to the values and interests of the most privileged Americans. Harder to pin down is the effect of disparities of influence on what government fails to do. Through much of U.S. history, our government has responded to the life circumstances of ordinary Americans by enacting major policies to spread opportunities and provide security to millions of individuals and families. Public education, Social Security and Medicare, the G.I. Bill, home-mortgage programs, certain farm programs, and many other efforts have enhanced the quality of life for millions of regular Americans.[43]

Class stratification in the United States is now a fundamental policy problem. Class stratification can help explain why the United States is unique when it comes to poverty in the industrialized free world. How can a country with such privilege be plagued with such relative poverty? In order to understand this phenomenon, a better understanding of the term "poverty" is in order.

Measuring Poverty in the United States

As Rebecca Blank noted in 2015,

Within a decade of its creation, the official poverty measure began to be criticized and suggestions for alternative measurement approaches began to be heard. All of its components were questioned—the definition of the resource-sharing unit, the use of pretax cash income, and the thresholds (which were thought to be too low). With improved data, analysts doubted that the threshold should be benchmarked to food alone. Moreover, the official poverty thresholds were criticized for not reflecting substantial differences in the costs of living across locations or increases in standards of living.

The absolute nature of the U.S. poverty threshold, based on data from the 1950s and adjusted for inflation over time, means that there is no conceptual justification to the current poverty line; it is simply an arbitrary dollar amount. Using a threshold calculated in 1964 (based on 1950s data) to estimate poverty in 2014 is to use a 50-year-old categorization. Because this measure is based on cash income, it is not affected by the many in-kind antipoverty programs initiated in the United States during the past five decades. Because tax measures do not affect the definition of pretax income, substantial increases in the after-tax income among low-income families due to the several expansions of the earned income tax credit over the years had no impact on the measure of poverty. In essence, the very definition created in the Johnson administration to help understand poverty has led to serious misunderstandings because of its growing inadequacy over time.[44]

There are serious public policy and human implications for the continued use of the Orshansky measure of poverty. It is an arbitrary dollar figure, as Professor Blank aptly described.[45] If the figure is too low, as many have maintained over the years, then the United States has a much more significant poverty issue than is presently envisioned by many.

John Schwarz has argued that "we need to recalibrate the poverty measure to make it true to Orshansky's measure."[46] Furthermore, he argued that

an honest poverty line would clarify how many Americans are poor and yet ineligible for assistance that would allow them to afford the very basics that the assistance programs were intended to provide. It would show that a far higher proportion of the poor than politicians or the public are aware of are hard workers; many millions of them are already in year-round full-time jobs. And perhaps most important, the large numbers of the poor, now and in relation to the past, would help us understand the serious harm inflicted on demand in the economy, which in turn limits business and contributes significantly to the economy's sluggish growth.[47]

Many policy makers accept the premise that typically between 11 and 15 percent of the nation's citizens live in poverty. Yet the data that are used to measure this phenomenon are suspect at best and reflective of a time long past. If elected officials and citizens alike wish to address the poverty problem in the United States, they must first understand the extent of the problem, which still needs to be identified over 50 years after the War on Poverty was launched.[48]

There have been a number of formal efforts to update and refine the poverty measure over the past few decades.[49] One such endeavor commenced in the early 1990s when the Panel on Poverty and Family Assistance was created by the National Academy of Sciences.[50]

Measuring Poverty: A New Approach was published in 1995.[51] By way of summary, the panel members concluded:

> The U.S. measure of poverty is an important social indicator that affects not only public perceptions of well-being in America, but also public policies and programs. The current measure was originally developed in the early 1960s as an indicator of the number and proportion of people with inadequate family incomes for needed consumption of food and other goods and services. At that time, the poverty "line" for a family of four had broad support. Since then, the poverty measure has been widely used for policy formation, program administration, analytical research, and general public understanding.
>
> Like other important indicators, the poverty measure should be evaluated periodically to determine if it is still serving its intended purposes and whether it could be improved. This report of the Panel on Poverty and Family Assistance provides such an evaluation. Our major conclusion is that the current measure needs to be revised: it no longer provides an accurate picture of the differences in the extent of economic poverty among population groups or geographic areas of the country, nor an accurate picture of trends over time. The current measure has remained virtually unchanged over the past 30 years. Yet during that time, there have been marked changes in the nation's economy and society and in public policies that have affected families' economic well-being, which are not reflected in the measure. Improved data, methods, and research knowledge make it possible to improve the current poverty measure.[52]

The panel participants recommended alterations to the definition of the poverty threshold and the adjustment of these thresholds for cost-of-living differences by geographical region as well as the urban/rural dichotomy. In addition, the researchers recommended a resource definition that measured after-tax income, since taxes are mandatory payments, plus imputed in-kind benefits from major welfare programs.[53] Bear in mind that some programs no longer exist in the same form as they did in the early to mid-1990s, especially Aid to Families with Dependent Children (AFDC). The precursor to the AFDC program was created by the original Social Security Act in 1935; it lasted until 1996, when it was replaced by the more restrictive Temporary Assistance to Needy Families program.[54]

The aforementioned recommendations led to further studies on the matter of measuring poverty in the United States.[55] In 2011, researchers at the U.S. Census Bureau began to regularly report a Supplemental Poverty Measure (SPM), which was somewhat an artifact of the recommendations of the Panel of Poverty and Family Assistance. To date, however, members of Congress have still not revised the poverty measure that Orshansky created.[56] As some have recently noted:

> The SPM is an effort to update poverty measurement, but its approach is conceptually similar to Orshansky's with a poverty threshold based on expenditures on necessities and a resource measure based on family resources. There are other approaches to poverty measurement that have been proposed that would measure poverty in fundamentally different ways. For example, many have suggested that poverty be defined as the share of the population below some point in the income distribution. Fuchs (1967) and Ruggles (1990) proposed a poverty threshold be set at 50 percent of median income. In contrast to the absolute poverty lines used in the official measure, a relative measure of poverty would remain constant even if all incomes are growing proportionally across the distribution. An alternative approach is to define a poverty threshold by estimating the cost of a comprehensive basket of necessary expenditures. Rather than using data on expenditures to determine a poverty threshold, such an approach would require an objective determination of what is "necessary" and what is a "reasonable cost" for those things deemed necessary. There have been efforts to create such baskets for the United States . . . A further alternative is focused on using expenditure data rather than income data in calculating the resource side of the poverty measure. Of course, this requires reliable measures of family expenditures (as opposed to income), which is not as frequently collected in many countries (although the United States has an annual expenditure survey) . . . A final alternative is to measure material hardship directly, rather than to assume that it is created by low income levels. Material hardship measures are only imperfectly correlated with income and clearly provide additional

information about economic need. This approach has been adopted by the EU, which supplements a poverty measure with multiple other measures of deprivation.[57]

Victor Fuchs, currently the Henry J. Kaiser Jr. Professor of Economics and Health Research and Policy Emeritus at Stanford University, authored a paper in 1967 that is referenced by these researchers.[58] In it, he offered his own poverty measure, four years after Orshansky's measure had been implemented:

> I propose that we define as poor *any family whose income is less than one-half the median family income* [italics in original]. No special claim is made for the precise figure of one-half; but the advantages of using a poverty standard that changes with the growth of real national income are considerable. First, it explicitly recognizes that all so-called "minimum" or "subsistence" budgets are based on contemporary standards which will soon be out of date. Second, it focuses attention on what seems to be a fundamental factor underlying the present concern about poverty—i.e., it represents a tentative groping toward a national policy with respect to the distribution of income. Finally, it provides a more realistic basis for appraising the success or failure of anti-poverty programs.[59]

Fuchs provided three questions with answers to his poverty measurement proposal. First, was his figure of one-half the median just as subjective as the Orshansky measure? He contended that in some ways his measure was subjective but that there were differences between the two measures. To him, the Orshansky measure purported to be objective because it was based on a budgetary analysis. His measure was preferable because it was akin to making a societal statement about poverty in the United States that would be created in a transparent manner through the traditional political process. Second, is it viable to use a single national median for all families in the United States? While it may be plausible to modify the national standard by accounting for such things as family size, geography, and other factors, it would be more facilitative to use a single standard and apply it evenly across the country. Third, do we need to bother to have a poverty measure at all? To some analysts, a measure was not an urgent need because they envisioned economic growth into the future with the median income steadily increasing over time. But as Fuchs noted in his article in the late 1960s, median income in 1965 was 60 percent higher than in 1947, but the poverty problem in the United States had not changed in spite of this reality. Since poverty is a dynamic phenomenon, it was incumbent upon successive generations of Americans to distinguish between luxury and necessity.[60]

Regardless of the outcome of any intellectual and moral debate about poverty, it is important to heed Fuchs's prophesy during the Johnson era:

> One point is clear. There is no costless way to help families out of poverty. If we think the goal is important, we must be prepared to pay the price. Thus far, the public has not been willing to do so. Indeed many of those who have been most vocal about helping the poor have been less than candid about indicating what the price is, or who should pay it. To raise the expectations of the poor, and to give the nonpoor the illusion that something significant is being accomplished when only token action has been undertaken, is to perform a disservice to all.[61]

Any debate about poverty will quickly illuminate ideological distinctions, values, and moral judgments. A half century after Fuchs's conclusion, it is entirely safe to contend that only token action has been taken in the campaign to combat poverty in the United States, which is sadly ironic given the status of the lone great superpower in the world.

Debates about measuring poverty in a wealthy nation inherently involve subjective judgments. By definition, they entail differential interpretations of capitalism, which will be discussed at greater length later in the book. As Patricia Ruggles (1990) delineated:

> The construction of an official poverty measure carries with it an implied judgment about social welfare. It says that it is not just the total welfare of all individuals in society that matters but also specifically the well-being of those who are least well-off. Although the problem of poverty is often seen by economists as a special subset of the problem of inequality—after all, if there were no inequality presumably there would also be no poverty— from the viewpoint of the policymaker a concern about poverty does not necessarily imply any interest at all in broader issues of distribution. Many policymakers start instead with the notion that underlay the War on Poverty—that there is some minimum "decent" standard of living, and a just society must attempt to ensure that all its members have access to at least this level of economic well-being.[62]

The crux of the poverty debate focuses on the creation of a measure that results in an acceptable and reasonable standard of living for the people involved. In other words, what level of income in the United States results in a "decent" (using Ruggles's term) quality of life? In the preface of her book, Ruggles maintains that "poverty is ultimately a normative concept, not a statistical one."[63] I very much concur with her assessment. All poverty measures have policy implications for society as a whole. A major increase in the Orshansky line today, for example, would mean that more people would be eligible for public assistance, and the costs of the programs would therefore increase. Members of Congress could change the rules of the public assistance programs, but they would obviously have to garner the political support to succeed. Yet having a poverty measure is absolutely essential, for it tracks the number of Americans who are living in economically deprived conditions over time. This is truly an accountability measure, for it provides an ongoing assessment of the extent to which the United States is plagued by an ongoing poverty reality in an otherwise affluent society.

But the accountability measure in question has to be reasonable. Back in 1974, Lee Rainwater made the following observation with regard to the status of poverty in the United States:

> Reflecting on the results of the war on poverty during its first decade reveals many paradoxes. The most central one is that while "poverty" has been reduced by almost half, we have no sense of an amelioration of the human problems associated with poverty. The proportion of the population living below the poverty line decreased from 22.4 percent in 1959 to 12.2 percent in 1969. In the 1970 recession this decline halted, and poverty increased slightly to 12.6 percent. Reductions in poverty seem to go hand in hand with increases in per capita personal income. No more elaborate explanation of the decline in poverty over the past decade is necessary than to say that the people at the bottom of the heap got their usual share of the increasing affluence, and this shift in their income moved almost half of them above the poverty line. If economic growth continues at its long term rate, it is not overly risky to predict the near elimination of poverty by around 1980. But we know that is ridiculous. Anyone who argues that in 1973 the poverty problem is almost half of what it was in 1959 is likely to meet with disbelief. His listeners will be quick to point to the undiminished intensity of a broad range of poverty-related human and social problems. Leaving aside the statistical indicators and looking instead at the quality of life of families at the lower end of the socioeconomic scale, one is impressed by how little the quality of the lives of these families seems to have changed over longer periods of time than a decade. The people who would have been considered poor on an "eyeball to eyeball" basis in 1959 still seem poor today.[64]

A measure of poverty must be reflective of societal values and mores. To me, it is truly a moral indicator, as it reflects a society's willingness to have an open and honest debate about what it means to be poor and what the society in question may be willing to do by way of public policy to assist the disadvantaged in their own communities and beyond.

New (But Old) Measure of Poverty in the United States along with the Orshansky Index

Professor Geoffrey Gilbert highlighted the reality that policy makers could use both an absolute measure of poverty (e.g., the Orshansky measure) and a relative poverty measure (e.g., the Fuchs measure):

> The poverty line adopted by the U.S. government in 1964 and still used today is sometimes called the Orshansky index, in honor of Mollie Orshansky, who devised it. Based on what it costs for a household to barely subsist, it is an absolute poverty standard. If general living conditions improve, the poverty line does not rise accordingly; it rises only with inflation. The economist Victor Fuchs proposed a different poverty standard in 1967. He argued for drawing the poverty line at one-half the national median income level. In 1967, the median household income in the United States was around $6,000, meaning there were as many households receiving more than that income as there were receiving less. Fuchs's proposal would have counted any household below $3,000 as poor. Coincidentally, in the mid-1960s, the Orshansky and Fuchs poverty lines both stood at roughly $3,000, but as time passed, the two lines spread apart, with the Fuchs standard rising faster. Thus, today we would count more Americans as poor if we applied the Fuchs standard than we do using the official (Orshansky) standard. Most other countries measure poverty in the relative manner that Fuchs proposed.[65]

Within an American context (not comparative) only, in reality there are two measures because the Orshansky and Fuchs measures have evolved greatly since the 1960s. The Orshansky poverty line is much lower today than the Fuchs measure. In operational terms, it is accurate to depict the Orshansky measure as an indicator of absolute poverty, as it is a fairly conservative measure of poverty; in that, about 15 percent of the people are living in poverty from one year to the next under this measure. Some would contend that the percentage of Americans living in poverty, at least in relative terms, is much higher than 15 percent. Again, in this scenario, the Fuchs measure is truly an indicator of relative poverty, as it evolves by definition as the overall household wealth of the nation changes and is significantly more "generous" than the Orshansky poverty line. This difference is depicted in table 1.11.

Throughout the late 1960s and 1970s, the two measures were fairly close, though the Fuchs measure has been higher than the Orshansky measure since 1967. In the 1980s, however, the gap between the two measures became more apparent. In 1986, for the first time, the difference was greater than $1,000 ($12,449 for the Fuchs line and $11,203 for the Orshansky line). In 1997, the gap increased to over $2,000 ($18,503 to $16,400). Just two years

Table 1.11   The Orshansky Poverty Line Versus the Fuchs Poverty Line, 1967–2015

Year	Median Household Income in the United States	Orshansky Poverty Line (Family of 4)	Fuchs Poverty Line (50% of Median Income)
1967	7,143	3,455	3,572
1968	7,743	3,597	3,872
1969	8,389	3,790	4,195
1970	8,734	3,970	4,367
1971	9,028	4,139	4,514
1972	9,697	4,277	4,849
1973	10,512	4,598	5,256
1974	11,197	5,103	5,599
1975	11,800	5,569	5,900
1976	12,686	5,890	6,343
1977	13,572	6,270	6,786
1978	15,064	6,747	7,532
1979	16,461	7,506	8,231
1980	17,710	8,414	8,855
1981	19,074	9,287	9,537
1982	20,171	9,862	10,086
1983	20,885	10,178	10,443
1984	22,415	10,609	11,208
1985	23,618	10,989	11,809
1986	24,897	11,203	12,449
1987	26,061	11,611	13,031
1988	27,225	12,092	13,613
1989	28,906	12,674	14,453
1990	29,943	13,359	14,972
1991	30,126	13,924	15,063
1992	30,636	14,335	15,318
1993	31,241	14,763	15,621
1994	32,264	15,141	16,132
1995	34,076	15,569	17,038
1996	35,492	16,036	17,746

Table 1.11   (*Continued*)

Year	Median Household Income in the United States	Orshansky Poverty Line (Family of 4)	Fuchs Poverty Line (50% of Median Income)
1997	37,005	16,400	18,503
1998	38,885	16,660	19,443
1999	40,696	17,029	20,348
2000	41,990	17,603	20,995
2001	42,228	18,104	21,114
2002	42,409	18,392	21,205
2003	43,318	18,810	21,659
2004	44,334	19,307	22,167
2005	46,326	19,971	23,163
2006	48,201	20,614	21,101
2007	50,233	21,203	25,117
2008	50,303	22,025	25,152
2009	49,777	21,954	24,889
2010	49,276	22,315	24,638
2011	50,054	23,021	25,027
2012	51,017	23,492	25,509
2013	51,939	23,834	25,970
2014	53,657	24,418	26,829
2015	56,516	24,447	28,258

Sources: U.S. Census Bureau. 2017. Poverty Thresholds. Accessed April 8, 2017, from https://www.census.gov/data/tables/time-series/demo/income-poverty/historical -poverty-thresholds.html;

U.S. Census Bureau. 2017. Median Annual Household Income (1967–2015). Accessed April 8, 2017, from https://www.census.gov/data/tables/time-series/demo/income -poverty/historical-income-households.html.

later, in 1999, the gap exceeded $3,000 ($20,348 to $17,029). As of 2015, the gap was still considerable and increased to just over $3,800 ($28,258 to $24,447). Bear in mind, this gap represents about a 15 percent difference in the two measures, meaning that the poverty rate would be significantly higher if policy makers had embraced and used the Fuchs measure years ago.

It would be virtually impossible in a political sense to replace the Orshansky measure altogether today. It has been in existence for over 50 years, and it allows leaders and policy makers to maintain a longitudinal understanding of poverty in the United States in absolute terms. Clearly, it is a limited esti-mate of poverty. In reality, the true extent of poverty in the United States is obfuscated by its continued use. In order to augment the collective under-standing of poverty in the United States, Fuchs's relative measure would result in greater awareness, as well as understanding, of the endemic nature of poverty in the United States.

There is complacency in this nation when it comes to poverty. Throughout American history, there have been "haves" and "have nots," which is to be expected in a capitalist system. The poverty rate in this country is unaccept-ably high for a nation of such vast wealth, and I am referring to the absolute Orshansky measure of poverty. By establishing a more progressive standard of poverty, using the Fuchs vision of the late 1960s, the more encompassing conception of poverty suggests that major challenges exist for policy makers who purport to make this a national public policy priority.

The number of people living in poverty in the United States is disgraceful. Children and women tend to be affected the most by this calamity. What kind of future is in store for children reared in poverty? What kinds of choices do parents with a substandard income have when it comes to such matters as dietary choices, clothing, health care, housing, education, utilities, transportation, insurance, and a plethora of other issues in contemporary society?

If our leaders truly wish to address poverty beyond impassioned rhetoric, adopting two measures of poverty would help. The Orshansky measure is destined for perpetuity well into the future; a rigorous national debate to change, alter, or delete it simply is not on the political agenda at the present time. Advocates of the poor in this society should fundamentally embrace the Fuchs relative measure as well, for it is reflective of a committed citizenry and group of leaders who are mission oriented and dedicated to the moral goal of reducing poverty so that the human condition can be enhanced for all Americans, not simply those who have been fortunate enough to have achieved the "American dream." We cannot assume that all those living in poverty, regardless of one's conception of the term, are lazy or ignorant, make bad choices, and are unwilling to take advantage of numerous oppor-tunities that are available to most people. Perhaps the examination of the evolution of poverty-relief efforts in American history that will ensue in chapter 2 will illuminate some lessons that can be extracted from the past in order to effectuate public policy making in a more positive and proactive manner. As John Cassidy reported in 2006:

> Mollie Orshansky, who is now ninety-one and living on Manhattan's East Side, never warmed to the idea of a relative-poverty line—she was too concerned about people actually starving—but she wasn't wedded to her method, either. "If someone has a better approach, fine," she said in 1999. "I was working with what I had and with what I knew."[66]

If Mollie Orshansky was amenable to differential measures of poverty many years after creating her poverty thresholds, then policy makers and researchers in our time should embrace her wisdom and do the same.

Notes

1. United Nations Educational, Scientific and Cultural Organization, "Poverty," http://www.unesco.org/new/en/social-and-human-sciences/themes/international-migration/glossary/poverty (accessed October 3, 2014).

2. Guy Palmer, "Relative Poverty, Absolute Poverty and Social Exclusion," http://www.poverty.org.uk/summary/social%20exclusion.shtml (accessed October 3, 2014).

3. Mollie Orshansky, "Perspectives on Poverty: How Poverty Is Measured," *Monthly Labor Review* 92, no. 2 (1969): 37.

4. Gordon M. Fisher, "Remembering Mollie Orshansky—The Developer of the Poverty Thresholds," *Social Security Bulletin* 68, no. 3 (2008): 79.

5. Fisher, "Remembering Mollie Orshansky—The Developer of the Poverty Thresholds," 79.

6. Fisher, "Remembering Mollie Orshansky—The Developer of the Poverty Thresholds," 79.

7. Fisher, "Remembering Mollie Orshansky—The Developer of the Poverty Thresholds," 79–80.

8. Fisher, "Remembering Mollie Orshansky—The Developer of the Poverty Thresholds," 80.

9. Fisher, "Remembering Mollie Orshansky—The Developer of the Poverty Thresholds," 80.

10. The American Presidency Project, "Lyndon B. Johnson: Annual Message to the Congress on the State of the Union, January 8, 1964," http://www.presidency.ucsb.edu/ws/?pid=26787 (accessed January 18, 2015).

11. The American Presidency Project, "Lyndon B. Johnson: Annual Message to the Congress on the State of the Union, January 8, 1964."

12. American Presidency Project, "President Lyndon B. Johnson's Remarks at the University of Michigan, May 22, 1964," http://www.presidency.ucsb.edu/ws/?pid=26262%20 (accessed April 8, 2017).

13. A more enhanced understanding of Mollie Orshansky's work can be obtained by reading the following: Mollie Orshansky, "Children of the Poor," *Social Security Bulletin* 26, no. 7 (1963): 3–13; Mollie Orshansky, "Counting the Poor: Another Look at the Poverty Profile," *Social Security Bulletin* 28, no. 1 (1965): 3–29; Mollie Orshansky, "Who's Who Among the Poor: A Demographic View of Poverty," *Social Security Bulletin* 28, no. 7 (1965): 3–32; Mollie Orshansky, *The Measure of Poverty (Technical Paper 1: Documentation of Background Information and Rationale for Current Poverty Matrix* (Washington, DC: U.S. Department of Health, Education, and Welfare, 1976); Mollie Orshansky, Harold Watts, Bradley R. Schiller, John J. Korbel, "Measuring Poverty: A Debate," *Public Welfare* 36, no. 2 (1978): 46–55; Mollie Orshansky,

"Commentary: The Poverty Measure," *Social Security Bulletin* 51, no. 10 (1988): 22–4.

14. Fisher, "Remembering Mollie Orshansky—The Developer of the Poverty Thresholds," 82.

15. Fisher, "Remembering Mollie Orshansky—The Developer of the Poverty Thresholds," 82.

16. Fisher, "Remembering Mollie Orshansky—The Developer of the Poverty Thresholds," 82.

17. Fisher, "Remembering Mollie Orshansky—The Developer of the Poverty Thresholds," 81–2.

18. U.S. Department of Health and Human Services, Office of the Assistant Secretary for Planning and Evaluation, "Frequently Asked Questions Related to the Poverty Guidelines and Poverty," http://aspe.hhs.gov/poverty/faq.cfm (accessed February 16, 2015).

19. U.S. Department of Health and Human Services, Office of the Assistant Secretary for Planning and Evaluation, "Frequently Asked Questions Related to the Poverty Guidelines and Poverty."

20. Tim Callen, "Back to Basics: What Is Gross Domestic Product?" *Finance and Development* (December 2008): 48.

21. World Bank, "World Development Indicators Database," http://databank.worldbank.org/data/download/GDP.pdf (accessed April 8, 2017).

22. Stockholm International Peace Research Institute, "Trends in World Military Expenditure, 2014," http://book.sipri.org/files/FS/SIPRIFS1504.pdf (accessed February 25, 2016), 1.

23. Stockholm International Peace Research Institute, "Trends in World Military Expenditure, 2014," 2.

24. Central Intelligence Agency, "The World Factbook," https://www.cia.gov/library/publications/the-world-factbook/rankorder/2119rank.html (accessed April 8, 2017).

25. Corrado Gini, "Variabilitá e mutabilitá: Contributo allo studio delle distribuzioni e delle relazioni statistiche," *Studi Economico-giurdici della Regia Facoltà Giurisprudenza* 3, no. 2 (1912): 3–159.

26. Tim F. Liao, "Measuring and Analyzing Class Inequality with the Gini Index Informed by Model-Based Clustering," *Sociological Methodology* 36 (2006): 201–03.

27. Liao, "Measuring and Analyzing Class Inequality with the Gini Index Informed by Model-Based Clustering," 202; Lidia Ceriani and Paolo Verme, "The Origins of the Gini Index: Extracts from Variabilitá e Mutabilitá (1912) by Corrado Gini," *Journal of Economic Inequality* 10 (2012): 421–22; Corrado Gini, "Measurement of Inequality of Incomes," *The Economic Journal* 31, no. 121 (1921): 124–26.

28. David R. James and Karl E. Taeuber, "Measures of Segregation," *Sociological Methodology* 15 (1985): 1–32; Brian L. Fife, *Desegregation in American Schools: Comparative Intervention Strategies* (New York: Praeger, 1992), 19–20.

29. National Poverty Center, "The GINI Coefficient and Segregation on a Continuous Variable," http://www.npc.umich.edu/publications/workingpaper05/paper02/Kim_Jargowsky_Gini_Segregation.pdf (accessed April 8, 2017); James and Taeuber, "Measures of Segregation"; Liao, "Measuring and Analyzing Class Inequality with the Gini Index Informed by Model-Based Clustering"; Ceriani and Verme, "The Origins of the Gini Index: Extracts from Variabilità e Mutabilità"; Lidia Ceriani and Paolo Verme, "Individual Diversity and the Gini Decomposition," https://openknowledge.worldbank.org/handle/10986/17315 (accessed April 8, 2017).

30. James and Taeuber, "Measures of Segregation," 5.

31. Freedom House, "Freedom in the World 2015," https://freedomhouse.org/sites/default/files/01152015_FIW_2015_final.pdf (accessed March 1, 2016). The nations categorized as "free" are as follows: Andorra, Antigua and Barbuda, Argentina, Australia, Austria, Bahamas, Barbados, Belgium, Belize, Benin, Botswana, Brazil, Bulgaria, Canada, Cape Verde, Chile, Costa Rica, Croatia, Cyprus, Czech Republic, Denmark, Dominica, Dominican Republic, El Salvador, Estonia, Finland, France, Germany, Ghana, Greece, Grenada, Guyana, Hungary, Iceland, India, Ireland, Israel, Italy, Jamaica, Japan, Kiribati, Latvia, Lesotho, Liechtenstein, Lithuania, Luxembourg, Malta, Marshall Islands, Mauritius, Micronesia, Monaco, Mongolia, Montenegro, Namibia, Nauru, Netherlands, New Zealand, Norway, Palau, Panama, Peru, Poland, Portugal, Romania, Saint Kitts and Nevis, Saint Lucia, Saint Vincent and Grenadines, Samoa, San Marino, São Tomé and Príncipe, Senegal, Serbia, Slovakia, Slovenia, South Africa, South Korea, Spain, Suriname, Sweden, Switzerland, Taiwan, Tonga, Trinidad and Tobago, Tunisia, Tuvalu, United Kingdom, United States, Uruguay, and Vanuatu.

32. World Bank, "World Development Indicators: Distribution of Income or Consumption," http://wdi.worldbank.org/table/2.9 (accessed March 1, 2016).

33. Freedom House, "Freedom in the World 2015."

34. United Nations Children's Fund, "Measuring Child Poverty: New League Tables of Child Poverty in the World's Rich Countries," http://www.unicef-irc.org/publications/660/ (accessed April 8, 2017).

35. United Nations Children's Fund, "Measuring Child Poverty: New League Tables of Child Poverty in the World's Rich Countries."

36. Megan E. Hatch and Elizabeth Rigby, "Laboratories of (In)equality? Redistributive Policy and Income Inequality in the American States," *Policy Studies Journal* 43, no. 2 (2015): 163.

37. Hatch and Rigby, "Laboratories of (In)equality? Redistributive Policy and Income Inequality in the American States," 181.

38. American Political Science Association, "American Democracy in an Age of Rising Inequality," http://www.apsanet.org/portals/54/Files/Task%20Force%20Reports/taskforcereport.pdf (accessed March 3, 2016). The members of the task force include Lawrence Jacobs (chair), University of Minnesota; Ben Barber, University of Maryland; Larry Bartels, Princeton University; Michael Dawson, Harvard University; Morris Fiorina, Stanford University; Jacob Hacker,

Yale University; Rodney Hero, Notre Dame University; Hugh Heclo, George Mason University; Claire Jean Kim, University of California, Irvine; Suzanne Metler, Syracuse University; Benjamin Page, Northwestern University; Dianne Pinderhughes, University of Illinois at Urbana-Champaign; Kay Lehman Schlozman, Boston College; Theda Skocpol, Harvard University; Sidney Verba, Harvard University.

39. American Political Science Association, "American Democracy in an Age of Rising Inequality."

40. American Political Science Association, "American Democracy in an Age of Rising Inequality," 1.

41. Brian L. Fife, "Congress and Electoral Reform in the Early Twenty-First Century," in *Working Congress: A Guide for Senators, Representatives, and Citizens,* ed. Robert Mann (Baton Rouge, LA: Louisiana State University Press, 2014), 62–78.

42. *Citizens United v. Federal Election Commission,* 558 U.S. 310 (2010).

43. American Political Science Association, "American Democracy in an Age of Rising Inequality," 15.

44. Rebecca Blank, "The Measurement of Poverty: An Evolving Story," *LaFollette Policy Report* 25, no. 1 (2015): 9.

45. Blank, "The Measurement of Poverty: An Evolving Story," 9.

46. John E. Schwarz, "Recalibrating the Poverty Line," *Los Angeles Times* (October 24, 2013), http://articles.latimes.com/2013/oct/24/opinion/la-oe-schwarz-poverty-line-income-gap-20131024 (accessed March 7, 2016).

47. Schwarz, "Recalibrating the Poverty Line."

48. Liana Fox, Christopher Wimer, Irwin Garfinkel, Neeraj Kaushal, and Jane Waldoger, "Waging War on Poverty: Poverty Trends Using a Historical Supplemental Poverty Measure," *Journal of Policy Analysis and Management* 34, no. 3 (2015): 567–92; Robert Haveman, Rebecca Blank, Robert Moffitt, Timothy Smeeding, and Geoffrey Wallace, "The War on Poverty: 50 Years Later," *Journal of Policy Analysis and Management* 34, no. 3 (2015): 593–638; Marianne P. Bitler and Lynn A. Karoly, "Intended and Unintended Effects of the War on Poverty: What Research Tells Us and Implications for Policy," *Journal of Policy Analysis and Management* 34, no. 3 (2015): 639–96.

49. Haveman, Blank, Moffitt, Smeeding, and Wallace, "The War on Poverty: 50 Years Later," 611.

50. Haveman, Blank, Moffitt, Smeeding, and Wallace, "The War on Poverty: 50 Years Later," 611. The Panel on Poverty and Family Assistance included Robert T. Michael (chair), University of Chicago; Anthony B. Atkinson, Oxford University; David M. Betson, University of Notre Dame; Rebecca M. Blank, Northwestern University; Lawrence Bobo, University of California, Los Angeles; Jeanne Brooks-Gunn, Columbia University; John F. Cogan, Stanford University; Sheldon H. Danziger, University of Michigan; Angus S. Deaton, Princeton University; David T. Ellwood, Harvard University; Judith M. Gueron, Manpower Demonstration Research Corporation; Robert M. Hauser, University of

Wisconsin; Franklin D. Wilson, University of Wisconsin; Constance F. Citro (study director); Nancy Maritato (research associate); Elaine Reardon (research associate); Agnes E. Gaskin (senior project assistant). See Constance F. Citro and Robert T. Michael (eds.), *Measuring Poverty: A New Approach* (Washington, DC: National Academy Press, 1995).

51. Citro and Michael, *Measuring Poverty: A New Approach*.

52. Citro and Michael, *Measuring Poverty: A New Approach*, 1.

53. Citro and Michael, *Measuring Poverty: A New Approach*; Haveman, Blank, Moffitt, Smeeding, and Wallace, "The War on Poverty: 50 Years Later," 611.

54. Social Security Administration, "The Social Security Act of 1935," https://www.ssa.gov/history/35act.html (accessed March 5, 2017); Public Law 104-193, August 22, 1996, "Personal Responsibility and Work Opportunity Reconciliation Act," https://www.gpo.gov/fdsys/pkg/PLAW-104publ193/pdf/PLAW-104publ193.pdf (accessed March 10, 2016).

55. Haveman, Blank, Moffitt, Smeeding, and Wallace, "The War on Poverty: 50 Years Later," 611–12.

56. Haveman, Blank, Moffitt, Smeeding, and Wallace, "The War on Poverty: 50 Years Later," 612.

57. Haveman, Blank, Moffitt, Smeeding, and Wallace, "The War on Poverty: 50 Years Later," 612–13.

58. Haveman, Blank, Moffitt, Smeeding, and Wallace, "The War on Poverty: 50 Years Later," 612–13; Victor R. Fuchs, "Redefining Poverty and Redistributing Income," *The Public Interest* 8 (1967): 88–95.

59. Fuchs, "Redefining Poverty and Redistributing Income," 89.

60. Fuchs, "Redefining Poverty and Redistributing Income," 93–4.

61. Fuchs, "Redefining Poverty and Redistributing Income," 95.

62. Patricia Ruggles, *Drawing the Line: Alternative Poverty Measures and Their Implications for Public Policy* (Washington, DC: Urban Institute Press, 1990), 15.

63. Ruggles, *Drawing the Line: Alternative Poverty Measures and Their Implications for Public Policy*, xv.

64. Lee Rainwater, *What Money Buys: Inequality and the Social Meanings of Income* (New York: Basic Books, 1974), 9.

65. Geoffrey Gilbert, *Rich and Poor in America: A Reference Handbook* (Santa Barbara, CA: ABC-CLIO, 2008), 135.

66. John Cassidy," Relatively Deprived: How Poor Is Poor?" *The New Yorker*, April 3, 2006, http://www.newyorker.com/magazine/2006/04/03/relatively-deprived (accessed April 13, 2016).

CHAPTER TWO

Historical Overview of Poverty-Relief Efforts in the United States

Regardless of political ideology, party affiliation, views of federalism, and the like, it is impossible to engage in welfare reform in the absence of sound theory. As I noted in an earlier work on education reform, "Plausible theory is essential in the pursuit of more scientific knowledge about education policy. In other words, a better command of ideas will promote the cause of education reform. Reform is not inevitable, and it does not systematically evolve by chance. In this noble campaign that we all universally endorse, our relative success is completely dependent on the human mind, the human spirit, and the political arena."[1] The oldest serving Supreme Court justice in history, Oliver Wendell Holmes Jr., once declared in the late 19th century:

> Theory is the most important part of the dogma of the law, as the architect is the most important man who takes part in the building of a house. The most important improvements in the last twenty-five years are improvements in theory. It is not to be feared as unpractical, for, to the competent, it simply means going to the bottom of the subject. For the incompetent, it sometimes is true, it has been said, that an interest in general ideas means an absence of particular knowledge. I remember in army days reading of a youth who, being examined for the lowest grade and being asked a question about squadron drill, answered that he never had considered the evolutions of less than ten thousand men. But the weak and foolish must be

left to their folly. The danger is that the able and practical minded should look with indifference or distrust upon the ideas the connection of which with their business is remote.[2]

In order to fully contend with the premise of reforming the social welfare system in the United States, a keen appreciation and understanding of theory are essential. Ultimately, if reform is to be achieved, it will be due to a sophisticated understanding and implementation of plausible theory in order to make the system more effective for citizens in the United States.

While Americans, both past and present, have typically been enamored with technological advancements, which are impressive to be sure, it is important to remember that many policy debates, including welfare reform, have been in existence for a very long time. We tend to think of such debates as novel, but this is oftentimes not the case. Indeed, many lessons can be extracted from history. What we decide to do with the knowledge in question is another matter altogether. Justice Holmes very succinctly identified the importance of history in law:

> At present, in very many cases, if we want to know why a rule of law has taken its particular shape, and more or less if we want to know why it exists at all, we go to tradition. We follow it in the Year Books, and perhaps beyond them to the customs of the Salian Franks, and somewhere in the past, in the German forests, in the needs of Norman kings, in the assumptions of a dominant class, in the absence of generalized ideas, we find out the practical motive for what now best is justified by the mere fact of its acceptance and that men are accustomed to it. The rational study of law is still to a large extent the study of history. History must be a part of the study, because without it we cannot know the precise scope of rules which it is our business to know. It is a part of the rational study, because it is the first step toward an enlightened skepticism, that is, toward a deliberate reconsideration of the worth of those rules. . . . For the rational study of the law the black-letter man may be the man of the present, but the man of the future is the man of statistics and the master of economics. It is revolting to have no better reason for a rule of law than that so it was laid down in the time of Henry IV. It is still more revolting if the grounds upon which it was laid down have vanished long since, and the rule simply persists from blind imitation of the past.[3]

The evolution of U.S. social welfare history is fairly replete and consistent. American policy makers have long struggled with addressing the vicissitudes of poverty. A remarkable account of this history was provided in 1978 by the social welfare historian James Leiby.[4]

The Evolution of Social Welfare in the United States

Leiby contends that from 1815 to 1845, a rural democracy prevailed in the United States, as an urban United States had not evolved yet:

> The urban-industrial style of life, which today has brought practically all Americans under the sway of its mass culture, began in a few scattered towns in a society that was agrarian, although it was already notably different from the more traditional agrarian societies of Europe. It took four or five generations for the new way of life to spread across the country. Occasionally, as in the case of San Francisco, a metropolis sprang into being and a hinterland grew up around it. More often, a crossroads market became the center of a specialized region. Before 1845 the characteristic interests and problems of urban-industrial life appeared in few places and not at all clearly; they came into view in the matrix of a rural democracy that seemed to embody essential norms of American life and provided a framework for our ideas about social welfare and its appropriate institutions.[5]

As Leiby notes, 1815 is a significant year, as it marked the end of the military phase of the War of 1812 following the signing of the Treaty of Ghent in late 1814.[6] Leiby offers the following summary for the period in question:

> To summarize the situation in the years 1815–1845, when the rural democracy was the unchallenged norm of American life, the basic idea of social justice was that of classical liberalism. Citizens were supposed to have equal rights (no legally privileged classes), substantially equal dignity of person, and equality of opportunity. Of course there were distinctions between rich and poor and inheritance was a factor, but these were matters of degree without sharp class divisions, and they were supposed to represent, in a rough, general way, differences of ability and effort. The ethical norm might be stated as follows: from each according to his inclination and talents, to each according to his achievements.
>
> In theory, the equality of rights applied to all adults; in fact, it was limited to men who shared European cultural backgrounds and norms of behavior. There were already movements toward a more inclusive definition in favor of equal rights for women, Africans, and Native Americans, but they did not have much support.
>
> The antecedents of modern social-welfare institutions came less from a secular ideal of social justice than from religious humanitarianism. To be sure, most people thought that social justice was a matter of following Christian moral precepts and that true Christianity, notably Protestantism, impelled society toward democratic values and forms (medieval Christianity, represented by Roman Catholicism, supported monarchy

and reaction, in this view). In fact American churches were democratic in their structure, dependent on the voluntary support of their members (no legally privileged or supported denomination), and politicians deferred to religious values if not to religious dogma.

For religious humanitarians the emphasis was on sympathy and duty. The unfortunate had a duty to bear up, to try to make the best of their situation. More to the point, the fortunate had a duty to help them.[7]

It is important to note that humanitarian reformers during the early decades of the 19th century focused on the individual, not on an entire class of people. Thus, the enemy of reformers was not the working class per se; the entity that needed to be addressed was ignorance and apathy in every social class.[8] Yet the context of the United States during this period is particularly noteworthy, for society then was very homogeneous; it was about to become more diverse and complicated by a number of operational measures.[9]

Post-1850 United States

The social order in the United States changed in the second half of the 19th century. The agrarian society that Thomas Jefferson envisioned was increasingly replaced by industrialization and urbanization. Throughout the 19th century, as the eminent historian Oscar Handlin highlighted in his many books, immigration continued from previous eras at an accelerated pace.[10] As he indicated in 1959:

Immigration had so long been a familiar aspect of American development that it was not until the end of the nineteenth century that any question was raised as to the propriety of its continuance. The whole history of the peopling of the continent had been one of immigration. The seventeenth century movement of population had brought the first settlements to the Atlantic seacoast. The eighteenth century newcomers had pushed those beyond the Alleghenys. And in the nineteenth century, a continued flow of new Americans had helped open the West and, at the same time, had contributed to the development of urban life and the growth of an industrial economy.

The nineteenth century migration to the United States had begun almost immediately after the restoration of peace in 1815. The first great, wave-like movement gathered strength steadily through the 1830's and 1840's, sweeping displaced Irish, German, and English peasants and laborers from the Old World to the New. Falling off in magnitude after 1854, the volume of new entries touched a low point in the mid-1860's. Then a second wave, made up primarily of Germans, Scandinavians, and Englishmen, reached its peak in 1882. Before the century was over, still a third wave was gathering momentum with a speed that was hardly checked when the outbreak of world war in 1914 brought it to a halt.[11]

For well over a century, immigration has been a contentious public policy issue. A comprehensive immigration policy has been debated by members of Congress for decades;[12] although legislative reform in this area has proven quite elusive. Immigration was a central issue in the 2016 presidential campaign, as Republican Donald Trump advocated building a wall that would cover 1,000 miles along the U.S.–Mexico border. To supporters, such a wall would reduce the number of illegal immigrants coming into the United States. Detractors of this measure contend that a wall of this magnitude would be a racist symbol, would be costly, and would denigrate the environment.[13]

Urban charities designed to assist the poor evolved due to the industrial revolution. Many workers were displaced from the factories as automated processes for creating a variety of goods were implemented. As a result, laborers found themselves competing with others for scarce jobs with very limited government regulations in place to protect workers from unsavory business practices.[14]

As Leiby details, urban charities were formulated in the United States between 1845 and 1900.[15] By 1850, immigrant slums were common in seaports in the United States, and state and city government officials did little by way of social policy to address the depravity that existed there. In the mid-19th century, it became clear that those with religious interests and motives were most inclined to create institutional responses to poverty. There were two broad intervention approaches: protestant groups, which were largely external to the immigrant groups in question, and the immigrants themselves, who attempted to create forms of mutual assistance for their peers. The groups tended to be hostile toward one another, which was ironic in that they shared many religious assumptions about humanity and spirituality.[16] It was during this time that organizations such as the Young Men's Christian Association (YMCA) and the Salvation Army were created.[17] The YMCA was organized in Boston in 1851, and the Salvation Army commenced in Philadelphia in 1880. Both organizations started in England initially.[18]

A common approach to attending to the needy in the 19th century was through an almshouse, which can be traced back to England in the 10th century.[19] According to a researcher at the Social Welfare History Project at Virginia Commonwealth University:

Between the 1820s and the late nineteenth century there was a huge growth in the number of poorhouses in America. Some were small, even homey, and held ten or twelve people with a superintendent and a matron, usually his unpaid wife. Large cities and some states had more notorious concrete block institutions which held thousands. Among the most notorious was the Tewksbury Almshouse in Massachusetts, near the large industrial center of Lowell. Bellevue Almshouse in New York City, now Bellevue Hospital, and Cook County Almshouse in Chicago, later Cook County Hospital, were other examples of large poorhouses. Over time, who entered the almshouse changed. For most of the nineteenth century, unemployed men came in and out of the poorhouses, and a large permanent population of people, including the aged, mentally and physically disabled, constituted the bulk of the "inmates." Reformers made efforts to remove from the poorhouses the mentally ill (an objective of the famous Dorothea Dix), children, the "feeble minded" (developmentally disabled) and "fallen women" (women perceived as immoral or prostitutes). As these reforms gained momentum, most people who had no choice but to stay in poorhouses were elderly. . . . Despite the horror that poorhouses conjured, the ingenuity of the poor and disabled and their resilience often undermined reformers' plans. Shortly after the Civil War, because of the 14th Amendment to the U.S. Constitution against "involuntary servitude," poorhouses became technically "voluntary," like today's homeless shelters. You could not be forced physically to remain there. Some people who were convicted of drinking or loitering could still be forced into an institution, but by the late nineteenth century, these were usually workhouses or houses of correction.[20]

A historian working in the Department of Health, Education, and Welfare noted in the late 1960s that almshouses provided poverty and medical relief for a number of citizens in the United States during the 19th century in particular. However, while it may be that some Americans at that time, especially those living in cities, benefitted from the existence of almshouses, there were others who quite literally experienced sheer misery in these institutions:

> During this period, the almshouse was extolled as the best means of caring for the destitute, albeit some were at pains to condemn it. Numbers of benevolent citizens were proud that their communities were presumably taking such good care of their dependents. Given the circumstances of the people the almshouses served and the fact that urban almshouses were largely free hospitals extending good medical care, these 19th Century communities *were* [italics in original] making admirable provision for their "worthy" and even their "unworthy" poor. . . .
>
> In rural areas the almshouse was likely to be bad, and often scandalously bad. Often it was nothing more than some poor farmer and his wife trying to manage some pitiful old sick people and cast-off children in a run-down house. Often no physician was in attendance. Even where housing, staff, and medical care were somewhat better, as would appear to have

been the case in the more prosperous townships and counties, almshouses were apt to be overcrowded and their facilities rapidly deteriorating, conditions that demoralized the staff and the dependents.

The idea that the "worthy" poor—the widows, the children, the sick, the aged—could be separated from the "unworthy" poor—the drunkards, the idlers, the thriftless, and the shiftless—persisted. But one is struck by the generally good intentions, the charitable spirit, the expression of community responsibility evident in the writings of politicians, of almshouses trustees, of physicians—in short those who came in direct contact with the poor.

Of course, the poor were forgotten for long stretches of time. They always are. . . . That not much in the way of improvement followed should not surprise our generation which has undoubtedly done better—but perhaps not much better.[21]

Coll's words almost 50 years ago are a reminder that, despite honorable intentions, humans are still struggling to find a way to assist those in need. A comprehensive history of almshouses in Philadelphia published in 1905 highlights that almshouses in that important seaport city date back to the early 1700s.[22] The conditions of these institutions designed to provide poverty relief to the less fortunate were deplorable in many instances:

The arrangements for heating and ventilating the Insane Department were very poor in 1849. Stoves were used for furnishing heat, but they did not accomplish the object. The poor unfortunates in that part of the institution suffered severely with the extreme cold. No one could imagine the effect it would have on them to be confined in wards where the temperature was below the freezing point; it certainly would not assist in their recovery. Feeble, demented creatures, whose bodies were not always properly covered with suitable clothing, could not endure it as well as the strong, healthier people, although it must have been very trying to all in the place.

The Board instructed Dr. Benedict to make tests with thermometers and to report the results. In February he presented a statement, in which he said: "On the first floor of the west wing of the Women's Lunatic Asylum, at about 9 o'clock A.M., found that a towel which a nurse was using to wipe one of the patients, in one of the cells, had frozen. The patient was a very delicate woman, and altogether unfit to be placed in such a temperature.

"This morning one of the patients was found under the bed, on the floor, wrapped up in the bedclothes. All water in the room was frozen. The thermometer stood at from 13 to 18 degrees. On the same day, at 2 o'clock P.M., the thermometer stood at 27 degrees in the cells, and 24 degrees in the open air. . . . What a horrible condition."[23]

The general conditions, for those afflicted with disease, mental challenges, and disabilities, never mind the plight of impoverished babies and children, would have been unimaginable by contemporary standards.

An account of a Philadelphia almshouse in 1856 by the chief resident physician illustrates the foresight of Coll's commentary of yesteryear:

> The following extracts from the report of the Chief Resident Physician show a terrible state of affairs, and reflect no credit upon any one connected with the management of the institution. The doctor said:
>
> "I have the honor to state: This institution, usually called the Almshouse, comprises within it a smallpox hospital, a lunatic asylum, a children's asylum, a lying-in department, a nursery, a hospital for medical, surgical, venerial and mania-a-potu cases; besides the Almshouse properly so called, which is in reality an infirmary for the blind, the lame, the superannuated, and other incurables so decrepit as not to be able to earn for themselves a livelihood.
>
> "The number of able-bodied men and women, although to the eye of the casual observer apparently large, is really comparatively small and consists chiefly of those vagrants who spend their lives in alternating between the low down dens of vice throughout the city, the county prison and this institution.
>
> "These are the ones who disgrace themselves and humanity, and by their presence bring a stigma upon the afflicted and the unfortunate, who are compelled here to seek relief and support, which would not attach to them if this place was in name, and, in the opinion of many in the community, what it is in reality, a hospital. These constitute the proper subjects for a House of Correction, which is so urgently required."[24]

Whether we consider the 19th century or the contemporary period, it would appear that solutions to the challenges inherent in the sheer existence of poverty have proven quite elusive.[25] A common theme that reverberates throughout the ages is that societal interventions are most definitely impacted by cultural beliefs, mores, and attitudes about the indigent.

Between 1850 and 1900, many character-building institutions were established in the United States.[26] These included prisons, mental institutions, houses of correction, and houses for wayward youth. The strategy of reformers was to change the moral behavior of individuals by modifying the environment in which they lived as well as by purposefully controlling their behavior.[27] Later, as the Progressive Era evolved, a different approach to social welfare would be implemented by social reformers.[28] A dominant paradigm in the 18th and 19th centuries was that humans were inclined to pursue pleasure and avoid work except when offered a material incentive. Reformers in the late 19th and early 20th centuries tended to emphasize that people are complicated and have diverse interests and a broad array of motives.[29] Rapid changes were also occurring in American society. A rural populist movement mobilized farmers in the Midwest and the South in the 1890s; farmers collectively opposed the low agricultural prices at that time, and they did not like being charged high rates by granary and railroad officials. They also opposed unsavory corporate leaders and Wall Street bankers.[30] Very significant changes occurred during this period of industrialization in American society:

> Immigrants bore the brunt of the negative consequences of industrialization in the northern and midwestern cities of the North. Roughly 21 million of the total population of 92 million Americans in 1911 were immigrants who had come to America between 1880 and 1914. Major American cities consisted of separate settlements, each with its own churches, political machines, and newspapers. Forty percent of the populations of the 12 largest cities consisted of immigrants, and another 20 percent of them were second-generation descendants; and 60 percent of the American labor force was foreign-born. The immigrants came from many European nations and possessed distinctive cultures.[31]

The end of the 19th and beginning of the 20th century was a fascinating time of social, political, cultural, and economic change in the United States.

The Progressive Era

A capsule summary of the Progressive Era (1890–1920) is provided below:

> Progressivism is the term applied to a variety of responses to the economic and social problems rapid industrialization introduced to America. Progressivism began as a social movement and grew into a political movement. The early Progressives rejected Social Darwinism. In other words, they were people who believed that the problems society faced (poverty, violence, greed, racism, class warfare) could be best addressed by providing good education, a safe environment, and an efficient workplace. Progressives lived mainly in the cities, were college educated, and believed that government could be a tool for change. Social reformers, like Jane Addams, and journalists, like Jacob Riis and Ida Tarbel, were powerful voices for progressivism. They concentrated on exposing the evils of corporate greed, combating fear of immigrants, and urging Americans to think hard about what democracy meant. Other local leaders encouraged Americans to register to vote, fight political corruption, and let the voting public decide how issues should best be addressed (the initiative, the referendum, and the recall). On a national level, progressivism gained a strong voice in the White House when Theodore Roosevelt became president in

1901. TR believed that strong corporations were good for America, but he also believed that corporate behavior must be watched to ensure that corporate greed did not get out of hand (trust-busting and federal regulation of business). Progressivism ended with World War I when the horrors of war exposed people's cruelty and many Americans associated President Woodrow Wilson's use of progressive language ("the war to make the world safe for democracy") with the war.[32]

The Democrat Woodrow Wilson was elected president in 1912 by garnering only 41.8 percent of the popular vote; in so doing, he received 435 electoral votes as he won 40 states. Former Republican president Theodore Roosevelt ran as a Progressive and finished second in the popular vote with 27.4 percent and second in the electoral college as well with 88 votes (he carried the states of Pennsylvania, Michigan, Minnesota, South Dakota, Washington, and California). The incumbent Republican president William Howard Taft only received 23.2 percent of the popular vote with 8 electoral votes (he won Vermont and Utah). The Socialist candidate, Eugene V. Debs, won 6 percent of the popular vote but no states.[33] Clearly, a split Republican Party had benefitted Wilson greatly; four years later, in 1916, the Republicans were unified. In spite of this reality, Wilson was able to narrowly secure reelection over Republican Charles Evans Hughes. He received 49.2 percent of the popular vote and 277 electoral votes; Hughes secured 46.1 percent of the popular vote and 254 electoral votes (Wilson won 30 out of 48 states).[34]

For many immigrants during the Progressive Era, life was often downright abysmal. Without food regulations and modern refrigeration, food poisoning was quite commonplace.[35] Published in 1906, Upton Sinclair's *The Jungle* exposed the brutal conditions of the meat-packing industry in the United States in the early 20th century:[36]

It was a long, narrow room, with a gallery along it for visitors. At the head there was a great iron wheel, about twenty feet in circumference, with rings here and there along its edge. Upon both sides of this wheel there was a narrow space, into which came the hogs at the end of their journey; in the midst of them stood a great burly Negro, bare-armed and bare-chested. He was resting for a moment, for the wheel had stopped while men were cleaning up. In a minute or two, however, it began slowly to revolve, and then the men upon each side of it sprang to work. They had chains which they fastened about the leg of the nearest hog, and the other end of the chain they hooked into one of the rings upon the wheel. So, as the wheel turned, a hog was suddenly jerked off his feet and borne aloft.

At the same instant the ear was assailed by a most terrifying shriek; the visitors started in alarm, the women pale and shrank back. The shriek was followed by another, louder and yet more agonizing—for once started upon that journey, the hog never came back; at the top of the wheel he was shunted off upon a trolley, and went sailing down the room. And meantime another was swung up, and then another, and another, until there was a double line of them, each dangling by a foot and kicking in frenzy— and squealing. The uproar was appalling, perilous to the ear-drums; one feared there was too much sound for the room to hold—that the walls must give way or the ceiling crack. There were high squeals and low squeals, grunts, and wails of agony; there would come a momentary lull, and then a fresh outburst, louder than ever, surging up to a deafening climax.[37]

Even though there were government meat inspectors, that did not mean that the food supply was safe. Sinclair's revelations would have a profound effect on American society. As he noted in Chicago in 1906:

The people of Chicago saw the government inspectors in Packingtown, and they all took that to mean that they were protected from diseased meat; they did not understand that these hundred and sixty-three inspectors had been appointed at the request of the packers, and that they were paid by the United States government to certify that all the diseased meat was kept in the state. They had no authority beyond that; for the inspection of meat to be sold in the city and state the whole force in Packingtown consisted of three henchmen of the local political machine! And shortly afterward one of these, a physician, made the discovery that the carcasses of steers which had been condemned as tubercular by the government inspectors, and which therefore contained ptomaines, which are deadly poisons, were left upon an open platform and carted away to be sold in the city; and so he insisted that these carcasses be treated with an injection of kerosene—and was ordered to resign the same week! So indignant were the packers that they went further, and compelled the mayor to abolish the whole bureau of inspection; so that since then there has not been even a pretense of any interference with the graft. There was said to be two thousand dollars a week hush-money from the tubercular steers alone; and as much again from the hogs which had died of cholera on the trains, and which you might see any day being loaded into box-cars and hauled away to a place called Globe, in Indiana, where they made a fancy grade of lard.[38]

In addition to the gruesome treatment of animals, as well as the unimaginable disregard to public health, workers were treated with vast indifference in the pursuit of profiteering:

There were men in the pickle-rooms, for instance, where old Antanas had gotten his death; scarce a one of these that had not some spot of horror on his person. Let a man so much as scrape his finger pushing a truck in the pickle-rooms, and he might have a sore that would put him out of the world; all the joints in his fingers might be eaten by the acid, one by one. Of the butchers and floorsmen, the beef-boners and trimmers, and all those who used knives, you could scarcely find a person who had the use of his thumb; time and time again the base of it had been slashed, till it was a mere lump of flesh against which the man pressed the knife to hold it. The hands of these men would be criss-crossed with cuts, until you could no longer pretend to count them or to trace them. They would have no nails,—they had worn them off pulling hides; their knuckles were swollen so that their fingers spread out like a fan. There were men who worked in the cooking-rooms, in the midst of steam and sickening odors, by artificial light; in these rooms the germs of tuberculosis might live for two years, but the supply was renewed every hour. . . . There were the "hoisters," as they were called, whose task it was to press the lever which lifted the dead cattle off the floor. They ran along the rafter, peering down through the damp and the steam; and as old Durham's architects had not built the killing-room for the convenience of the hoisters, at every few feet they would have to stoop under a beam, say four feet above the one they ran on; which got them into the habit of stooping, so that in a few years they would be walking like chimpanzees. Worst of any, however, were the fertilizer-men, and those who served in the cooking-rooms. These people could not be shown to the visitor,—for the odor of a fertilizer-man would scare any ordinary visitor at a hundred yards, and as for the other men, who worked in tank-rooms full of steam, and in some of which there were open vats near the level of the floor, their peculiar trouble was that they fell into the vats; and when they were fished out, there was never enough of them left to be worth exhibiting,—sometimes they would be overlooked for days, till all but the bones of them had gone out to the world as Durham's Pure Leaf Lard![39]

The Progressives succeeded in persuading members of Congress to pass legislation regulating product quality between 1906 and 1915. Among the key acts passed were the Pure Food and Drug Act (1906), the Federal Meat Inspection Act (1906), the Federal Trade Commission (1914), and the Clayton Act (1914).[40] Clearly, President Theodore Roosevelt was influenced by Sinclair as he relied on his account of the packinghouses in Chicago to protect the poor and society in general. In his own words: "There were many other things that we did in connection with corporations. One of the most important was the passage of the meat inspection law because of scandalous abuses shown to exist in the great packing-houses of Chicago and elsewhere."[41]

It is noteworthy that public opinion and leaders such as presidents Theodore Roosevelt and Woodrow Wilson prompted the members of the various sessions of Congress to respond to national calamities; these actions suggest that though Americans tend to indicate to pollsters that they do not like "big government," they nevertheless expect congressional action in a time of crisis.[42] This reality has been evidenced since Congress created the Interstate Commerce Commission in 1887, which was basically the beginning of the Progressive Era.[43]

Beyond the Progressive Era

The United States reverted to a conservative disposition following the departure of Woodrow Wilson from the White House in 1921. In the 1920 presidential election, Republican Warren Harding defeated Democrat James Cox by a significant margin. Harding received 60.3 percent of the popular vote and 404 electoral votes; Cox garnered 34.1 percent of the popular vote and 127 electoral votes.[44] Harding died unexpectedly in 1923; Americans would later become aware of many scandals involving some of his key officials, although Harding himself was not involved in any criminal misdeeds.[45] Vice-President Calvin Coolidge became president and was subsequently elected to his own term in 1924 by a wide margin over Democrat John W. Davis. Coolidge garnered 54 percent of the popular vote and 382 electoral votes; Davis won 28.8 percent of the popular vote and 136 electoral votes; Progressive Robert LaFollette received 16.6 percent of the popular vote, and he prevailed in Wisconsin with its 13 electoral votes.[46] In 1928, Coolidge chose not to seek reelection. The Republicans nominated Herbert Hoover, and he defeated Democrat Alfred Smith handily. He garnered 58.2 percent of the popular vote and 444 electoral votes; Smith's tally of the popular vote was 40.8 percent with 87 corresponding electoral votes.[47] The United States' repudiation of the progressive policies of the past was replete with three consecutive conservative Republican presidential electoral landslides. The Roaring Twenties were famously captured by a noteworthy author in 1925.[48] In *The Great Gatsby*, F. Scott Fitzgerald provided an account of the fabulously wealthy Jay Gatsby, who seemingly represented the wealth of the period, at least for a select few:

> There was music from my neighbor's house through the summer nights. In his blue gardens men and girls came and went like moths among the whisperings and the champagne and the stars. At high tide in the afternoon I watched his guests driving from the tower of his raft, or taking the sun on the hot sand of his beach while his two motor- boats slit the waters of the Sound, drawing aquaplanes over cataracts of foam. On week-ends his Rolls-Royce became an omnibus, bearing parties to and from the city between nine in the morning and long past midnight, while his station wagon scampered like a brisk yellow bug to meet all trains. And on

Mondays eight servants, including an extra gardener, toiled all day with mops and scrubbing-brushes and hammers and garden- shears, repairing the ravages of the night before. . . .

At least once a fortnight a corps of caterers came down with several hundred feet of canvas and enough colored lights to make a Christmas tree of Gatsby's enormous garden. On buffet tables, garnished with glistening hors d'oeuvre, spiced baked hams crowded against salads of harlequin designs and pastry pigs and turkeys bewitched to a dark gold. In the main hall a bar with a real brass rail was set up, and stocked with gins and liquors and with cordials so long forgotten that most of his female guests were too young to know one from another.[49]

Fitzgerald documented the substantial divide between most Americans' daily lives and the extreme wealth experienced by the very few. As history would have it, the beauty, romance, and mysticism depicted by Fitzgerald was temporal and short-lived, ending when the stock market crashed in October of 1929.[50] It was described in the following manner by one source:

The Roaring Twenties roared loudest and longest on the New York Stock Exchange. Share prices rose to unprecedented heights. The Dow Jones Industrial Average increased six-fold from sixty-three in August 1921 to 381 in September 1929. After prices peaked, economist Irving Fisher proclaimed, "stock prices have reached 'what looks like a permanently high plateau.'"

The epic boom ended in a cataclysmic bust. On Black Monday, October 28, 1929, the Dow declined nearly 13 percent. On the following day, Black Tuesday, the market dropped nearly 12 percent. By mid-November, the Dow had lost almost half of its value. The slide continued through the summer of 1932, when the Dow closed at 41.22, its lowest value of the twentieth century, 89 percent below its peak. The Dow did not return to its pre-crash heights until November 1954.[51]

The stock market crash would plunge the nation into the Great Depression, which was the worst economic calamity of the 20th century. As a result of the very serious and sobering realities of poverty and unemployment that followed the crash, the Republicans were rebuked in the next several presidential elections, beginning with Franklin D. Roosevelt's first victory in 1932.

The Republicans nominated the incumbent Hoover for another term. Roosevelt, who was James Cox's vice-presidential running mate in 1920, was the Democratic nominee. He promised Americans a "New Deal" if elected.[52] Hoover was routed out of office by 57.4 percent to 39.6 percent in the popular vote and 472 to 59 in the electoral college.[53] One explanation for Hoover's defeat was as follows:

> As the Depression worsened in the 1930s, causing severe hardships for millions of Americans, many looked to the federal government for assistance. When the government failed to provide relief, President Herbert Hoover (1874–1964) was blamed for the intolerable economic and social conditions, and the shantytowns that cropped up across the nation, primarily on the outskirts of major cities, became known as Hoovervilles.[54]

Roosevelt prevailed in the next three presidential elections (1936, 1940, and 1944) by sizable margins.[55] In 1936, he defeated Alfred Landon in the popular vote, 60.8 percent to 36.5 percent. It is exceedingly rare for a U.S. presidential candidate to garner more than 60 percent of the popular vote. The electoral tally was 523 to 8.[56] In 1940, Roosevelt won an unprecedented third term over Wendell Willkie by garnering 54.7 percent of the popular vote to 44.8 percent, which corresponded to an electoral margin of 449 to 82.[57] Four years later, during World War II, Roosevelt won a fourth term over Thomas Dewey, 53.4 percent to 45.9 percent, and 432 to 99 in the electoral college.[58] Thus, none of Roosevelt's four Republican opponents achieved 100 or more electoral votes in their campaigns against him. Shortly into his fourth term, on April 12, 1945, however, Roosevelt died, leaving his vice-president at the time, Harry Truman, to become the new president.[59]

The transition from the Progressive Era to the eventual New Deal was abrupt. Following the ratification of the 19th Amendment in 1920, Progressives would not have another major political victory until the New Deal era. As one historian of the time period noted:

> The 1920s were, Jane Addams sadly concluded, "a period of political and social sag." Progressive activists achieved a few victories such as the Sheppard-Towner Act of 1921, which provided modest federal funds to support instruction in hygiene for expectant and new mothers. But reformers by and large had to sit back and watch the Republican administrations of Warren G. Harding, Calvin Coolidge, and Herbert Hoover pursue a politics of individualism and laissez-faire. Influenced by his experiences in the Wilson government, Hoover tried to promote collaborative "association" between government and businessmen. Yet, essentially the Republicans gutted the economic accomplishments of the Progressive Era by cutting the hated income tax, ignoring organized labor and the poor, and allowing big business to dominate federal regulatory agencies. The 1920s made clear that the progressives had seriously overestimated the power and the will of the state to limit corporations.[60]

As demonstrated in their electoral behavior in the three presidential elections in the 1920s, Americans reverted to a time of deregulation, libertarianism, and relative inwardness. Ironically, this approach to federalism and regulatory matters is what prompted the advent of the Progressive Era and certainly illustrates the general tendency of Americans to take a cyclical approach to questions of federalism and the role of government in the economy and society. Simply put, the pendulum shifted back to the right during the 1920s. There was also a religious component to the shift back to conservatism in the 1920s:

> Republican conservatives were just as sure that God had in fact blessed the world—or at least America—once again. "The radicalism which had tinged our whole political and economic life from soon after 1900 to the World War period was passed," Calvin Coolidge contentedly observed. "There were still echoes of it, and some of its votaries remained, but its power was gone." Looking back years later, Coolidge explained that "the demobilization of the country was practically complete, people had found themselves again, and were ready to undertake the grand work of reconstruction in which they have since been so successfully engaged." Caught up in the joy of that moment, Coolidge—taciturn in public, acerbic in private—allowed himself to talk like a progressive. "In that work we have seen the people of America create a new heaven and a new earth," Coolidge rhapsodized. "The old things have passed away, giving place to a glory never before experienced by any people of our world." For many years, it was the progressives who had imagined utopia—"a new heaven and a new earth"—and summoned the nation to build it. Now Coolidge and the conservatives claimed the right to dream and lead. The "old things" had indeed "passed away": progressive ideas would linger, occasional progressive legislation would still pass; but the Progressive Era was over.[61]

The events that occurred during the Hoover administration, particularly between 1929 and 1932, would change the return to "normalcy" that Warren Harding promulgated in 1920:

> America's present need is not heroics, but healing; not nostrums but normalcy; not revolution, but restoration; not agitation, but adjustment; not surgery, but serenity; not the dramatic, but the dispassionate; not experiment, but equipoise; not submergence in internationality, but sustainment in triumphant nationality. It is one thing to battle successfully against world domination by military autocracy, because the infinite God never intended such a program, but it is quite another thing to revise human nature and suspend the fundamental laws of life and all of life's acquirements.[62]

Confronted with the realities of dramatic unemployment, lost fortunes and savings, significantly depressed stock prices, and rampant poverty, Americans grew wary of Hoover's pleas for patience and insistence that the marketplace would largely correct itself.[63] Even though many reforms would be implemented during the New Deal, it is important to note that in the 1932 presidential campaign, Franklin Roosevelt did not run as a Progressive or Liberal. He did offer more rhetorical and policy support for the unemployed, and Americans ultimately repudiated Hoover's policies and decided to give Roosevelt, and the Democrats, a chance to revive the bleak economy.[64]

The New Deal Era

Leiby captured the essence of Herbert Hoover's thinking during the early years of the Depression during his tenure as president:

> Just as Hoover thought of the Depression as a temporary emergency, pending recovery, so he thought that unemployment relief was properly a temporary emergency that called for a special organization. It was like a flood, famine, or war. Hoover was disposed to think in these terms because he had made his first great public reputation in the World War and its aftermath as an administrator of war relief, and in 1927, as Secretary of Commerce, he had masterfully organized a major flood relief effort in the Mississippi Valley. He had a wide acquaintance and following among philanthropists and social workers of the sort that turned up in the American Red Cross, which mobilized resources for disasters, and community chests, which furnished a nucleus of professional staff for local disaster relief. As for administrative organization, he thought it should be largely volunteer and local. Of course outside help was necessary, but it should be channeled through a makeshift arrangement of local people. It should help local people help each other, drawing extensively on their firsthand knowledge of the situation and the resources available.[65]

Under duress, Americans rejected Hoover's conservative ideology and adherence to social Darwinism. Hoover equated federal social programs with the socialist ideology; Americans at the time, however, expected federal intervention due to the size and magnitude of the economic calamities that persisted over time.[66]

To put Roosevelt's 1932 victory into historical context, his victory in the electoral college ranks him 11 out of 58 presidential elections, capturing almost 89 percent of the electoral votes. His victory in the popular vote, where he won by about 18 percent, ranks him 9 out of 49 elections.[67] In 1933, however, the inauguration date for new presidents was still March 4. Thus, Roosevelt had to wait about four months after his decisive victory before he could implement policies to address the numerous economic and social challenges that existed in the country at the time. Due to the implementation of the 20th Amendment, however, the inauguration date was changed to January 20; Roosevelt would be the first president inaugurated on this date (in 1937, following his second election victory).[68]

In order to provide poverty relief for the American people, Roosevelt persuaded members of Congress to pass, and he signed, 15 major bills in his first 100 days of presidential action (March 9 to June 16, 1933). In terms of financial reforms, the following laws were passed during this time: Emergency Banking Act (March 9), Government Economy Act (March 20), Abandonment of the Gold Standard (April 19), Securities Act (May 27), Abrogation of Gold Payment Clause (June 5), Home Owners Loan Act (June 13), and Glass-Steagall Banking Act (June 16). With regard to jobs and economic relief, the following laws were created: Creation of Civilian Conservation Corps (March 31), Federal Emergency Relief Act (May 12), National Industrial Recovery Act (June 16), and Emergency Railroad Transportation Act (June 16). Rural reforms were pursued through the following laws: Agricultural Adjustment Act (May 12), Emergency Farm Mortgage Act (May 12), Tennessee Valley Authority Act (May 18), and Farm Credit Act (June 16).[69] The economy in the United States was in shambles. Unemployment was approximately 25 percent of the adult population.[70] The situation in the United States was quite bleak:

> The strongest pressure for reform derived, however, from the magnitude of human suffering that existed during the decade of the 1930s. . . . Persons of all social classes were devastated by economic suffering and resorted to desperate and improvisational survival strategies. Some persons moved into tents in the countryside during the summer; three or more families shared apartments; groups of single women shared apartments and lived from the wages of a single worker; persons tried to grow produce in gardens; and teenagers roamed the countryside when their families could not support them. Lorena Hickok, a woman reporter who was commissioned by Eleanor Roosevelt to tour the country in a car, wrote daily letters to her in which she documented the suffering of members of all social classes. White-collar Americans feared foreclosure or evictions, had to pawn family possessions, feared their neighbors would discover they were on relief, and shunned wearing clothes that were made in the sewing rooms of relief programs. Malnutrition and starvation were widely reported; in some cases, thousands of children were placed in summer camps to give them adequate food. Medical care was lacking for members of all classes since many physicians and hospitals refused service to destitute persons. Many persons lacked funds, even when on welfare, to heat or light their homes or to purchase clothing. Foreclosures, evictions, layoffs, family disruption, and suicides were commonplace. When touring major American cities in 1932, Harry Hopkins observed that the hundreds of thousands of

Americans who lined the streets to watch FDR's procession did not protest, yell, or applaud but stood in stunned silence.[71]

In addition to the high level of unemployment, it is estimated that during the 1930s, the poverty rate in the United States was 60 percent of the population or higher (recall that poverty was not officially measured in the United States at this time—see chapter 1).[72] Thus, Roosevelt had to put Americans back to work in order to have any hope of alleviating the dramatic poverty challenges that existed at the time. In addition to the jobs programs delineated above, a central act in American history, designed in large part to alleviate poverty, was signed in the summer of 1935.

The Social Security Act of 1935

Roosevelt signed the Social Security Act on August 14, 1935.[73] It was largely the product of the Committee on Economic Security (CES), which was created by Executive Order 6757 on June 29, 1934.[74] According to the order, "The Committee shall study problems relating to the economic security of individuals and shall report to the President not later than December 1, 1934, its recommendations concerning proposals which in its judgment will promote greater economic security."[75] The primary participants of the committee included the chair, Frances Perkins (secretary of labor from 1933 to 1945), Henry Morgenthau (secretary of treasury from 1934 to 1945), Homer Cummings (U.S. attorney general from 1933 to 1939), Henry Wallace (secretary of agriculture from 1933 to 1940 and later vice-president), Harry Hopkins (director of the Federal Emergency Relief Administration from 1933 to 1935), and Professor Edwin Witte (executive staff director and an economist at the University of Wisconsin).[76] Basically, the committee members were charged with creating a social insurance program in half a year.[77] In early January 1935, the members of the CES submitted their report to Roosevelt.[78]

The social insurance movement did not begin with Franklin Roosevelt or his subordinates. By the time the members of Congress passed the Social Security Act in late 1935, there were already 34 nations with some form of social insurance program in operation. The first was adopted in Germany in 1889 at the urging of Chancellor Otto von Bismarck.[79] While the definition of social insurance can vary, it is basically premised on insuring people in some manner against a discernible risk; typically the program is created not to address the needs of a specific individual per se but to address broader social policy objectives.[80]

Some contend that Frances Perkins was the primary architect not only of the New Deal but of the Social Security Act as well.[81] Others label Edwin Witte as the father of the Social Security Act.[82] As Perkins would later recall about her experience on the CES,

I've always said, and I still think we have to admit, that no matter how much fine reasoning there was about the old-age insurance system and the unemployment insurance prospects—no matter how many people were studying it, or how many committees had ideas on the subject, or how many college professors had written theses on the subject—and there were an awful lot of them—the real roots of the Social Security Act were in the great depression of 1929. Nothing else would have bumped the American people into a social security system except something so shocking, so terrifying, as that depression.[83]

Ultimately, the Social Security Act was passed in the U.S. House of Representatives on April 19, 1935, by a vote of 372 to 33. Two people voted present and 25 members did not vote. Of the 372 affirmative votes, 284 were Democrats, 81 were Republicans, and 7 were affiliated with other parties. This translates into a 91.4 percent affirmation rate of all those who voted. The negative votes were evenly split between Democrats and Republicans (15 each) and were joined by 3 members from other parties. Two months later, on June 19, 1935, the members of the Senate endorsed the measure by a vote of 77 to 6. Sixty Democrats and 16 Republicans supported it along with 1 member from another party, 5 Republicans and 1 Democrat voted against it, and 12 senators did not vote. This translates into a 92.8 percent affirmation vote of all senators who voted. Since the bills were different, a conference committee was created to work out the differences between the two versions of the bill. The conferees met throughout the month of July. The conference report was passed by voice vote in the House on August 8, 1935, and in the Senate on August 9, 1935.[84]

A basic summary of the Social Security Act is as follows:

The Act created several programs that, even today, form the basis for the government's role in providing income security, specifically, the old-age insurance, unemployment insurance, and Aid to Families with Dependent Children (AFDC) programs. The old-age program is, of course, the precursor to today's Old-Age, Survivors, and Disability Insurance, or Social Security, program. Unemployment insurance continues to this day, and AFDC is the forerunner to the current Temporary Assistance for Needy Families program. The original Act also provided federal support for means-tested old-age assistance programs run by the states, which were eventually transformed into the current Supplemental Security Income (SSI) program. The original Act also contained provisions allowing for research on the topic of health insurance, but the Medicare program would not come into existence until 30 years later.[85]

Under the initial rules of the program, a 1 percent tax on both employees and employers (thus 2 percent total) was assessed on the first $3,000 in annual earnings. In the original law, benefits would not be sent to citizens until 1942. This allowed the program to build a reserve fund in advance of sending money to beneficiaries.[86] After many subsequent changes over the last 80 years, the Social Security tax in 2017 is 7.65 percent for both the employee and employer (thus, 15.3 percent total) on the first $127,200 in annual earnings.[87]

The Social Security Act was an omnibus bill containing seven different programs: old-age assistance (federal financial support and oversight of state-based social welfare programs for older Americans), federal retirement benefits (Social Security), unemployment insurance (national unemployment insurance that provided federal funding and state administration of the program), Aid to Dependent Children (state-based social welfare for children in need; it would later be called Aid to Families with Dependent Children), grants to states covering maternal and child welfare (federal funding of state programs for expectant mothers and newborn babies), public health work (federal funding of state public health programs), and aid to the blind (federal funding of state programs to aid the blind).[88] Aid to Dependent Children (ADC) has been described in the following manner:

> Aid to Dependent Children or ADC (later renamed Aid to Families with Dependent Children [AFDC]) was Title IV of the Social Security Act of 1935. At first it functioned mainly to provide federal grants to help the states maintain their mothers' aid laws that had been passed in 40 states between 1910 and 1920. With the federal government providing 1/3 of costs, the program offered aid to poor parents, imagined at that time to be always female, caring for children without a husband.
>
> The ADC plan was written by the previous and current directors of the U.S. Children's Bureau in the Department of Labor, Grace Abbott and Katherine Lenroot. They lobbied hard to get this program added to the Social Security bill, which was aimed at male breadwinners, reflecting the masculinist assumptions and composition of the Committee on Economic Security (CES) that wrote the bill. The Children's Bureau's goal was to provide aid to all children whose mothers lacked the support of a breadwinner, no matter how they got to that position. Moreover, Abbott and Lenroot designed it to operate with the highest social work standards, offering personal casework services to lone mothers as well as cash stipends. They sought casework both because they wanted to remove ADC recipients from the stigma of public assistance, and because they believed that mother-headed families were problematic and needed support and guidance.[89]

The original ADC program was in existence until 1961.[90] ADC was formally changed to AFDC for cultural reasons, and the program took effect under its new name in 1962:

Although the ADC subsidy was originally intended to allow mothers to stay at home to care for their children, a series of cultural, demographic, and policy shifts related to marriage, poverty, and women's employment began to undermine public support for that goal. Concerns about whether the ADC subsidy inadvertently encouraged unwed motherhood arose early on in some states. From a federal perspective, these concerns were short circuited by the perception that ADC was a program for families headed by widows. In 1939, however, Survivors Benefits were added to the mainstream Social Security program that separately aided widows—the most "deserving" of mothers—and left the ADC program to serve a caseload of apparently less deserving single mothers.

The original title of the program was Aid to Dependent Children. The stated purpose of Title IV was to provide financial assistance to needy dependent children. The federal program made no provision for assisting a parent or other relative in the household although it did specify that the child must live with a parent or other close relatives to be eligible for federal aid. It was not until 1950 that the federal government began to share in the maintenance costs of a caretaker relative[,] the child of an unemployed parent and that parent (AFDC-Unemployed Parent), effective in 1961; a second parent in a family with an incapacitated or unemployed parent was allowed effective in 1962 and the name of the program was changed to Aid to Families with Dependent Children.[91]

In a relatively short time, cultural perceptions about the AFDC program would also evolve. Ironically, both AFDC, and ADC before it, seemingly experienced similar issues once the respective programs were created by Congress.

The AFDC program lasted from 1962 to 1996. Along with its precursor, ADC, the promise of federal assistance to those in need (mostly children) that was established by Roosevelt and the members of Congress in 1935 effectively lasted for 61 years:

The Aid to Families with Dependent Children (AFDC) program was for 60 years the nation's most visible cash assistance program for the poor. As its name suggests, the program was created to aid children whose parents could not financially support them, and about two-thirds of AFDC recipients were children. In August 1996, Congress passed welfare reform legislation abolishing AFDC in favor of a Temporary Assistance to Needy Families (TANF) block grant that passes funds for cash assistance to the states to use in welfare programs they design themselves. Even though AFDC no longer formally exists, most of what is known about U.S. welfare policy and its effects on families and children has been learned by studying that program and efforts to modify it.[92]

AFDC grant levels had a wide variance during the program's existence. For example, the median state grant for a family of three in 1994 with no earned income was $366 per month. The least generous state benefit was Mississippi's $120 per month for a family of that size; the most generous state benefit was Alaska's $923 per month. Despite significant differences between and among the states, one stark reality was that no state's benefit level kept pace with the rate of inflation. The median state grant declined in value by 47 percent from 1970 to 1994.[93]

The AFDC program was officially terminated by Public Law 104-193 (Personal Responsibility and Work Opportunity Reconciliation Act of 1996—PRWORA).[94] It was replaced by the Temporary Assistance for Needy Families (TANF) program on July 1, 1997.[95] In 1992, Bill Clinton pledged to "end welfare as we know it."[96] In 1996, he ended the promise of federal assistance for those who qualify established by Franklin Roosevelt when he signed the "welfare reform" bill that was crafted by Republicans. On July 18, 1996, the measure passed in the House by a 256 (226 Republicans and 30 Democrats) to 170 (4 Republicans, 165 Democrats, and 1 Independent) margin. Eight members did not vote. The Senate subsequently passed its measure with changes on July 23, 1996, by a 74 (51 Republicans and 23 Democrats) to 24 (1 Republican and 23 Democrats) margin. Two members did not vote. A conference report was endorsed by the House on July 31, 1996, by a 328 (230 Republicans and 98 Democrats) to 101 (2 Republicans, 98 Democrats, and 1 Independent) tally. Five members did not vote. A day later, the Senate agreed to the conference report, 78 (53 Republicans and 25 Democrats) to 21 (21 Democrats). One member did not vote. Clinton signed the bill on August 22, 1996, and he would later be reelected to a second term over Bob Dole in November of that year.[97]

The PRWORA made it impossible for most legal immigrants to obtain food stamps. Among its major provisions included terminating welfare as an entitlement program, requiring recipients to begin working after two years of receiving benefits, placing a lifetime limit of five years of benefits paid by federal funds, and encouraging two-parent families and discouraging out-of-wedlock births.[98] To supporters of the bill, the federal government would stop promoting a culture of dependency for welfare recipients. To opponents, the bill was based on sexist and racist stereotypes about welfare recipients, and there was a general sense of dismay and disappointment that Roosevelt's social contract with Americans was basically ended by a Democratic president.[99] Frances Fox Piven and Richard Cloward explained the political realities that resulted in the demise of the New Deal social welfare compact:

> Sober people should wonder whether it makes much sense to force the mothers of young children into the search for work at a time when postindustrial restructuring of the labor market has already displaced many

existing workers. But these policies are not driven by visions of a better collective future. They are driven by the economic and political interests that have coalesced in the assault on the social compact. In part, the motivation is simply greed. Business groups and their politician allies push for tax cuts for the best-off, and reconcile this with fiscal prudence by also pushing for cuts in spending for the worst-off. Not incidentally, the worst-off are ordinarily, in the absence of protest, least able to defend the programs on which they depend. Attacking programs for the poorest of the poor also meshes with the interests of politicians who have adapted to the new business–Christian political machine on the Republican side, and the shriveling infrastructure and constituencies of the New Deal Democrats on the other side, by resorting to a scapegoat politics which singles out the poor, especially poor women, immigrants, and minorities. The singular focus on the poor and their programs as somehow to blame for what is wrong with America has so far succeeded in distracting the attention of the mass of working people from the steady erosion of their wages and working conditions.[100]

Perhaps a significant distraction occurred in the 2016 presidential election when sufficient numbers of working-class Americans voted for Donald Trump. Similar to Piven and Cloward's point, some would contend that it is counterintuitive for working-class citizens to support a candidate who was openly in favor of tax cuts for the wealthy and corporations while being opposed to collective bargaining. While many politicians have hailed the welfare reform bill of 1996 as a great success, others would dispute the claim and contend that the proportion of Americans living in abject poverty has increased due, in part, to the draconian requirements established in the PRWORA.[101]

The Great Society Era

The food stamp program was another major poverty-relief program that was established in the 1960s when Lyndon Johnson was president. It was not the first food stamp program in the United States, however. In 1939, a "Food Stamps Plan" was implemented by the Roosevelt administration as part of the New Deal. The vision behind it largely emanated from Henry Wallace, the secretary of agriculture. Food assistance was made available to low-income citizens through the purchase of food stamps. The program ended in 1943, however, as during World War II the economic boom associated with the war effort resulted in a significant reduction in indigence in the United States.[102] The vision of a food stamp program was formalized by Congress on August 31, 1964, when President Johnson signed the Food Stamp Act of 1964 into law.[103] The measure passed in the U.S. House on April 8, 1964, by a vote of 229 to 189 (216 Democrats and 13 Republicans voted for it; 163 Republicans and 26 Democrats voted against it; 10 voted present, and 5 members did not vote).[104] The House bill was basically in the same form as a measure that was proposed in 1963 by the Kennedy administration. The Johnson administration requested $550 million for four years; the House authorized $400 million over four years, and it was later reduced by the Senate to $375 million over three years. Unlike the House, there was little opposition to the bill in the Senate. On June 30, 1964, the bill was passed by a voice vote in the Senate but returned to the House due to the change in funding. On August 11, 1964, the House passed the altered bill by a voice vote.[105] When he signed the bill into law, Johnson made the following remarks:

> I am proud to sign the Food Stamp Act of 1964 because it is a realistic and responsible step toward the fuller and wiser use of our agricultural abundance. I believe the Food Stamp Act weds the best of the humanitarian instincts of the American people with the best of the free enterprise system. Instead of establishing a duplicate public system to distribute food surplus to the needy, this act permits us to use our highly efficient commercial food distribution system. It is one of many sensible and needed steps we have taken to apply the power of America's new abundance to the task of building a better life for every American. . . . As a permanent program, the food stamp plan will be one of our most valuable weapons for the war on poverty.[106]

Participation in the food stamp program increased from over 560,000 in 1965 to 15 million in 1974.[107] In 2016, the revised program had more than 44.2 million participants with total costs of the program approaching $71 billion.[108]

The "food stamp" name was dropped on October 1, 2008, when Congress passed the Food, Conservation, and Energy Act of 2008 (Public Law 110-246).[109] The name of the program was changed to Supplemental Nutrition Assistance Program (SNAP).[110] On May 22, 2008, the House passed the bill by a 306 (216 Democrats and 90 Republicans) to 110 (12 Democrats and 98 Republicans) margin. Nineteen members did not vote. On June 5, 2008, the Senate passed the same bill in identical form, 77 (34 Republicans, 41 Democrats, and 2 Independents) to 15 (13 Republicans and 2 Democrats). Eight senators did not vote. On June 18, 2008, President George W. Bush vetoed the bill. That same day members of both chambers voted to override Bush's veto (317–109 in the House and 80–14 in the Senate).[111]

Besides the food stamp program, the War on Poverty included at least three other major initiatives.[112] The other major laws passed under the guise of the War on Poverty in the mid-1960s included the Economic Opportunity Act of 1964, the Elementary and Secondary Education Act of 1965, and the

Social Security Amendments of 1965, which created, among other things, the Medicare and Medicaid programs.[113]

The Economic Opportunity Act of 1964 passed in the U.S. Senate on July 23, 1964, after only two full days of debate.[114] It was approved by a 61 (51 Democrats and 10 Republicans) to 34 (12 Democrats and 22 Republicans) vote. Four senators did not vote.[115] Final passage in the U.S. House only took a couple of days, but the debate was much more contentious.[116] On August 8, 1964, the measure was passed by a 226 (204 Democrats and 22 Republicans) to 185 (40 Democrats and 145 Republicans) margin. Seven House members voted present, and 13 did not vote.[117] Johnson signed the bill into law on August 20, 1964. At the time, the president remarked:

> On this occasion the American people and our American system are making history. For so long as man has ever lived on this earth poverty has been his curse. On every continent in every age men have sought escape from poverty's oppression. Today for the first time in all the history of the human race, a great nation is able to make and is willing to make a commitment to eradicate poverty among its people. Whatever our situation in life, whatever our partisan affiliation, we can be grateful and proud that we are able to pledge ourselves this morning to this historic course. We can be especially proud of the nature of the commitments we are making. This is not in any sense a cynical proposal to exploit the poor with a promise of a handout or a dole. We know—we learned long ago—that answer is no answer. The measure before me this morning for signature offers the answer that its title implies—the answer of opportunity. For the purpose of the Economic Opportunity Act of 1964 is to offer opportunity, not an opiate. For the million young men and women who are out of school and who are out of work, this program will permit us to take them off the streets, put them into training programs, to prepare them for productive lives, not wasted lives. In this same sound, sensible, and responsible way we will reach into all the pockets of poverty and help our people find their footing for a long climb toward a better way of life. We will work with them through our communities all over the country to develop comprehensive community action programs—with remedial education, with job training, with retraining, with health and employment counseling, with neighborhood improvement. We will strike at poverty's roots. This is by no means a program confined just to our cities. Rural America is afflicted deeply by rural poverty, and this program will help poor farmers get back on their feet and help poor farmers stay on their farms. It will help those small businessmen who live on the borderline of poverty. It will help the unemployed heads of families maintain their skills and learn new skills.[118]

The Economic Opportunity Act of 1964 was an omnibus bill.[119] This act provided the legislative foundation for the creation of the Office of Economic

Opportunity, the Job Corps, Volunteer Services in America, Upward Bound, Head Start, Legal Services, the Neighborhood Youth Corps, and the Community Action Program. Passage of this law launched the War on Poverty; its focus was on providing economic opportunity, and the ultimate goal was to guide its beneficiaries to independence and sustainability.[120]

In the following year, another important initiative of the War on Poverty was passed by members of Congress: the Elementary and Secondary Education Act (ESEA) of 1965. On March 26, 1965, the U.S. House passed the ESEA by a tally of 263 (228 Democrats and 35 Republicans) to 153 (57 Democrats, 95 Republicans, and 1 Independent). Seventeen members did not vote.[121] The bill was passed in the U.S. Senate on April 9, 1965, 73 (55 Democrats and 18 Republicans) to 18 (3 Democrats, 14 Republicans, and 1 Independent). Nine members did not vote.[122] On April 11, 1965, Johnson signed the bill into law.[123] In Johnson City, Texas, he declared at the site of his early childhood school:

> In this one-room schoolhouse Miss Katie Deadrich taught eight grades at one and the same time. Come over here, Miss Katie, and sit by me, will you? Let them see you. I started school when I was four years old, and they tell me, Miss Kate, that I recited my first lessons while sitting in your lap. From our very beginnings as a nation, we have felt a fierce commitment to the ideal of education for everyone. It fixed itself into our democratic creed. . . . Now, within the past three weeks, the House of Representatives, by a vote of 263–153, and the Senate, by a vote of 73 to 18, have passed the most sweeping educational bill ever to come before Congress. It represents a major new commitment of the federal government to quality and equality in the schooling that we offer our young people. I predict that all of those of both parties of Congress who supported the enactment of this legislation will be remembered in history as men and women who began a new day of greatness in American society.[124]

The ESEA established Title I programs, which provided federal funding for programs and projects designed to meet the educational needs of children in school attendance areas where a high concentration of families are poverty stricken.[125]

In order to further combat poverty, Johnson signed the Social Security Amendments of 1965 on July 30, 1965.[126] This bill created Medicare and Medicaid and also expanded Social Security benefits for retirees, widows, the disabled, and college students. It was financed by an increase in the payroll tax cap and rates.[127] Johnson chose to sign this bill in Independence, Missouri, the longtime home of President Harry Truman, who was in attendance. Johnson shared the following commentary on that day:

> The people of the United States love and voted for Harry Truman, not because he gave them hell—but because he gave them hope. I believe

today that all America shares my joy that he is present now when the hope that he offered becomes a reality for millions of our fellow citizens. I am so proud that this has come to pass in the Johnson Administration. But it was really Harry Truman of Missouri who planted the seeds of compassion and duty which have today flowered into care for the sick, and serenity for the fearful. Many men can make many proposals. Many men can draft many laws. But few have the piercing and humane eye which can see beyond the words to the people that they touch. Few can see past the speeches and the political battles to the doctor over there that is tending the infirm, and to the hospital that is receiving those in anguish, or feel in their heart painful wrath at the injustice which denies the miracle of healing to the old and to the poor. And fewer still have the courage to stake reputation, and position, and the effort of a lifetime upon such a cause when there are so few that share it. But it is just such men who illuminate the life and history of a nation. And so, President Harry Truman, it is in tribute not to you, but to the America that you represent, that we have come here to pay our love and our respects to you today. For a country can be known by the quality of the men it honors. By praising you, and by carrying forward your dreams, we really affirm the greatness of America.[128]

When the program was initially created, Medicare had two parts (A and B). Part A covered hospital insurance (inpatient hospital stays, care in a skilled nursing facility, hospice care, and some home health care). Part B covered medical insurance (certain doctors' services, outpatient care, medical supplies, and preventive services).[129]

Bill Clinton and George W. Bush Era

In 1997, Part C (Medicare Advantage Plans) was added to Medicare through the Balanced Budget Act of 1997.[130] Part C is a type of plan offered by a private company that contracts with Medicare to provide citizens with their Part A and B benefits. Medicare Advantage Plans include health maintenance organizations, preferred provider organizations, private fee-for-service plans, special needs plans, and Medicare Medical Savings Account Plans.[131] On June 25, 1997, the bill passed in the U.S. House, 270 (219 Democrats and 51 Republicans) to 162 (154 Democrats, 7 Republicans, and 1 Independent). Three House members did not vote.[132] It passed the U.S. Senate the same day by unanimous consent. Because the bills were not identical, a conference committee was created, and its report was endorsed by the House members on July 30, 1997, by a 346 (193 Republicans and 153 Democrats) to 85 vote (32 Republicans, 52 Democrats, and 1 Independent). Four members did not vote. A day later, the senators approved the conference report, 85 (43 Republicans and 42 Democrats) to 15 (12 Republicans and 3 Democrats). President Bill Clinton signed the measure on August 5, 1997.[133]

Part D of Medicare provided prescription drug coverage.[134] Part D was created by the Medicare Prescription Drug, Improvement, and Modernization Act (Public Law 108-173).[135] On June 27, 2003, the U.S. House passed the bill by one vote, 216 (207 Republicans and 9 Democrats) to 215 (19 Republicans, 195 Democrats, and 1 Independent). One member voted present, and 3 did not vote. The measure was changed in the Senate and passed by unanimous consent on July 7, 2003. Subsequently, the conference report passed in the House by a 220 (204 Republicans and 16 Democrats) to 215 (25 Republicans, 189 Democrats, and 1 Independent) margin on November 22, 2003. The measure passed in the Senate on November 25, 2003, 54 (42 Republicans, 11 Democrats, and 1 Independent) to 44 (9 Republicans and 35 Democrats). Two senators did not vote.[136] President George W. Bush signed the bill on December 8, 2003.[137]

According to the Kaiser Family Foundation,

> Medicare Part D is a voluntary outpatient prescription drug benefit for people on Medicare that went into effect in 2006. All 57 million people on Medicare, including those ages 65 and older and those under age 65 with permanent disabilities, have access to the Part D drug benefit through private plans approved by the federal government; in 2016, nearly 41 million Medicare beneficiaries are enrolled in Medicare Part D plans. During the Medicare Part D enrollment period, which runs from October 15 to December 7 each year, beneficiaries can choose to enroll in either stand-alone prescription drug plans (PDPs) to supplement traditional Medicare or Medicare Advantage prescription drug (MA-PD) plans (mainly HMOs and PPOs) that cover all Medicare benefits including drugs. Beneficiaries with low incomes and modest assets are eligible for assistance with Part D plan premiums and cost sharing.[138]

Officials in the Congressional Budget Office estimate that spending on Part D benefits will cost about $94 billion in 2017, which accounts for 15.6 percent of net Medicare outlays.[139] The prescription drug benefit helps to reduce the financial burden of out-of-pocket drug expenditures for those who are enrolled in the program. This is particularly important to people with modest incomes as well as those who are compelled to purchase very expensive drugs due to their health challenges.[140]

It is interesting to note that the creation of Medicaid in the mid-1960s garnered much less attention than the Medicare benefit:

> When passed, as part of the Social Security Amendments of 1965, the Medical Assistance program—more commonly known as Medicaid—was not high profile legislation. Unlike Medicare, there was no strong lobby pushing for its enactment. Its inclusion as one slab of the "three-layer"

cake was almost fortuitous. A legislative draftsman said that he doubted that more than half a day was devoted to consideration of its provisions. Nor did it occasion much discussion in committee or floor debate.

As legislation, Medicaid was often characterized as an "afterthought"— a casual and belated inclusion once the main business of Medicare was settled. Yet, within a few months after its initial implementation the program was being described as a "sleeping giant," because of its phenomenal capacity for growth. Although casual afterthoughts can often have big, unforeseen consequences, these two views of Medicaid seem in conflict. Yet each reflects a truth about the program. Though Medicaid came late in the legislative process, after other major structural decisions had been made, for Wilbur Mills—chairman of the House Ways and Means Committee and the most important legislative sponsor—the Medical Assistance Program was a significant benefit for the poor and structurally important as part of his overall design for health benefits in the Social Security Amendments of 1965. Medicaid was considerably more than an "afterthought" for him. And for Wilbur Cohen—the most active and influential member of the administration—Medicaid was the culmination and ratification of a project begun almost twenty years earlier: to create a health benefit for the poor by incremental expansion, using the Social Security Act as a legislative vehicle.[141]

Medicaid is a public assistance program that serves low-income citizens of all ages. Patients typically pay no part of the direct costs for covered medical expenses. At times a small copayment is required. Medicaid is a joint federal–state program, and it varies from state to state. Basically, the program is run by state and local officials within prescribed federal guidelines.[142] Thirty-two states and the District of Columbia currently provide Medicaid benefits to people who are eligible for Supplemental Security Income (SSI) benefits. In these states, the SSI application is also the Medicaid application. Seven states (Alaska, Idaho, Kansas, Nebraska, Nevada, Oregon, and Utah) use the same rules for Medicaid and SSI but require a separate application. Eleven states have their own eligibility rules for Medicaid, which are different from SSI rules (Connecticut, Hawaii, Illinois, Indiana, Minnesota, Missouri, New Hampshire, North Dakota, Ohio, Oklahoma, and Virginia).[143]

Like Social Security, the funding for Medicare emanates from social insurance payroll taxes. The Social Security tax has been 6.2 percent of income since 1990 (matched by the employer). The Medicare tax has been 1.45 percent since 1986, but unlike Social Security, there is no cap, so citizens pay the tax the entire calendar year.[144] An additional Medicare tax, however, began in 2013. A surcharge Medicare tax of 0.9 percent began on wages in excess of $200,000 or $250,000 for married couples filing jointly. Thus, for wages in excess of these respective amounts, the Medicare tax in effect increased from 1.45 to 2.35 percent.[145]

Barack Obama Era

When President Obama signed the Patient Protection and Affordable Care Act (PPACA) into law on March 23, 2010 (Public Law 111-148), he opined,

I'm signing this bill for all the leaders who took up this cause through the generations, from Teddy Roosevelt to Franklin Roosevelt, from Harry Truman to Lyndon Johnson, from Bill and Hillary Clinton to one of the deans who's been fighting this so long, John Dingell, to Senator Ted Kennedy—and it's fitting that Ted's widow, Vicki, is here—it's fitting Teddy's widow, Vicki, is here and his niece Caroline, his son Patrick, whose vote helped make this reform a reality. I remember seeing Ted walk through that door in a summit in this room a year ago, one of his last public appearances. And it was hard for him to make it. But he was confident that we would do the right thing.

Our presence here today is remarkable and improbable. With all the punditry, all of the lobbying, all of the game-playing that passes for governing in Washington, it's been easy at times to doubt our ability to do such a thing, such a complicated thing, to wonder if there are limits to what we as people can still achieve. It's easy to succumb to the sense of cynicism about what's possible in this country.

But today we are affirming that essential truth, a truth every generation is called to rediscover for itself, that we are not a nation that scales back its aspirations. We are not a nation that falls prey to doubt or mistrust. We don't fall prey to fear. We are not a nation that does what's easy. That's not who we are. That's not how we got here.

We are a nation that faces its challenges and accepts its responsibilities. We are a nation that does what is hard, what is necessary, what is right. Here in this country, we shape our own destiny. That is what we do. That is who we are. That is what makes us the United States of America.

And we have just enshrined, as soon as I sign this bill, the core principle that everybody should have some basic security when it comes to health care. And it is an extraordinary achievement that has happened because of all of you and all the advocates all across the country.[146]

Obama suggested that passage of the PPACA was a difficult and daunting challenge politically. The debate and votes in Congress are reflective of that reality. The bill was first introduced in the U.S. House on September 17, 2009, about nine months after Obama was inaugurated. After extensive debate in both chambers, the bill was passed in the U.S. Senate by a 60 (58 Democrats and 2 Independents) to 39 (39 Republicans) tally. One senator did not vote. The Senate bill was later approved in the U.S. House by a 219 (all Democrats) to 212 (34 Democrats and 178 Republicans) margin.[147] No Republicans in either chamber were willing to vote in favor of the bill, though the bill's advocates in Congress and in the administration attempted to coax some moderates in the GOP to support it, ultimately to no avail.

There are a number of key coverage provisions in the PPACA that are intended to expand access to health insurance, increase consumer protections, emphasize prevention and wellness, curb the rate of rising health care costs, and improve quality and system performance.[148] A primary goal of the law, and an important focal point in this historical overview, is to extend health insurance coverage to about 32 million Americans who are uninsured by expanding both private and public insurance. Many of the key provisions of the law were implemented on January 1, 2014. These include, among other things, the following:

- requiring employers to cover their workers or pay penalties (with some exceptions)
- providing tax credits to small businesses that covered specified costs of health insurance for employees
- requiring individuals to purchase health insurance, with some exceptions
- requiring the creation of state-based health insurance exchanges to help citizens and employers purchase insurance
- expanding Medicaid to cover people with incomes below 133 percent of federal poverty guidelines
- requiring the creation of temporary high-risk pools for those who could not purchase health insurance on the private market due to preexisting conditions
- requiring insurance plans to cover young adults on parents' policies up to the age of 26[149]

In addition to addressing the access to health insurance issue, the PPACA also established a number of protections for citizens, including a prohibition of lifetime and annual monetary caps on insurance coverage, of excluding coverage for children with preexisting conditions, and of cancelling health coverage (except in the case of fraud).[150]

The Republicans in the House have voted to repeal or delay implementation of parts of the PPACA, commonly referred to as "Obamacare" by critics, dozens of times since the law was passed.[151] To date, such measures have not been acted upon in the Senate. With Republicans controlling the House, Senate, and the presidency as of early 2017, the fate of the PPACA is very much an ongoing debate in American politics.

The Lessons of History

The prominent social welfare policy researcher Bruce Jansson aptly entitled a book on the history of social welfare policies in the United States in the late 1980s *The Reluctant Welfare State*.[152] He explained why he selected this particular title:

Profound ambivalence toward the victims of social problems has existed in American society since the Colonial Period. On one hand, Americans have often exhibited compassion toward hungry, destitute, ill, and transient Americans as illustrated by a host of ameliorative public policies as well as a rich tradition of private philanthropy. But they have also demonstrated a callous disregard for persons who suffered deprivation as demonstrated by the late development of federal programs, oppressive treatment of racial and other groups, and coupling of assistance with punitive and demeaning regulations. The term *reluctant welfare state* expresses this paradox of punitiveness and generosity.[153]

Indeed, the United States has a history of contradictions when it comes to assisting those in need. While some citizens rebuke the notion of what they perceive to be wasteful social welfare spending, others are very quick to help those in need, particularly when a natural disaster occurs in this country or somewhere else in the world.

There are a number of lessons to extract from historical efforts to provide poverty relief. First and perhaps most importantly, there is no singular conception or universal understanding of what can be done by way of public policy in order to lower the poverty rate in the United States. Poverty relief can be accomplished through a number of different mechanisms: direct public assistance, education, health coverage, economic opportunities, skills training, child care, and housing assistance, among other interventions.

Another fundamental lesson is that politics matters. Some of the laws and programs that have been established historically, such as Social Security and the ESEA, came to fruition because key leaders at the time, particularly at the national level, had the requisite vision and were politically effective at operationalizing their vision into tangible public policies. Of course, a number of key factors are intertwined as the United States is a democratic republic. Public opinion is important when it comes to the politics of poverty relief. When the public is receptive to assisting those in need through government intervention, the reality is that programmatic changes can be ushered through the two chambers of Congress, particularly when the political will to do so exists at 1600 Pennsylvania Avenue.

As a corollary to the premise that politics matters, elections have consequences. Under the Constitution, federal elections are held every two years. Thus, all 435 members are elected in the U.S. House every two years, and members of the House have two-year terms. One-third of the U.S. Senate is contested every two years, as Senate elections were staggered by the framers when the institution was established, and senators were assigned six-year terms. A midterm election occurs when the presidency is not being contested. Presidents have four-year terms, so two years after they begin their terms, a referendum of sorts occurs on their leadership through the midterm election. Though I will discuss this more later, suffice it to say at this juncture that voter turnout in the United States is shockingly low. One can only wonder what the implications might be if the United States had voter turnout rates on par with most of the rest of the free world.

History also illuminates the importance of political ideology in American politics. The assumptions and beliefs about the proper role of government in a capitalist society affect the political debate about the plight of the poor in the United States. An analysis of this debate and the general divide about issues related to government intervention has been a bit of a wedge issue throughout U.S. history, from the time of the Federalists versus Democratic Republicans to the present with regard to Democrats and Republicans.

Another lesson from history is the importance of context. Why is it that more policies to alleviate the challenges inherent in the existence of poverty were passed during certain periods as opposed to others? Sometimes external issues dominate the political agenda, whether in a historical sense or when analyzing the politics of the here and now. When a tangible crisis exists, the issues related to that conflict are likely to dominate what may or may not be politically tenable. In other words, even effective public managers cannot always control what is on their agenda as external forces may to a large extent impact what people do and do not talk about.

I believe that the fundamental lesson that can be extracted from history and applied to poverty-relief efforts is theoretical in nature. There are always diverse opinions and perceptions about the poor and what role, if any, government officials should play to reduce the harmful effects of poverty on society in general. To some people, the state has a responsibility to provide at least minimal assistance for those in need, regardless of what choices those afflicted may have made to contribute to their existing plight. Such individuals are presumably motivated by a sense of morality and compassion, and they believe that tax revenue should be redirected to the impoverished because it is simply the right thing to do. To others, the welfare state encourages people to be lazy and make poor choices in their lives without suffering the consequences, and it generally encourages cultural dependency (citizens who are perceived to be dependent on the government for money as opposed to working for their own wages). Undoubtedly, a large majority of Americans may fall somewhere in the middle of these polar extremes. As Jansson succinctly noted:

> A challenge for contemporary Americans consists not only in understanding the evolution and nature of the American responses (or nonresponses)

to social problems but in making moral judgments about them. Do we wish to evolve a welfare state that is more like those in European nations, or do we want to severely limit its size? Policy developments of the past two centuries suggest that these questions will not be resolved for generations and that reformers will encounter many obstacles along the way.[154]

To some political leaders, there is no urgent need to reform the welfare system because members of Congress and President Bill Clinton successfully reduced the culture of dependency by establishing a limit on how long able-bodied people could receive benefits from the government. To others, the United States should have a more expansive and less punitive welfare state, and, at some point, the United States will have the leadership and political acumen to expand what presently exists. Regardless of the differing perspectives on poverty, it is fairly easy to predict that a more expansive welfare state in the United States is highly unlikely at the present time. Helping the poor has not been on the top of the political agenda for a generation or more, and there is little reason to believe that it will become an urgent priority in the short term.

Notes

1. Brian L. Fife, *Old School Still Matters: Lessons from History to Reform Public Education in America* (Santa Barbara, CA: Praeger, 2013), 8.

2. Oliver Wendell Holmes, "The Path of the Law," *Harvard Law Review* 10, no. 8 (1897): 477–78.

3. Holmes, "The Path of the Law," 469.

4. James Leiby, *A History of Social Welfare and Social Work in the United States, 1815–1972* (New York: Columbia University Press, 1978); Paul Adams, "Social Policy and the Working Class," *Social Service Review* (September 1985): 387–402.

5. Leiby, *A History of Social Welfare and Social Work in the United States, 1815–1972*, 6–7.

6. Leiby, *A History of Social Welfare and Social Work in the United States, 1815–1972*, 7; History Channel, "January 8, 1815: Jackson Leads Troops to Victory at New Orleans," http://www.history.com/this-day-in-history/jackson-leads-troops-to-victory-at-new-orleans (accessed January 8, 2017).

7. Leiby, *A History of Social Welfare and Social Work in the United States, 1815–1972*, 68–9.

8. Leiby, *A History of Social Welfare and Social Work in the United States, 1815–1972*, 70.

9. Leiby, *A History of Social Welfare and Social Work in the United States, 1815–1972*, 70.

10. For information about Oscar Handlin's life, see American Historical Association, "Perspectives on History: Oscar Handlin (1915–2011)," https://www.historians.org/publications-and-directories/perspectives-on-history/january-2012/in-memoriam-oscar-handlin (accessed January 13, 2017). For more information about immigration in U.S. history, consult the following works by Professor Handlin: *Race and Ethnicity in American Life* (Boston: Little, Brown and Company, 1948); *The Uprooted: The Epic Story of the Great Migrations that Made the American People* (Boston: Little, Brown and Company, 1951); *The American People in the Twentieth Century* (Cambridge, MA: Harvard University Press, 1954); *Immigration as a Factor in American History* (Englewood Cliffs, NJ: Prentice-Hall, 1959); *Boston's Immigrants: A Study in Acculturation* (New York: Atheneum, 1969).

11. Handlin, *Immigration as a Factor in American History*, 1.

12. Council on Foreign Relations, "The U.S. Immigration Debate," http://www.cfr.org/immigration/us-immigration-debate/p11149 (accessed January 13, 2017).

13. Council on Foreign Relations, "The U.S. Immigration Debate." The U.S.–Mexican border is about 1,900 miles long. About 650 miles of the border already has a series of fences, concrete slabs, and other structures. A study commissioned by *The Washington Post* estimated that the cost of Donald Trump's wall would be approximately $25 billion. In addition, some environmentalists maintain that the border region is a delicate ecosystem where many birds and animals migrate between the two countries. A wall could threaten a number of species, including black bears and the American jaguar.

14. Some of the leading industrialists during the 19th and early 20th centuries were able to profit from a general lack of federal regulation over the workplace. Chief among them are undoubtedly John D. Rockefeller and Andrew Carnegie. See Ron Chernow, *Titan: The Life of John D. Rockefeller, Sr.* (New York: Random House, 1998); David Nasaw, *Andrew Carnegie* (New York: Penguin, 2006).

15. Leiby, *A History of Social Welfare and Social Work in the United States, 1815–1972,* 71–89.

16. Leiby, *A History of Social Welfare and Social Work in the United States, 1815–1972,* 75.

17. Young Men's Christian Association, "The Story of Our Founding," http://www.ymca.net/history/founding.html (accessed January 14, 2017); Salvation Army, "History of the Salvation Army," http://www.salvationarmyusa.org/usn/history-of-the-salvation-army (accessed January 14, 2017).

18. Young Men's Christian Association, "The Story of Our Founding"; Salvation Army, "History of the Salvation Army."

19. Almshouse Association, "Historical Summary," http://www.almshouses.org/history/historical-summary/ (accessed January 16, 2017).

20. Virginia Commonwealth University, Social Welfare History Project, "Poor Relief and the Almshouse," http://socialwelfare.library.vcu.edu/issues/poor-relief-almshouse/ (accessed January 16, 2017).

21. Blanche D. Coll, *Perspectives in Public Welfare: A History* (Washington, DC: Government Printing Office, 1969), 27–8.

22. Charles Lawrence, *History of the Philadelphia Almshouses and Hospitals from the Beginning of the Eighteenth to the Ending of the Nineteenth Centuries, Covering a Period of Nearly Two Hundred Years, Showing the Mode of Distributing Public Relief through the Management of the Board of Overseers of the Poor, Guardians of the Poor and the Directors of the Department of Charities and Correction* (Philadelphia: Compiled and Published by Author, 1905).

23. Lawrence, *History of the Philadelphia Almshouses and Hospitals from the Beginning of the Eighteenth to the Ending of the Nineteenth Centuries, Covering a Period of Nearly Two Hundred Years, Showing the Mode of Distributing Public Relief through the Management of the Board of Overseers of the Poor, Guardians of the Poor and the Directors of the Department of Charities and Correction*, 165–66.

24. Lawrence, *History of the Philadelphia Almshouses and Hospitals from the Beginning of the Eighteenth to the Ending of the Nineteenth Centuries, Covering a Period of Nearly Two Hundred Years, Showing the Mode of Distributing Public Relief through the Management of the Board of Overseers of the Poor, Guardians of the Poor and the Directors of the Department of Charities and Correction*, 198–99.

25. The reader may benefit from a more recent study of almshouses in the United States from the New England region. See David Wagner, *The Poorhouse: America's Forgotten Institution* (Lanham, MD: Rowman & Littlefield, 2005).

26. Bruce C. Jansson, *The Reluctant Welfare State: A History of American Social Welfare Policies* (Belmont, CA: Wadsworth Publishing, 1988), 57.

27. Jansson, *The Reluctant Welfare State: A History of American Social Welfare Policies*, 57.

28. Leiby, *A History of Social Welfare and Social Work in the United States, 1815–1972*, 136–62. In his book, Leiby accentuates the time period from 1900 to 1919.

29. Leiby, *A History of Social Welfare and Social Work in the United States, 1815–1972*, 137–38.

30. Leiby, *A History of Social Welfare and Social Work in the United States, 1815–1972*, 87.

31. Jansson, *The Reluctant Welfare State: A History of American Social Welfare Policies*, 87.

32. George Washington University, Eleanor Roosevelt Papers Project, "The Progressive Era (1890–1920)," https://www2.gwu.edu/~erpapers/teachinger /glossary/progressive-era.cfm (accessed January 30, 2017). An analysis of the ascendancy and the termination of the Progressive movement can be obtained in Michael McGerr, *A Fierce Discontent: The Rise and Fall of the Progressive Movement in America* (New York: Oxford University Press, 2003).

33. American Presidency Project, "Election of 1912," http://www.presidency .ucsb.edu/showelection.php?year=1912 (accessed January 29, 2017). A description of the 1912 Progressive Party is available in George Henry Payne's, who was Theodore Roosevelt's campaign manager, *The Birth of the New Party or Progressive Party* (Naperville, IL: J. L. Nichols & Company, 1912).

34. American Presidency Project, "Election of 1916," http://www.presidency .ucsb.edu/showelection.php?year=1916 (accessed January 30, 2017). For a brief

discussion of the 1912 and 1916 presidential elections, see University of Virginia, Miller Center of Public Affairs, "Woodrow Wilson: Campaigns and Elections," http://millercenter.org/president/biography/wilson-campaigns-and-elections (accessed January 29, 2017).

35. Jansson, *The Reluctant Welfare State: A History of American Social Welfare Policies*, 88.

36. Upton Sinclair, *The Jungle* (New York: The Heritage Press, 1965).

37. Sinclair, *The Jungle*, 35.

38. Sinclair, *The Jungle*, 93.

39. Sinclair, *The Jungle*, 95–6.

40. See Kenneth Warren, *Administrative Law in the Political System*, 5th ed. (Boulder, CO: Westview Press, 2011), 41; James Q. Wilson, "The Rise of the Bureaucratic State," in *Bureaucratic Power in National Politics*, 3rd ed., ed. Francis E. Rourke (Boston: Little, Brown and Company, 1978), 54–78; Public Law 59-242 (June 30, 1906), "Federal Meat Inspection Act," https://www.loc.gov/law/help/statutes-at-large/59th-congress/session-1/c59s1ch3913.pdf (accessed February 12, 2017); Public Law 59-384 (June 30, 1906), "Pure Food and Drug Act," https://www.loc.gov/law/help/statutes-at-large/59th-congress/session-1/c59s1ch3915.pdf (accessed February 12, 2017); Public Law 63-212 (September 26, 1914), "Federal Trade Commission Act," https://www.loc.gov/law/help/statutes-at-large/63rd-congress/session-2/c63s2ch311.pdf (accessed February 12, 2017); Public Law 63-212 (October 15, 1914), "Clayton Act," https://www.loc.gov/law/help/statutes-at-large/63rd-congress/session-2/c63s2ch323.pdf (accessed February 12, 2017).

41. Theodore Roosevelt, *Theodore Roosevelt: An Autobiography* (New York: Macmillan, 1914), 458.

42. For example, see Gallup Poll, "Americans Still See Big Government as Top Threat," http://www.gallup.com/poll/201629/americans-big-government-top-threat.aspx (accessed February 12, 2017).

43. Warren, *Administrative Law in the Political System,* 5th ed., 15.

44. American Presidency Project, "Election of 1920," http://www.presidency.ucsb.edu/showelection.php?year=1920 (accessed February 24, 2017).

45. History.com, "Warren G. Harding," http://www.history.com/topics/us-presidents/warren-g-harding (accessed February 24, 2017).

46. American Presidency Project, "Election of 1924," http://www.presidency.ucsb.edu/showelection.php?year=1924 (accessed February 24, 2017).

47. American Presidency Project, "Election of 1928," http://www.presidency.ucsb.edu/showelection.php?year=1928 (accessed February 24, 2017).

48. History.com, "The Roaring Twenties," http://www.history.com/topics/roaring-twenties (accessed February 24, 2017).

49. F. Scott Fitzgerald, *The Great Gatsby* (New York: Scribner, 2004), 39–40.

50. History.com, "Stock Market Crash of 1929," http://www.history.com/topics/1929-stock-market-crash (accessed February 24, 2017).

51. Federal Reserve History, "Stock Market Crash of 1929," http://www.federalreservehistory.org/Events/DetailView/74 (accessed February 25, 2017).

52. Living New Deal, "The New Deal," https://livingnewdeal.org/what-was -the-new-deal/ (accessed February 25, 2017).

53. American Presidency Project, "Election of 1932," http://www.presidency .ucsb.edu/showelection.php?year=1932 (accessed February 24, 2017).

54. History.com, "Hoovervilles," http://www.history.com/topics/hoovervilles (accessed February 25, 2017).

55. Presidents have had limited terms since the passage of the 22nd Amendment in 1951.

56. American Presidency Project, "Election of 1936," http://www.presidency .ucsb.edu/showelection.php?year=1936 (accessed February 24, 2017).

57. American Presidency Project, "Election of 1940," http://www.presidency .ucsb.edu/showelection.php?year=1940 (accessed February 24, 2017).

58. American Presidency Project, "Election of 1944," http://www.presidency .ucsb.edu/showelection.php?year=1944 (accessed February 24, 2017).

59. History.com, "Franklin D. Roosevelt," http://www.history.com/topics/us -presidents/franklin-d-roosevelt (accessed February 25, 2017).

60. McGerr, *A Fierce Discontent: The Rise and Fall of the Progressive Movement in America*, 315.

61. McGerr, *A Fierce Discontent: The Rise and Fall of the Progressive Movement in America*, 312–13.

62. Warren G. Harding, "Back to Normal: Address Before Home Market Club," in *Rededicating America: Life and Recent Speeches of Warren G. Harding*, ed. Frederick E. Schortemeier (Indianapolis, IN: Bobbs-Merrill, 1920), 223–24.

63. Jansson, *The Reluctant Welfare State: A History of American Social Welfare Policies*, 115.

64. Jansson, *The Reluctant Welfare State: A History of American Social Welfare Policies*, 116–17.

65. Leiby, *A History of Social Welfare and Social Work in the United States, 1815– 1972*, 221.

66. Jansson, *The Reluctant Welfare State: A History of American Social Welfare Policies*, 116.

67. *New York Times*, "Trump's Electoral College Victory Ranks 46th in 58 Elections," https://www.nytimes.com/interactive/2016/12/18/us/elections/donald -trump-electoral-college-popular-vote.html?_r=0 (accessed February 28, 2017).

68. History.com, "Why Does Inauguration Day Fall on January 20?," http:// www.history.com/news/ask-history/why-does-inauguration-day-fall-on-january-20 (accessed February 28, 2017).

69. Franklin D. Roosevelt Presidential Library and Museum, "Action, and Action Now: FDR's First 100 Days," https://fdrlibrary.org/documents/356632 /390886/actionguide.pdf/07370301-a5c1-4a08-aa63-e611f9d12c34 (accessed March 4, 2017).

70. Franklin D. Roosevelt Presidential Library and Museum, "Action, and Action Now: FDR's First 100 Days."

71. Jansson, *The Reluctant Welfare State: A History of American Social Welfare Policies*, 118.

72. Thomas Corbett, "The Rise and Fall of Poverty as a Policy Issue," http://www .irp.wisc.edu/publications/focus/pdfs/foc302b.pdf (accessed March 5, 2017).

73. Public Law 74-271 (August 14, 1935), "The Social Security Act of 1935," http://www.legisworks.org/congress/74/publaw-271.pdf (accessed March 5, 2017); Social Security Administration, "The Social Security Act of 1935," https://www .ssa.gov/history/35act.html (accessed March 5, 2017).

74. The American Presidency Project, "Franklin Roosevelt: Executive Order 6757: Initiating Studies on Social and Economic Security, June 29, 1934," http://www .presidency.ucsb.edu/ws/index.php?pid=14707 (accessed March 14, 2017).

75. The American Presidency Project, "Franklin Roosevelt: Executive Order 6757: Initiating Studies on Social and Economic Security, June 29, 1934," http://www .presidency.ucsb.edu/ws/index.php?pid=14707 (accessed March 14, 2017).

76. Social Security Administration, "Brief History: The Committee on Economic Security," https://www.ssa.gov/history/ces.html (accessed March 14, 2017).

77. Social Security Administration, "Brief History: The Committee on Economic Security."

78. Social Security Administration, "Social Security: Historical Background and Development of Social Security," https://www.ssa.gov/history/briefhistory3 .html (accessed March 14, 2017).

79. Social Security Administration, "Social Security: Historical Background and Development of Social Security."

80. Social Security Administration, "Social Security: Historical Background and Development of Social Security."

81. Frances Perkins Center, "Her Life: The Woman Behind the New Deal," http://francesperkinscenter.org/life-new/ (accessed March 14, 2017).

82. Social Security Administration, "Edwin E. Witte: The Beginnings of Social Security," https://www.ssa.gov/history/cohenwitte.html (accessed March 14, 2017).

83. Social Security Administration, "The Roots of Social Security, by Frances Perkins, Delivered at Social Security Administration Headquarters—Baltimore, Maryland, October 23, 1962," https://www.ssa.gov/history/perkins5.html (accessed March 14, 2017).

84. Social Security Administration, "1935 Congressional Debates on Social Security," https://www.ssa.gov/history/tally.html (accessed March 15, 2017).

85. Patricia P. Martin and David A. Weaver, "Social Security: A Program and Policy History," *Social Security Bulletin* 66, no. 1 (2005): 2.

86. Public Law 74-271 (August 14, 1935), "Social Security Act."

87. Social Security Administration, "Fact Sheet: 2017 Social Security Changes," https://www.ssa.gov/news/press/factsheets/colafacts2017.pdf (accessed March 15, 2017).

88. Larry DeWitt, "The Development of Social Security in America," *Social Security Bulletin* 70, no. 3 (2010): 5.

89. Linda Gordon and Felice Batlan, "The Legal History of the Aid to Dependent Children Program," http://socialwelfare.library.vcu.edu/public-welfare/aid -to-dependent-children-the-legal-history/ (accessed March 16, 2017).

90. John E. Hansan, "Public Welfare: Aid for Dependent Children (ADC: 1935-61)," http://socialwelfare.library.vcu.edu/public-welfare/public-welfare-aid-for-dependent-children/ (accessed March 16, 2017).

91. Hansan, "Public Welfare: Aid for Dependent Children (ADC: 1935-61)."

92. Stephen B. Page and Mary B. Larner, "Introduction to the AFDC Program," *The Future of Children: Welfare to Work* 7, no. 1 (1997): 20.

93. Page and Larner, "Introduction to the AFDC Program," 21–2.

94. Public Law 104-193 (August 22, 1996), "Personal Responsibility and Work Opportunity Reconciliation Act of 1996," https://www.gpo.gov/fdsys/pkg/PLAW-104publ193/pdf/PLAW-104publ193.pdf (accessed March 10, 2016).

95. Public Law 104-193 (August 22, 1996), "Personal Responsibility and Work Opportunity Reconciliation Act of 1996."

96. Alana Semuels, "The End of Welfare as We Know It: America's Once-Robust Safety Net Is No More," *The Atlantic* (April 1, 2016), https://www.theatlantic.com/business/archive/2016/04/the-end-of-welfare-as-we-know-it/476322/ (accessed March 18, 2017).

97. GovTrack.Us, "H.R. 3734 (104th): Personal Responsibility and Work Opportunity Reconciliation Act of 1996," https://www.govtrack.us/congress/bills/104/hr3734 (accessed March 18, 2017).

98. Public Law 104-193 (August 22, 1996), "Personal Responsibility and Work Opportunity Reconciliation Act of 1996."

99. Frances Fox Piven and Richard A. Cloward, *The Breaking of the American Social Compact* (New York: The New Press, 1997).

100. Piven and Cloward, *The Breaking of the American Social Compact*, 171.

101. Alana Semuels, "The End of Welfare as We Know It: America's Once-Robust Safety Net Is No More."

102. SNAP to Health Organization, "The History of SNAP," https://www.snaptohealth.org/snap/the-history-of-snap (accessed March 18, 2017).

103. Public Law 88-525 (August 31, 1964), "The Food Stamp Act of 1964," https://fns-prod.azureedge.net/sites/default/files/PL_88-525.pdf (accessed March 18, 2017).

104. GovTrack.Us, "H.R. 10222 Passage," https://govtrack.us/congress/votes/88-1964/h149 (accessed March 18, 2017).

105. *CQ Almanac 1964*, "Permanent Food Stamp Program Set Up," https://library.cqpress.com/cqalmanac/document.php?id=cqal64-1303932 (accessed March 18, 2017).

106. American Presidency Project, "Lyndon B. Johnson, Remarks upon Signing the Food Stamp Act, August 31, 1964," http://www.presidency.ucsb.edu/ws/?pid=26472 (accessed March 18, 2017).

107. U.S. Department of Agriculture, "Supplemental Nutrition Assistance Program (SNAP)," https://www.fns.usda.gov/snap/short-history-snap (accessed March 18, 2017).

108. U.S. Department of Agriculture, "Supplemental Nutrition Assistance Program Participation and Costs," https://www.fns.usda.gov/sites/default/files/pd/SNAPsummary.pdf (accessed March 18, 2017).

109. Public Law 110-246 (June 18, 2008), "Food, Conservation, and Energy Act of 2008," https://www.gpo.gov/fdsys/pkg/PLAW-110publ246/pdf/PLAW-110publ246.pdf (accessed March 19, 2017).

110. U.S. Department of Agriculture, "Supplemental Nutrition Assistance Program (SNAP)."

111. GovTrack.Us, "H.R. 6124 (110th): Food, Conservation, and Energy Act of 2008," https://www.govtrack.us/congress/bills/110/hr6124 (accessed March 20, 2017).

112. Dylan Matthews, "Everything You Need to Know about the War on Poverty," *The Washington Post*, January 8, 2014, https://www.washingtonpost.com/news/wonk/wp/2014/01/08/everything-you-need-to-know-about-the-war-on-poverty/?utm_term=.477a95b56a76 (accessed March 20, 2017).

113. Matthews, "Everything You Need to Know about the War on Poverty."

114. Martha J. Bailey and Nicolas J. Duquette, "How Johnson Fought the War on Poverty: The Economics and Politics of Funding at the Office of Economic Opportunity," *Journal of Economic History* 74, no. 2 (2014): 356.

115. GovTrack.Us, "S. 2642 Passage," https://www.govtrack.us/congress/votes/88-1964/s452 (accessed March 21, 2017).

116. Bailey and Duquette, "How Johnson Fought the War on Poverty: The Economics and Politics of Funding at the Office of Economic Opportunity," 356.

117. GovTrack.Us, "S. 2642 Passage," https://www.govtrack.us/congress/votes/88-1964/h201 (accessed March 21, 2017).

118. American Presidency Project, "Lyndon B. Johnson: Remarks Upon Signing the Economic Opportunity Act, August 20, 1964," http://www.presidency.ucsb.edu/ws/?pid=26452 (accessed March 21, 2017).

119. Public Law 88-452 (August 20, 1964), "Economic Opportunity Act of 1964," https://www.gpo.gov/fdsys/pkg/STATUTE-78/pdf/STATUTE-78-Pg508.pdf (accessed March 21, 2017).

120. Connecticut Association for Community Action, "History," http://www.cafca.org/history (accessed March 21, 2017).

121. GovTrack.Us, "To Pass H.R. 2362, the Elementary and Secondary Education Act of 1965." https://www.govtrack.us/congress/votes/89-1965/h26 (accessed March 27, 2017).

122. GovTrack.Us, "To Pass H.R. 2362, the Elementary and Secondary Education Act of 1965."

123. Public Law 89-10 (April 11, 1965), "Elementary and Secondary Education Act of 1965," http://files.eric.ed.gov/fulltext/ED017539.pdf (accessed March 27, 2017).

124. Lyndon Baines Johnson Presidential Library, "Johnson's Remarks on Signing the Elementary and Secondary Education Act, Johnson City, Texas, April 11, 1965," http://www.lbjlibrary.org/lyndon-baines-johnson/timeline/johnsons-remarks-on-signing-the-elementary-and-secondary-education-act (accessed March 27, 2017).

125. Public Law 89-10 (April 11, 1965), "Elementary and Secondary Education Act of 1965."

126. Public Law 89-97 (July 30, 1965), "Social Security Amendments of 1965," https://www.gpo.gov/fdsys/pkg/STATUTE-79/pdf/STATUTE-79-Pg286 .pdf (accessed March 27, 2017).

127. Wilbur J. Cohen and Robert M. Ball, "Social Security Amendments of 1965: Summary and Legislative History," *Social Security Bulletin* 28, no. 9 (1965): 3–21.

128. Social Security Administration, "Social Security History: President Lyndon B. Johnson," https://www.ssa.gov/history/lbjstmts.html (accessed March 30, 2017).

129. Medicare.gov, "What's Medicare?" https://www.medicare.gov/sign-up -change-plans/decide-how-to-get-medicare/whats-medicare/what-is-medicare .html (accessed March 30, 2017).

130. Public Law 105-33 (January 7, 1997), "Balanced Budget Act of 1997," https://www.gpo.gov/fdsys/pkg/PLAW-105publ33/pdf/PLAW-105publ33.pdf (accessed March 30, 1997).

131. Medicare.gov, "What's Medicare?"

132. GovTrack.us, "H.R. 2015 (105th): Balanced Budget Act of 1997," https:// www.govtrack.us/congress/bills/105/hr2015 (accessed March 27, 2017).

133. GovTrack.us, "H.R. 2015 (105th): Balanced Budget Act of 1997."

134. Medicare.gov, "What's Medicare?"

135. Public Law 108-173 (December 8, 2003), "Medicare Prescription Drug, Improvement, and Modernization Act of 2003," https://www.gpo.gov/fdsys/pkg /PLAW-108publ173/pdf/PLAW-108publ173.pdf (accessed March 30, 2017).

136. GovTrack.us, "H.R. 1 (108th): Medicare Prescription Drug, Improvement, and Modernization Act of 2003," https://www.govtrack.us/congress /bills/108/hr1 (accessed March 30, 2017).

137. For a history of the prescription drug benefit, see Thomas R. Oliver, Philip R. Lee, and Helene L. Lipton, "A Political History of Medicare and Prescription Drug Coverage," *The Milbank Quarterly* 82, no. 2 (2004): 283–354.

138. Kaiser Family Foundation, "The Medicare Part D Prescription Drug Benefit, September 26, 2016," http://kff.org/medicare/fact-sheet/the-medicare -prescription-drug-benefit-fact-sheet/ (accessed March 30, 2017).

139. Kaiser Family Foundation, "The Medicare Part D Prescription Drug Benefit, September 26, 2016."

140. Kaiser Family Foundation, "The Medicare Part D Prescription Drug Benefit, September 26, 2016."

141. David G. Smith and Judith D. Moore, *Medicaid Politics and Policy, 1965– 2007* (New Brunswick, NJ: Transaction Publishers, 2008), 21.

142. U.S. Department of Health and Human Services, "What Is the Difference between Medicare and Medicaid?" https://www.hhs.gov/answers/medicare-and -medicaid/what-is-the-difference-between-medicare-medicaid/index.html (accessed March 30, 2017).

143. Social Security Administration, "Medicaid Information," https://www .ssa.gov/disabilityresearch/wi/medicaid.htm (accessed March 30, 2017).

144. Social Security Administration, "Social Security and Medicare Tax Rates," https://www.ssa.gov/oact/progdata/taxRates.html (accessed March 30, 2017).

145. Internal Revenue Service, "Questions and Answers for the Additional Medicare Tax," https://www.irs.gov/businesses/small-businesses-self-employed /questions-and-answers-for-the-additional-medicare-tax (accessed March 30, 2017).

146. Public Law 111-148 (March 23, 2010), "Patient Protection and Affordable Care Act of 2010," https://www.ssa.gov/OP_Home/comp2/F111-148.html (accessed March 30, 2017); American Presidency Project, "Barack Obama: Remarks on Signing the Patient Protection and Affordable Care Act, March 23, 2010," http://www .presidency.ucsb.edu/ws/?pid=87660 (accessed March 31, 2017).

147. GovTrack.us, "H.R. 3590 (111th): Patient Protection and Affordable Care Act," https://www.govtrack.us/congress/bills/111/hr3590 (accessed March 30, 2017).

148. National Conference of State Legislatures, "The Affordable Care Act: A Brief Summary, March 2011," http://www.ncsl.org/portals/1/documents/health /hraca.pdf (accessed March 31, 2017).

149. National Conference of State Legislatures, "The Affordable Care Act: A Brief Summary, March 2011."

150. National Conference of State Legislatures, "The Affordable Care Act: A Brief Summary, March 2011." For more analysis of the PPACA, see Kaiser Family Foundation, "Summary of Coverage Provisions in the Patient Protection and Affordable Care Act, July 17, 2012," http://kff.org/health-costs/issue-brief/sum mary-of-coverage-provisions-in-the-patient (accessed March 30, 2017); Michael T. French, Jenny Homer, Gulcin Gumus, and Lucas Hickling, "Key Provisions of the Patient Protection and Affordable Care Act (ACA): A Systematic Review and Presentation of Early Research Findings," *Health Services Research* 51, no. 5 (2016): 1735–71.

151. *The Washington Post*, "The House Has Voted 54 Times in Four Years on Obamacare. Here's the Full List," March 21, 2014, https://www.washingtonpost .com/news/the-fix/wp/2014/03/21/the-house-has-voted-54-times-in-four-years -on-obamacare-heres-the-full-list/?utm_term=.f15371c83a0b (accessed March 31, 2017).

152. Jansson, *The Reluctant Welfare State: A History of American Social Welfare Policies*.

153. Jansson, *The Reluctant Welfare State: A History of American Social Welfare Policies*, 1.

154. Jansson, *The Reluctant Welfare State: A History of American Social Welfare Policies*, 245.

CHAPTER THREE

The Widening Gap between Rich and Poor in the United States

Thomas Jefferson articulated a long time ago the inherent dangers of an aristocratic class in the United States. In a letter to John Adams in 1813, Jefferson declared:

> For I agree with you that there is a natural aristocracy among men. The grounds of this are virtue and talents. Formerly bodily powers gave place among the aristoi. But since the invention of gunpowder has armed the weak as well as the strong with missile death, bodily strength, like beauty, good humor, politeness and other accomplishments, has become but an auxiliary ground of distinction. There is also an artificial aristocracy founded on wealth and birth, without either virtue or talents; for with these it would belong to the first class. The natural aristocracy I consider as the most precious gift of nature for the instruction, the trusts, and government of society. And indeed it would have been inconsistent in creation to have formed man for the social state, and not to have provided virtue and wisdom enough to manage the concerns of the society. May we not even say that that form of government is the best which provides the most effectually for a pure selection of these natural aristoi into the offices of government? The artificial aristocracy is a mischievous ingredient in government, and provision should be made to prevent its ascendancy. On the question, What is the best provision, you and I differ; but we differ as rational friends, using the free exercise of our own reason, and mutually indulging its errors. *You* think it best to put the Pseudo-aristoi into a

separate chamber of legislation where they may be hindered from doing mischief by their coordinate branches, and where also they may be a protection to wealth against the Agrarian and plundering enterprises of the Majority of the people. I think that to give them power in order to prevent them from doing mischief, is arming them for it, and increasing instead of remedying the evil.[1]

In this communiqué between the third and second president of the republic, the former executive leaders highlighted a key concern of the early founders of the country. They abhorred the European aristocracy and were troubled by the lack of opportunities for people who were not born into economic, political, or social privilege. An aristocracy, to them, ran counter to republican principles and the dual notions that Americans were self-governed and that all citizens were equal. While equality was obviously not afforded to all people at the time, the repudiation of aristocratic rule is clear.

Jefferson provided the following synopsis on the subject:

With respect to Aristocracy, we should further consider that, before the establishment of the American states, nothing was known to History but the Man of the old world, crouded within limits either small or overcharged, and steeped in the vices which that situation generates. A government adapted to such men would be one thing; but a very different one that for the Man of these states. Here every one may have land to labor for himself if he chuses; or, preferring the exercise of any other industry, may exact for it such compensation as not only to afford a comfortable subsistence, but wherewith to provide for a cessation from labor in old age. Every one, by his property, or by his satisfactory situation, is interested in the support of law and order. And such men may safely and advantageously reserve to themselves a wholesome controul over their public affairs, and a degree of freedom, which in the hands of the Canaille of the cities of Europe, would be instantly perverted to the demolition and destruction of every thing public and private.[2]

To Jefferson, a republic afforded men the opportunity to succeed on their own terms. Not being born into affluence did not necessarily doom a person to a laborious life without the opportunity to advance one's social circumstance, at least in the New World.

The historian Gabriel Kolko published a book on wealth in the United States in 1962.[3] In it, he refutes a common assumption about U.S. wealth distribution:

Most recent studies of American society assume that since the end of the Great Depression, in 1939, the nation's wealth has been redistributed and prosperity has been extended to the vast majority of the population. The authors of these works—popular and academic alike—are virtually unanimous in their conviction that our society has attained a substantial measure of social and economic democracy. They hail our economy for its triumphs in eliminating poverty and in creating the life of abundance for the many, not the few.

This assumption of economic equality has become the foundation of broad new theories in the social sciences, the common impression of millions of intelligent laymen—and even the basis of specific political and social policies on taxes, aid to the elderly, poverty, and other areas of economic significance.

But this assumption is nonetheless fallacious, for despite the obvious increase in prosperity since the abysmal years of the Great Depression, the basic distribution of income and wealth in the United States is essentially the same now as it was in 1939, or even 1910. Most low-income groups live substantially better today, but even though their real wages have mounted, their percentage of the national income has not changed.[4]

Kolko embraced a similar view as Thomas Jefferson when it comes to an aristocracy in the United States:

Thomas Jefferson feared and distrusted "an aristocracy of wealth [as] of more harm and danger than benefit to society." Traditionally, it has been recognized that the danger of excessive concentration of wealth arises from the economic power it brings. This has an enormous potential; it can be used to influence the mass media, to affect the political order, to stimulate economic cycles—to name just a few of its consequences. Although the equalitarian goal has never been challenged as an American ideal, the economic revolution that followed the Civil War brought the economy largely under the control of a small number of individuals who acquired vast fortunes and economic power. Sharing Jefferson's fear and accepting his goal, advocates of the income-redistribution theory rejoice that the post–Civil War inequities have been righted. But it is highly questionable whether the economic power arising from the possession or control of savings, economic assets, and income, and a voice in corporate policy has become more diffused since the early days of the New Deal. Now, when political democracy is challenged by a totalitarian way of life that also holds out the promise of economic equality, it is of crucial importance for us to evaluate the structure of the American economy and decide whether it has, in fact, achieved the equalitarian goal set forth by Jefferson.[5]

The extent to which wealth is concentrated in the United States will be examined in order to ascertain the plausibility of applied Jeffersonian theory in the early 21st century.

Aggregate Income in the United States Today

Every year, officials in the U.S. Census Bureau provide data estimates on the shares of aggregate income by percentile. The figures for 2015 are available in table 3.1. The highest quintile possesses over half the wealth in the country. The top 5 percent control over 22 percent of the money in the United States. Conversely, over 25 percent of Americans are in the middle, second, and lowest quintile.[6] Accordingly, the Gini index of income inequality is 48, which could mean that almost half the people share all the income in the United States while the remaining citizens have nothing. Since that is highly unlikely, it could mean that the top 10 percent of the population is very affluent, and the next 48 percent is more or less equal, while the remaining 42 percent are very poor.[7] At a comparative level, it certainly indicates that wealth is more stratified in the United States between the haves and the have-nots than in other democratic nations. Nevertheless, the growing gap between rich and poor is a global phenomenon, as highlighted by Branko Milanovic and Shlomo Yitzhaki:

> 78 percent of world population is poor, 11 percent belongs to the middle class, and 11 percent are rich. Thus, world seems—any way we consider it—to lack middle class. It looks like a proverbial hourglass: thick on the bottom, and very thin in the middle. Why does the world not have a middle class? First—an obvious answer—is that it is because world inequality is extremely high. When the Gini coefficient is 66 . . . it is simply numerically impossible to have a middle class. But what may be the substantive cause for the absence of the middle class? We conjuncture that this is because there is no agency whose mandate would be to care about it, and

Table 3.1   Shares of Aggregate Income by Percentile, 2015

Percentile	Money Income
Lowest quintile	3.1
Second quintile	8.2
Middle quintile	14.3
Fourth quintile	23.2
Highest quintile	51.1
Top 5 percent	22.1
Gini index of income inequality	0.479

Source: Proctor, Bernadette D., Jessica L. Semega, and Melissa A. Kollar. September 2016. *Income and Poverty in the United States: 2015.* Accessed May 2, 2017, from https://www.census.gov/content/dam/Census/library/publications/2016/demo/p60-256.pdf.

which would be elected by world citizens (in other words, there is no world government as distinct from inter-national agencies), and because national authorities understandably care about their own first and foremost. They heavily discount, or do not care, about the poverty of others, perhaps because foreigners are not their voters, or because of both psychological and physical distance between people in different countries. . . . Thus people can escape, but only a little bit, the curse or the blessing of their countries' mean income. Migration might, in many cases, represent a better option for many people from the poor countries. Their incomes would, almost in a flash, increase. But that's where impediments to migration come into the play. Today's definition of citizenship is access to a number of welfare benefits that keep even the bottom of income distribution in the rich countries well off. Thus the poor people from the poor countries will either have to be absorbed and their incomes increased, or they have to be kept out.[8]

The plight of the poor continues to be a significant public policy, human, and moral dilemma. Whether in the United States or beyond its borders, a relatively small percentage of the population owns a significant share of the wealth, while the share controlled by the impoverished continues to shrink.

Based on economic analysis provided by a number of researchers, Paul Krugman contends that the gap between rich and poor is, in fact, widening at an alarming rate:

The other day I found myself reading a leftist rag that made outrageous claims about America. It said that we are becoming a society in which the poor tend to stay poor, no matter how hard they work; in which sons are much more likely to inherit the socioeconomic status of their father than they were a generation ago.

The name of the leftist rag? *Business Week*, which published an article titled "Waking Up From the American Dream." . . .

Thirty years ago we were a relatively middle-class nation. It had not always been thus: Gilded Age America was a highly unequal society, and it stayed that way through the 1920s. During the 1930s and '40s, however, America experienced what the economic historians Claudia Goldin and Robert Margo have dubbed the Great Compression: a drastic narrowing of income gaps, probably as a result of New Deal [Depression relief programs] policies. And the new economic order persisted for more than a generation: Strong unions; taxes on inherited wealth, corporate profits and high incomes; close public scrutiny of corporate management—all helped to keep income gaps relatively small. The economy was hardly egalitarian, but a generation ago the gross inequalities of the 1920s seemed very distant . . .

Now they're back. According to estimates by the economists Thomas Piketty and Emmanuel Saez—confirmed by data from the Congressional Budget Office—between 1973 and 2000 the average real income of the bottom 90 percent of American taxpayers actually fell by 7 percent. Meanwhile, the income of the top 1 percent rose by 148 percent, the income of the top 0.1 percent rose by 343 percent and the income of the top 0.01 percent rose 599 percent. . . . The distribution of income in the United States has gone right back to Gilded Age levels of inequality.[9]

Mark Twain called the period roughly from the 1870s to 1900 the Gilded Age. In fact, he published a book in 1873, along with Charles Dudley Warner, entitled *Gilded Age: A Tale of Today*.[10] His perception of the period was that the United States was becoming a booming economy after the Civil War, at least in terms of outward appearances. The reality, however, as depicted by Twain in his book, is that there was a great deal of corruption and greed in American society where the few lived a life of extravagance at the expense of the many. As the noted biographer of Mark Twain, Justin Kaplan, put it:

The Gilded Age echoes the sounds of its times—the rustle of greenbacks and the hiss of steam, pigs grunting in the village mud, the clang of railroad iron and the boom of blasting charges, the quiet talk of men in committee rooms and bankers' offices. Its raw materials are disaster, poverty, blighted hopes, bribery, hypocrisy, seduction, betrayal, blackmail, murder, and mob violence. Written at a time when each day brought news of some revelation in the Beecher affair or the Crédit Mobilier investigation, its subject is democracy gone off the tracks.

In January, 1873, yet another scandal broke on an already hard-pressed Grant administration. It supplied Clemens and Warner with their basic situation, and it set them to working six days a week to rush the book to completion. In the wisdom of his fifty-sixth year, Senator Samuel C. Pomeroy, Radical Republican and Lincoln opponent who had represented Kansas in Washington since 1861, was seeking a third term. Before a joint session of the legislature in Topeka this tireless worker in the cause of temperance and the Sunday School was charged with having offered another politician $8,000 for his nominating vote, and the charge was supported with evidence that was altogether damning. In two previous campaigns Pomeroy had been under suspicion of vote-buying. This time the convention refused to believe his story that the money was not a bribe but a loan to help a friend—he even insisted that there was nothing unusual in making large and unreceipted loans in greenbacks from hotel rooms at midnight—and unanimously declined to support him for the nomination. . . . He subsided into private life, emerging briefly eleven years later as the presidential nominee of the prohibition party.[11]

There is much about the Gilded Age that contemporary citizens would abhor. Yet by comparison, we are still plagued by poverty, money still plays a fundamental role in American politics, the gap between rich and poor is widening, violence is endemic in society, and political scandals still persist. Twain was truly appalled by the state of American society and politics during his time:

> Mark Twain looked at his times not only through a window but in a mirror as well. In his later years, reflecting on his boyhood in Hannibal, he said that the California Gold Rush of 1849 was the watershed dividing an age of high morality and lofty impulses from an age of money-lust, hardness, and cynicism. In his simplified view of history, the Golden Age of his boyhood was followed by an age which cared about gold only, and then by a Gilded Age, to whose squalid values money gave a specious luster. In "The Revised Catechism," published in the *New York Tribune* in September, 1871, he summed up the bitter credo of the age:
>
>> What is the chief end of man?—to get rich. In what way?—dishonestly if we can; honestly if we must. Who is God, the one only and true? Money is God. Gold and greenbacks and stock—father, son, and the ghost of same—three persons in one; these are the true and only God, mighty and supreme; and William Tweed is his prophet.[12]

In the current age, when Donald Trump ascended to the presidency in part by flaunting his ability to make money, I am not so sure that the 2010s are that markedly different from the 1870s.

Uri Dadush and three colleagues have studied income equality extensively and have made the following conclusion about the United States:

> Income inequality has increased dramatically in the United States since the late 1970s. The great economic and financial crisis that hit in 2008 and the persistent high unemployment that has come with it have drawn greater attention to the trend toward marked concentration of income at the top, little or no progress for the middle, and precariousness at the bottom of the income distribution. The problem is now squarely at the center of the political debate. Even among those who view inequality neutrally— or even positively—as the way in which markets reward performance, most agree that some of the features that accompany it, such as reduced opportunity and low social mobility, increased prevalence of poverty, and the stagnation of median household income, are undesirable. Those who traditionally are more concerned about high inequality worry that increased concentration of income is also leading to the concentration of political power, which impedes efforts to mitigate inequality and even may promote policies that exacerbate it. Meanwhile, a number of economists have argued recently that the extreme concentration of income at the top may undermine macroeconomic and financial stability by making it

harder to sustainably maintain strong aggregate demand or by encouraging excessive borrowing.[13]

Income inequality is a fundamental challenge to the financial solvency of the U.S. federal government. It has long been perceived by many in this country that the poor have manipulated and exploited program rules and policies to their advantage, and the result is that taxpayers subsidize their lifestyles and poor choices. What many do not realize is that the most affluent in this society have benefitted from government policies to the detriment of most. Such policies cannot be sustained for a host of reasons that will be analyzed to a greater extent in chapters 4 and 5.

Sobering findings were promulgated by a team of researchers at the Economic Policy Institute in a recent study:

> Income inequality has risen in every state since the 1970s and in many states is up in the post–Great Recession era. In 24 states, the top 1 percent captured at least half of all income growth between 2009 and 2013, and in 15 of those states, the top 1 percent captured all income growth. In another 10 states, top 1 percent incomes grew in the double digits, while bottom 99 percent incomes fell. For the United States overall, the top 1 percent captured 85.1 percent of total income growth between 2009 and 2013. In 2013 the top 1 percent of families nationally made 25.3 times as much as the bottom 99 percent.
>
> Rising inequality is not just a story of those in the financial sector in the greater New York City metropolitan area reaping outsized rewards from speculation in financial markets. While New York and Connecticut are the most unequal states (as measured by the ratio of top 1 percent to bottom 99 percent income in 2013), nine states, 54 metropolitan areas, and 165 counties have gaps wider than the national gap. In fact, the unequal income growth since the late 1970s has pushed the top 1 percent's share of all income above 24 percent (the 1928 national peak share) in five states, 22 metro areas, and 75 counties.[14]

These findings suggest that income inequality is an endemic reality in the United States. A number of other evaluators have shared similar conclusions. A group of researchers at the Center on Budget and Policy Priorities (CBPP) studied income inequality over the past 60 years (or three generations) and made the following conclusions:

> The years from the end of World War II into the 1970s were ones of substantial economic growth and broadly shared prosperity.
>
> Incomes grew rapidly and at roughly the same rate up and down the income ladder, roughly doubling in inflation-adjusted terms between the late 1940s and early 1970s.

The income gap between those high up the income ladder and those on the middle and lower rungs—while substantial—did not change much during this period.

Beginning in the 1970s, economic growth slowed and the income gap widened.

Income growth for households in the middle and lower parts of the distribution slowed sharply, while incomes at the top continued to grow strongly.

The concentration of income at the very top of the distribution rose to levels last seen more than 80 years ago (during the "Roaring Twenties").

Wealth—the value of a household's property and financial assets, minus the value of its debts—is much more highly concentrated than income. The best survey data show that the top 3 percent of the distribution hold over half of all wealth. Other research suggests that most of that is held by an even smaller percentage at the *very* top, whose share has been rising over the last three decades.[15]

An apt description of the Roaring Twenties is as follows:

The 1920s were an age of dramatic social and political change. For the first time, more Americans lived in cities than on farms. The nation's total wealth more than doubled between 1920 and 1929, and this economic growth swept many Americans into an affluent but unfamiliar "consumer society." People from coast to coast bought the same goods (thanks to nationwide advertising and the spread of chain stores), listened to the same music, did the same dances and even used the same slang! Many Americans were uncomfortable with this new, urban, sometimes racy "mass culture"; in fact, for many—even most people in the United States, the 1920s brought more conflict than celebration.[16]

The 1920s ended in a very abrupt and tumultuous manner with the stock market crash and the ensuing Great Depression, and the consequences across the United States were devastating. What is even more troublesome now is that the CBPP researchers have determined that wealth is even more concentrated than income in the United States today (see table 3.2).

According to these data presented by the CBPP researchers, in 2013, the top 3 percent of Americans had 31 percent of the before-tax income in the United States. The next 7 percent had 17 percent of the income, while the bottom 90 percent had slightly more than half (53 percent) of the income. Contrast the data on before-tax income with wealth, however. The top 3 percent controlled over half (54 percent) of the wealth in the country and the next 7 percent over one-fifth (21 percent). The bottom 90 percent of Americans controlled only

Table 3.2   Distribution of Before-Tax Income and Wealth, 2013

	Distribution of Before-Tax Income*	Distribution of Wealth*
Bottom 90 percent	53%	25%
Top 3 percent	31%	54%
Next 7 percent	17%	21%

* Percentages may not add up to 100 due to rounding.

Source: Adapted from Stone, Chad, Danilo Trisi, Arloc Sherman, and Emily Horton. November 7, 2016. *A Guide to Statistics on Historical Trends in Income Inequality.* Accessed May 16, 2017, from http://www.cbpp.org/sites/default/files/atoms/files/11-28-11pov_1.pdf.

one-fourth of the wealth (25 percent).[17] Basically, while the top 10 percent of Americans received a little less than half of all income (48 percent), this same group controlled 75 percent of all wealth. At this juncture of American history, it would be prudent to consider the Jeffersonian perspective when it comes to a landed aristocracy in the United States.

Lane Kenworthy and Timothy Smeeding provided a status update as well as a future assessment of inequality in the United States:

> In the 1970s the United States had one of the most unequal (possibly the most unequal) income distributions among the world's rich nations. In the ensuing decades it has become even more unequal, and the pace of growth of inequality has been faster than almost anywhere else. If we exclude the top 1 percent, as do the data for other countries in this project, income inequality rose rapidly in the 1980s and slowly in the 1990s and 2000s. If we include the top 1 percent, it rose rapidly in all three decades.
>
> The causes of America's high level and rapid growth in income inequality since the 1970s are multiple: weak and weakening unions, stagnant educational attainment, a surge in globalization, an increase in competition in mainly domestic industries, skill-biased technological change, a shift in corporate governance toward emphasis on "shareholder value" and short-run profits, growing use of pay-for-performance, an increase in low-skilled immigration, a stall in the real value of the statutory minimum wage, deregulation (particularly in finance), growing use of stock options to reward CEOs coupled with a sharp run-up in stock values, the spread of winner-take-all markets in various industries, and reductions in effective tax rates for households at the top. There is no single culprit. Indeed, there is little agreement among scholars on even the top handful of causes, save labor market inequality which forms the majority of market incomes in the United States. But then many of these same arguments can be made about the causes of labor market inequality.[18]

The duo do not expect any reversal in income inequality in the United States at any time in the foreseeable future. In fact, it may accelerate:

> Perhaps the most damning indicator of rising inequality is falling intergenerational mobility. America is not a country which is terribly fixated on overall 'outcome' inequality, be it wealth, consumption or income inequality. Poverty is often blamed on the lack of initiative of the poor rather than on social malaise. And individual effort, self-reliance, and the importance of the work ethic are widely seen as the ways to get ahead in the United States. But the United States is also widely supportive of the principle of equal opportunity. Increasingly people are finding links between declining opportunity and inequality, especially for the middle class. How this sharp contrast between inequality of outcome or results, and inequality of opportunity plays itself out is likely the most important social question before our country today.[19]

The focus of chapter 4 will be on theory and ideas as to why poverty persists in the richest country on the planet. The aforementioned researchers pose a fundamental question in American society today: Does equality of opportunity currently exist in the United States? The essence of the American Dream for countless generations is that hard work, plausible choices, and conformance to society's rules will result in a good life with an abundance of opportunities available for those willing to sacrifice to achieve some modicum of material success. In recent decades, an important choice for many has been the pursuance of a college degree. In addition to the quest to gain new knowledge, a college education is still considered by many to be instrumental to gaining entry to the profession of choice as well as to a higher wage with more duties and responsibilities. Statisticians and data analysts at the U.S. Bureau of Labor Statistics consistently track unemployment rates and earnings by educational attainment. The data for 2016 are illuminating (see table 3.3).

People with more formal education make substantially more than less-educated Americans, and the differences are substantial. In terms of median weekly earnings, those with a doctorate make $1,160 more each week than those who do not have a high school diploma. Americans with a professional degree fare even better, as they make $1,241 more per week than their counterparts who lack a high school diploma. Perhaps intuitively, this same trend applies to unemployment rates by educational attainment. While the unemployment rate for all workers was 4 percent in 2016, it was 1.6 percent for those with a doctorate or a professional degree, but those lacking a high school diploma correspondingly had an unemployment rate of 7.4 percent.[20] Clearly, in a country where income inequality is increasing, access to higher education is absolutely critical to children born in working- and middle-class families, as a deficient formal educational background increases the probability of a relatively low-paying career with uncertain job security.

Table 3.3   Earnings and Unemployment Rates by Educational Attainment, 2016*

	Median Usual Weekly Earnings	Unemployment Rate
Doctoral degree	$1664	1.6%
Professional degree	$1745	1.6%
Master's degree	$1380	2.4%
Bachelor's degree	$1156	2.7%
Associate's degree	$819	3.6%
Some college, no degree	$756	4.4%
High school diploma	$692	5.2%
Less than a high school diploma	$504	7.4%

* Data are for persons 25 years of age and older. Earnings are for full-time wage and salary workers.

Source: U.S. Bureau of Labor Statistics, Office of Occupational Statistics and Employment Projections. 2017. Employment Projections: Unemployment Rates and Earnings by Educational Attainment, 2016. Accessed May 22, 2017, from https://www.bls.gov/emp/ep_chart_001.htm.

A number of scholars have contributed to the scholarship on income inequality. A diverse array of thinkers will be presented so as to place this issue in its proper context in contemporary American politics and society.

The Challenge of Income Inequality in the United States

Robert Reich is Chancellor's Professor and Carmel P. Friesen Chair in Public Policy at the University of California. He worked in the Ford, Carter, and Clinton administrations, where he was secretary of labor from 1993 to 1997.[21] Reich published a seminal book in the early 1990s entitled *The Work of Nations: Preparing Ourselves for 21st-Century Capitalism.*[22] In it, he offered the following synopsis of income inequality:

Many reasons have been offered to explain the trend toward income inequality. Some people blame the tax system. During the 1980s, Social Security payroll taxes, state and local sales taxes, and so-called user fees such as highway tolls and water charges all increased. These types of taxes inevitably claim a higher portion of the earnings of the poor than of the rich. The Social Security payroll tax, it should be remembered, works exactly like the income tax but in reverse. Rather than exempt low incomes, it exempts high incomes. The tax must be paid even on the first dollar earned, but only up to a certain ceiling . . . Above the ceiling, no more payments need be made for the year . . . Social Security also exempts investment income, like interest on capital gains. . . . Meanwhile, wealthy Americans—armed with the cleverest symbolic-analytic tax specialists that money could buy—discovered ever more decorous ways of sheltering their incomes.[23]

The affluent have much at their disposal—including resources, the political process itself, and the ability to influence the political process—that middle- and working-class Americans simply do not possess. It is no wonder that laws and policies created particularly since the 1980s have been advantageous to them and discernibly disadvantageous to other groups in society. As Reich explained in a later work:

> As inequality has widened, the means America once used to temper it— progressive income taxes, good public schools, trade unions that bargain for higher wages—have eroded. As the risks of sudden loss of job or income have grown, the social safety net has become less reliable. More of us lack health insurance. As a nation, we seem incapable of doing what is required of us to reduce climate change. Many Americans are also concerned about the crassness and coarseness of much of contemporary culture, and about the loss of Main Streets and their surrounding communities. In all these respects, democracy has been unable to take effective action, or even articulate the tradeoffs and sacrifices doing so would entail. Capitalism has become more responsive to what we want as individual purchasers of goods, but democracy has grown less responsive to what we want together as citizens.[24]

A plethora of public policy and moral challenges confront contemporary Americans; an assessment of political ideology and capitalism will ensue in chapter 4.

Professor Stephen Haseler, director of the Global Policy Institute, provided an apt description of the experience of countless middle- and working-class citizens in the United States:

> Postwar capitalism—that mix of private and public, social and market that operated from the 1950s to the late 1970s—was a great Western success story. It created the most historically elusive of outcomes: rising profits and a rise in the income and living standards of almost everyone. Inequality was not banished, but it was a political economy in which "a rising tide lifted all ships". Socially it saw the emergence of a mass Western middle class and the dream of mass prosperity. In such an optimistic environment only extreme egalitarians worried overly about inequalities and the riches of the wealthy.
>
> Unfortunately, in today's new, rawer, global capitalism the metaphor of the rising tide that lifts all ships no longer holds. A more suitable metaphor

would now be a superliner (where those who can scramble aboard are safe, secure and becoming increasingly wealthy) surrounded by little ships in trouble, with many sinking. This "sinking" was confirmed by the most powerful economic player in the US government in the late 1990s, US Federal Reserve chairman Alan Greenspan, who conceded that the 1990s had witnessed an absolute decline—sometimes quite steeply—in the living standards of millions of US individuals and families; a similar worrying decline to that which had occurred in that other highly global-friendly nation, Britain.[25]

Economic insecurity is a measurable phenomenon. Officials at the Gallup Poll have asked the following question consistently since 2001: "Thinking about the job situation in America today, would you say it is now a good time or a bad time to find a quality job?" The results of the time-series analysis are presented in table 3.4.

Americans have not been confident in their collective employment outlook. Since 2001, on average, 68 percent report that it is a bad time to find a quality job, while only 28.4 percent believe that it is a good time to do so. Only a small percentage (3.6 percent) reported no opinion on the question, meaning that there is a stark dichotomy in that people either believe it is a good or bad time to find a quality job and not much in between. In short, since this century began, almost 7 in 10 adult Americans typically believe that good quality jobs are outside the realm of the possible. This is hardly a ringing endorsement of the status quo when it comes to the economic confidence of the masses.

Haseler provides a distinct understanding of history with his description of the "super rich":

> The end of the forty years of Cold War was more than the political triumph of the West over the Soviet Union. It was also more than the victory of freedom and pluralism over command communism. When the Berlin Wall cracked open and the iron curtain fell a new form of capitalism came into its own—global capitalism—and with it new global elite, a new class.

Table 3.4   American Attitudes about Finding a Quality Job, 2001–2017*
"Thinking about the Job Situation in America Today, would You Say It is a Good Time or a Bad Time to Find a Quality Job?"

	Good Time	Bad Time	No Opinion
Mean	28.4%	68%	3.6%
Standard Deviation	12.2	13.1	1.4

* The data cover surveys between August 2001 and May 2017 (198 surveys).

Source: Adapted from Gallup Poll. 2017. Economy. Accessed May 24, 2017, from http://www.gallup.com/poll/1609/consumer-views-economy.aspx.

This new class already commands wealth beyond the imagination of ordinary working citizens. It is potentially wealthier than any super-rich class in history (including the robber barons, those "malefactors of great wealth" criticised by Teddy Roosevelt, and the nineteenth-century capitalists who inspired the opposition of a century of Marxists). The new class of super-rich are also assuming the proportions of overlordship, of an overclass—as powerful, majestic and antidemocratic as the awesome, uncompromising imperial governing classes at the height of the European empires.

The awesome new dimension of today's super-rich—one which separates them sharply from earlier super rich—is that they owe no loyalty to community or nation. The wealthy used to be bounded within their nations and societies—a constraint that kept aggregations of wealth within reason and the rich socially responsible. Now, though, the rich are free: free to move their money around the world. In the new global economy super-rich wealth (capital) can now move their capital to the most productive (or high profit, low cost) haven, and with the end of the Cold War— and the entry into global economy of China, Russia, Eastern Europe and India—these opportunities have multiplied. The super-rich are also free to move themselves. Although still less mobile than their money, they too are becoming less rooted, moving easily between many different locations.[26]

While some criticize the leading capitalists of the late 19th and early 20th centuries for the manner in which they amassed their fortunes (e.g., John D. Rockefeller Sr., Andrew Carnegie, and Henry Ford), consider the contemporary era. Is avarice today any different than it was during the Progressive Era? While the context of the global economy is obviously different, some industrial owners' drive to keep wages and benefits down for employees, while maximizing profits, is a relative constant for those who are less attentive, or indifferent, to the plight of workers and their families and more focused on the pursuit of material entities and economic, political, and social power.[27]

From 1988 to 1990, Jonathan Kozol visited and studied schools across the United States. He interviewed children, teachers, principals, and school superintendents. He determined that schools for the rich and the poor were anything but equal, and the divide between the two extremes was actually widening. The urban schools that he investigated were overcrowded, understaffed, and lacked the basic requirements that students need to learn. By way of conclusion, he offered the following bleak assessment:

Standing here by the Ohio River, watching it drift west into the edge of the horizon, picturing it as it flows onward to the place three hundred miles from here where it will pour into the Mississippi, one is struck by the sheer beauty of this country, of its goodness and unrealized goodness, of the limitless potential that it holds to render life rewarding and the spirit clean. Surely there is enough for everyone within this country. It is a tragedy that these good things are not more widely shared. All our children ought to be allowed a stake in the enormous richness of America. Whether they were born to poor white Appalachians or to wealthy Texans, to poor black people in the Bronx or to rich people in Manhasset or Winnetka, they are all quite wonderful and innocent when they are small. We soil them needlessly.[28]

Given the existence of income inequality in the United States, and the reality that a significant portion of public K–12 education is funded through local property taxes, Kozol has a valid point about the implications of inequality for public education. Children in this country are not afforded equality of opportunity because of the collective choices made by the adult population. This unsavory denial in the United States today runs counter to the fundamental idea that public education should serve all children in a republic and that it should be funded by the citizens. This vision traces back to Thomas Jefferson, Benjamin Rush, Noah Webster, and the person largely responsible for the implementation of public education in the United States in the 19th century, Horace Mann.[29]

The late sociologist Lee Rainwater expressed the inherent complexities that exist with regard to the inequality debate in the United States in 1974:

During the past decade, as issues of social inequality have come to dominate domestic policy debate, social science theories, perspectives, and data have assumed an increasingly central role in these discussions. Basic stratification categories such as race and ethnic status and social class status have provided a background for thinking through many policy issues. Terms like "poverty," "lower-class culture," "Middle America," "the working class," and so on, have become staples of media and political rhetoric. Equally, or perhaps more, important for much social policy activity have been the understandings and assumptions of policy makers concerning the social meanings and uses of resources (financial resources, entitlements, services) that are provided by or affected by public policies. As the "welfare state" has become increasingly established and elaborated, policies that define where families and individuals stand in the stratification system have become increasingly fateful for them. Yet the correspondence between the way stratification operates in the real world and the images of the stratification system portrayed by social science and carried in the heads and writings of policy makers and executives must be taken as quite problematic. The situation becomes even more confusing when policy aims to change the way the stratification system operates—for example, by seeking to achieve greater equality of opportunity. The validity of beliefs about the stratification system, so problematic at the static level, becomes even more problematic when the focus shifts to the dynamics of how the system operates and how it might change.[30]

Indeed, a number of policy interventions have been attempted in U.S. history presumably to assist those in need (see chapter 2). The philosophical assumptions inherent in the public policies in question will be scrutinized in chapter 4.

The vicissitudes of poverty were captured by Peter Edelman in a sobering, but highly familiar, manner in 2012:

> Many . . . will be thoroughly familiar with the terminology and the reality of the cradle-to-prison pipeline. The over-incarceration of African American and Latino young men is a national scandal. Low-income young men of color—especially those growing up in high-poverty neighborhoods—are fated under current circumstances to end up in prison in percentages that far exceed their share of the population. I saw this happening in the late 1970s when I was the head of the youth corrections agency in New York State, and it has gotten much, much worse since then. We are losing generation after generation.
>
> Check the boxes: father in and out of prison or whereabouts unknown or never known. Mother struggling to find steady work and often not succeeding. Drugs or alcohol in the parental picture somewhere. Violence in the home. Early childhood inattention or worse. Terrible schools. No caring adult other than the mother or grandmother in the boy's life. Street culture that valorizes defiance and denigrates educational achievement. Police all too willing to arrest.
>
> Result: time in prison, likely fathering children and not marrying the mother, and difficulty in finding work for the rest of his life. Poverty in childhood makes these young men strong candidates for getting into trouble with the law in the first place, and time in prison makes them even stronger candidates for lives of poverty and disenfranchisement from the democratic process, pushing the arithmetic of politics to the right and shrinking the constituency for support of low-income communities.[31]

The widening gap between rich and poor has devastating consequences in a democratic republic. The United States is unique in the free world in that the level of poverty is so much higher in this country than in other democracies. What are the implications for the have-nots? Edelman, the former advisor to Senator Robert Kennedy, later served as assistant secretary of Health and Human Services under President Clinton. He and another colleague, Mary Jo Bane, resigned their positions at HHS to protest Clinton's endorsement of the Republican welfare reform bill in 1996.[32] The accuracy of Edelman's characterization of poverty in the United States cannot be challenged. The political will to change the status quo has been lacking for a number of generations.

It was during this same period (the beginning of Clinton's second term as president) that Denny Braun published a book entitled *The Rich Get Richer: The Rise of Income Inequality in the United States and the World*.[33] Braun described the historical nature of income inequality this way:

> It seems that people have always argued about how resources in society are to be shared. Disagreement usually centers around whether the share we get is an equitable and fair reward for our hard work, effort, and sacrifice. One school of thought believes that those who receive more must somehow deserve their higher incomes. Another view sees society as basically unfair . . . This privileged class is often accused of cruel indifference toward the suffering of the masses they dominate. A famous quote attributed to Marie Antoinette just prior to the bloody French Revolution in the eighteenth century illustrates this attitude. The story is told that as queen of France, at the apex of an incredibly opulent and decadent court society, she was informed that the peasants had no bread, that they were literally starving to death. Her alleged offhand quote, "Let them eat cake," earned her a place of infamy in history.
>
> There is evidence that she never voiced such incredible indifference. Yet even if she lacked concern for the poor, this may not have stemmed from genuine cruelty. Marie Antoinette was simply ignorant of the true condition of the poor within French society. Being so out of touch with her starving subjects literally cost her her head! The parallel message for any society with an economic elite which bleeds the very financial life from its citizenry ought to be crystal clear. To continue—through chicanery, fraud, and naked force—to steal from the poor to enrich those who are already abundantly wealthy eventually carries an extreme penalty. To follow a path of economic gluttony while those around us literally starve all but guarantees some form of "French Revolution" for contemporary society.[34]

Extreme income inequality is a reckless leadership model even for a despot; history is replete with examples where the masses ultimately revolted from their plight and changed the leadership structure in their societies through violent means. A society where hope is absent is one in which chaos will ultimately prevail. A significant gap between rich and poor should not be tolerated in a democracy, for it suggests that equality of opportunity does not exist. For some corporate leaders in this country, their corporations come first and foremost, ahead of their own country. Braun explained:

> We can no longer assume that U.S. corporations doing a land-office business abroad will have the best interests of the American people and their government at heart. In fact, there is evidence to the contrary. The heads of multinational firms have been remarkably candid in admitting that their corporations come first. These global enterprises are now shedding any

vestige of American identity as they develop world markets and reduce their dependency on home sales . . . In effect, our country has helped to pay for the overseas expansion of multinationals through generous tax policies. As a result, investment capital needed at home is now pouring out of the country at an alarming rate. Along with the capital flight have gone the countless jobs that would have been available if more modern, up-to-date, competitive factories had been built inside our borders. Deindustrialization has set in. One direct consequence has been a decline in our standard of living. Personal income in America is in a tailspin, especially in comparison to other industrial countries. A tide of income inequality is sweeping over us as a result.[35]

In reality, our leaders have encouraged corporate leaders to engage in unabashed avarice by creating policies that assisted them to maximize profits at the expense of American workers. This path is not sustainable and must be reversed by a concerted national effort to put the needs of the many, the American people, ahead of corporate interests, which tend to be extremely narrow and self-serving.

One very prominent Supreme Court justice in U.S. history who understood the link between public policy and income differentials was Louis Brandeis (1856–1941). Brandeis was nominated by President Woodrow Wilson and confirmed by the U.S. Senate in 1916, and he was the first Jewish American to serve on the court; he retired from the bench in 1939.[36] Melvin Urofsky expressed Brandeis's understanding of income inequality before the Great Depression ever ensued:

As early as 1922, Brandeis recognized that the so-called boom had very weak underpinnings. In the nineteenth century, innovations in production and transportation had led to cost reductions that had been passed on in the form of lower prices to the consumer. Since 1900, quite the opposite development had taken place, with production costs and consumer prices rising, not for lack of invention, but because large companies increased their profit margins. Distribution had become the job of middlemen, whose costs added to the final price of every product. Consumers paid more, but workers did not see an equivalent rise in their wages. As a result, a small percentage of the population realized great wealth, while the majority of Americans paid more for their costs of living on wages that failed to increase. As the decade wore on, the discrepancy in income distribution grew worse.

The following year Brandeis complained about the tax policies of the Harding administration and Secretary of the Treasury Andrew W. Mellon, which benefited large corporations and railroads at the expense of the middle class. If bigger companies were as efficient as they claimed to be, they could easily afford to pay higher taxes and should consider it a sort of excess profits tax.[37]

Brandeis's vision during the Progressive Era could easily be applied to contemporary society. Corporate profits are up substantially, but not wages for most American workers. This schism is simply not sustainable.

In 1930, the influential historian Charles A. Beard reflected on Brandeis's views on social and economic justice:

> Mr. Justice Brandeis, like every other judge, entered upon his responsibilities with a fairly coherent picture in his mind of what he wished American society to represent and become. It is true that he wrote no systematic treatise on sociology before taking on the ermine. Nor was he given to that logical perfection which usually eventuates in Utopia. Yet from his writings and activities so briefly surveyed above can be constructed in bold outlines a mosaic of the convictions and facts that largely determined his approach to controversial questions before the Court.
>
> American society, as Mr. Brandeis then conceived it, should not be dominated by huge monopolies and trusts, but should be the home of "the new freedom," in which small, individual enterprises can flourish under the defensive arm of the government. The relations of the great utilities and the public should be adjusted on principles of prudent investment, efficient capitalization, scientific management, and fair earnings equitably shared with the public under sliding-scale rules. Trade unions are necessary to the upholding of decent living standards among the mass of workers, and in the weighting of judicial opinion they should be given the benefit of the doubt unless the mandate of the law is too clear to be mistaken or the end sought is undesirable as ascertained by an inquiry into facts. The weakness of wage-earners in our industrial society must be offset by state and federal legislation of a social character, and since the Constitution is blessed by "a convenient vagueness," such legislation should be sustained if the facts indicate that it is fairly calculated to accomplish a reasonable purpose.[38]

In the late 19th century, Brandeis's views about American workers were greatly influenced by his own observations and experiences as a young man:

> The great mass of Jewish immigration from eastern Europe after 1880 had flooded into New York, and both workers and shop owners in the garment business had gotten off the boats together. Many of the bosses had been workers themselves, and the negotiations amazed Brandeis as workers and manufacturers shouted at each other across the table in Yiddish, which he more or less understood because of his fluency in German. Some of the workers may have complained about the serflike status that they, and especially the women, endured in the shops, but at the conference table Brandeis saw more of what he termed "industrial democracy" than he had ever witnessed before. These workers, many of them literate and articulate, felt no sense of inferiority to their employers and treated them as equals.

Certainly in Boston he had never heard a labor man yell at his boss, "Ihr darft sich shemen! Passt dos far a Idn?"—Shame on you! Is this worthy of a Jew?" Workers and shop owners quoted the Bible and the Talmud at each other, and he heard one man shout at his employer in the words of Isaiah, "It is you who have devoured the vineyard, the spoil of the poor is in your house. What do you mean by crushing My people, by grinding the face of the poor?" Later, when he joined the Zionist movement . . . and people asked him how he had come to that decision, he insisted that he had come back to his people through his Americanism, and cited the democracy he saw at work in the garment strike.[39]

Labor unrest was particularly high in the late 19th and early 20th centuries, as McGerr succinctly reported:

The "greatest conflict between capital and labor ever waged in the history of the world" began in stillness on the morning of May 12, 1902. That day, at a call from the United Mine Workers (UMW), more than 140,000 laboring men abandoned their jobs in the anthracite coal fields of northeastern Pennsylvania. In mine after mine across Wyoming, Lehigh, and Schuykill districts, the hard, noisy work of blasting, digging, and hauling coal gave way to "absolute quiet."[40]

Yet there were other strikes before and after this infamous strike:

The anthracite coal strike was one of the soaring number of work stoppages that made the United States the most strike-torn nation in the world. In 1898, there had been 1,098 strikes and lockouts across the country. The number jumped to 1,839 in 1900 and jumped again to 3,012 in 1901. These battles testified to the intensity of class conflict in industrial America. With the return of prosperity, with the continuing mechanization of the workplace, with the growth of labor organization, workers and employers naturally continued their ongoing struggle to control manual labor and its rewards. The deep ideological divide between the two sides, the chasm between individualism and mutualism, intensified the conflict. In the 1900s, no one knew what the outcome would be.[41]

Many strikes became violent, and the divide between the workers and management was comparatively high in the annals of American history. When the gap between the haves and have-nots increases beyond some threshold, the lessons of history are abundantly clear. Discord no longer is extraordinary but the norm.

Thomas Piketty and Emmanuel Saez studied income inequality in the United States from 1913 to 1998.[42] In comparing the United States, United Kingdom, and France, the researchers provided the following conclusions:

Some important differences, however, need to be emphasized. First, the shock of World War II was more pronounced in France and in the United Kingdom than in the United States. This is consistent with the fact that capital owners suffered from physical capital losses during the war in Europe, while there was no destruction on U.S. soil. Second, the World War II wage compression was very short-lived in France, while it had long-lasting effects in the United States. In France, wage inequality, measured both in terms of top wage shares and in terms of interdecile ratios, appears to have been extremely stable over the course of the twentieth century. The U.S. history of wage inequality looks very different: the war compression had long-lasting effects, and then wage inequality increased considerably since the 1970s, which explains the U.S. upturn of top income shares since the 1970s. The fact that France and the United States display such diverging trends is consistent with our interpretation that technical change alone cannot account for the U.S. increase in inequality. . . .

In France, top incomes are still composed primarily of dividend income, although wealth concentration is much lower than what it was one century ago. In the United States, due to the very large rise of top wages since the 1970s, the coupon-clipping rentiers have been overtaken by the working rich. Such a pattern might not last for very long because our proposed interpretation also suggests that the decline of progressive taxation observed since the early 1980s in the United States could very well spur a revival of high wealth concentration and top capital incomes during the next few decades.[43]

Indeed, Piketty and Saez's prophesy was quite accurate in the early part of the 21st century. The tax cuts advocated by President George W. Bush and passed by the members of Congress in 2001 and 2003 actually exacerbated the problem of income inequality in the United States. As Emily Horton of the Center on Budget and Policy Priorities reported:

The largest benefits from the Bush tax cuts flowed to high-income taxpayers. From 2004–2012 (the years for which comparable estimates are available), the top 1 percent of households received average tax cuts of more than $50,000 each year. On average, these households received a total tax cut of over $570,000 over this period.

High-income taxpayers also received the largest tax cuts as a share of their after-tax incomes. The Tax Policy Center estimated that in 2010, the year the tax cuts were fully phased in, they raised the after-tax incomes of the top 1 percent of households by 6.7 percent, while only raising the after-tax incomes of the middle 20 percent of households by 2.8 percent. The bottom 20 percent of households received the smallest tax cuts, with their after-tax incomes increasing by just 1.0 percent due to the tax cuts.[44]

Many economists, historians, political scientists, and sociologists alike have been making the same contention for some time. The growing inequality in the United States is not a coincidence; it is, in part, the product of direct government intervention on the part of past presidents and members of Congress. Since the early 1980s, the rise of regressive taxation has resulted in a significant shift in wealth away from the vast majority of Americans to the most affluent in this society. In this context, it is hardly surprising that the gap between rich and poor has widened so much in the United States compared to our democratic peers across the globe.

Miles Corak conducted a study of a number of Western nations, including the United States, to determine the relationship between income inequality and intergenerational economic mobility.[45] Similar to a plethora of other studies, his findings suggest a continuance of the divide between the haves and have-nots in the United States:

> Relatively less upward mobility of the least advantaged is one reason why intergenerational mobility is lower in the United States than in other countries to which Americans are often compared. But it is not the only reason. Intergenerational mobility is also lower because children of top-earning parents are more likely to become top earners in their turn. An era of rising inequality will be more likely to heighten these differences than diminish them. . . . Inequality lowers mobility because it shapes opportunity. It heightens the income consequences of innate differences between individuals; it also changes opportunities, incentives, and institutions that form, develop, and transmit characteristics and skills valued in the labor market; and it shifts the balance of power so that some groups are in a position to structure policies or otherwise support their children's achievement independent of talent. . . .
>
> While the imagined prospect of upward mobility for those in the lower part of the income distribution shares little in common with the generational dynamics of the top 1 percent, the latter may continue to be an important touchstone for those in, say, the top fifth of the US income distribution. After all, this group too has experienced significant growth in its relative standing, which partly reflects an increasing return to the graduate and other higher degrees for which they exerted considerable effort but is also linked to a background of nurturing families and select colleges. . . . For them, the "American Dream" lives on, and as a result they are likely not predisposed, with their considerable political and cultural influence, to support the recasting of American public policy to meet its most pressing need, the upward mobility of those at the bottom.[46]

The conclusions rendered in this intergenerational mobility analysis are most disconcerting. They suggest that, at best, the notion of the "American Dream," which will be scrutinized in chapter 4, exists for 20 percent of the population, but the reality for the remaining 80 percent is that upward mobility is unlikely. For much of U.S. history, Americans have subscribed to the idea that through hard work, good choices, and following the rules, opportunities for upward mobility abound. What happens in a society where a fairly rigid class system exists? To what extent will the United States, the only superpower on earth, prosper into the future when so few of its citizens are destined to advance their class existence in a society with limited upward mobility? The juxtaposition between the United States and other global democracies presented in this chapter does not reflect well on a country that emerged as one of two superpowers after World War II and became the only superpower when the Soviet Union dissolved. If people lose hope and no longer believe they can change their own plight in this world, and worse, that their children are destined to struggle just to maintain their current existence, they may engage in nontraditional and perhaps extremist activities, and they may find the political messages of fringe candidates appealing (e.g., Donald Trump in 2016).

In a book originally published in 1975, the late economist Arthur Okun contended that capitalism created disparities between and among citizens. Efficiency is the penultimate principle in economic institutions. The pursuit of efficiency can produce income inequality, as Okun explained:

> American society proclaims the worth of every human being. All citizens are guaranteed equal justice and equal political rights. Everyone has a pledge of speedy response from the fire department and access to national monuments. As American citizens, we are all members of the same club.
>
> Yet at the same time, our institutions say "find a job or go hungry," "succeed or suffer." They prod us to get ahead of our neighbors economically after telling us to stay in line socially. They award prizes that allow the big winners to feed their pets better than the losers can feed their children.
>
> Such is the double standard of a capitalist democracy, professing and pursuing an egalitarian political and social system and simultaneously generating gaping disparities in economic well-being. This mixture of equality and inequality sometimes smacks of inconsistency and even insincerity. Yet I believe that, in many cases, the institutional arrangements represent uneasy compromises rather than fundamental inconsistencies. The contrasts among American families in living standards and in material wealth reflect a system of rewards and penalties that is intended to encourage effort and channel it into socially productive activity. To the extent that the system succeeds, it generates an efficient economy. But that pursuit of efficiency necessarily creates inequalities. And hence society faces a tradeoff between equality and efficiency.[47]

Okun died in 1980. In the most recent edition of *Equality and Efficiency: The Big Tradeoff*, Lawrence Summers wrote the foreword and explains how Okun's views may have evolved in the post-Reagan era. Summers is currently the Charles W. Eliot University Professor of Harvard University. He previously served as president of Harvard and was the U.S. treasury secretary from 1999 to 2001.[48] In the context of Okun's time, the regressive income tax policies, especially during the Reagan and George W. Bush eras, had not yet been implemented. Summers hypothesizes that Okun would have responded to the changing economic and political dynamics in the following manner:

> First, Okun would recognize the stagnation in middle-class incomes is a central issue for democracies. He would emphasize the importance of constructive supply-side agenda that embraces the development of human capital, scientific knowledge, public infrastructure, and business investment. . . .
>
> Second, Okun would have been very disturbed by the rapid growth in incomes at the top of the distribution. I am quite confident that if he were writing today he would have been even more emphatic in urging reform to make taxes more progressive. . . .
>
> Third, Okun would, I suspect, have had great sympathy for those who pointed out the adverse impacts of globalization on disadvantaged workers. He would have empathized with complaints that outsourcing leads to the hollowing out of traditional industrial sectors. But, in line with his generally balanced approach, I suspect that he would nonetheless have supported well-designed policy packages that promoted trade . . .
>
> Fourth, Okun would have been both surprised and appalled that deflation had become as much an American economic challenge as inflation. And he would have been very troubled by the retreat from work by middle-aged men. The idea that even when the economy is near full employment, more than one in seven men between the ages of 25 and 54 are not working would have left him profoundly dissatisfied. . . .
>
> Fifth, Okun would, I imagine, have engaged in some way with the widespread loss of confidence in government and other institutions that has become manifest over the last long generation. I am not sure what he would have concluded. . . . I suspect he would have been sympathetic to the objective of improving government performance to restore the faith of citizens.[49]

Obviously, economists, just like other social scientists, draw normative conclusions that vary.[50] Other scholars may not concur with Summers's assessment of Okun. Nevertheless, it is important to remember that all analysts are influenced by a plethora of factors, including their interpretation of history, vision, and the context of the time in which they lived.

Income Inequality and Poverty

The United States' capitalist tradition is deeply rooted in its history (see chapter 4). I am not suggesting that everyone should have an equal outcome (i.e., all adults in the United States have the same annual income). There are a plethora of reasons why that vision would be both implausible and impractical. The notion of equality of opportunity, however, is a rich tenet of the American tradition. Benjamin Page and James Simmons offered a profound commentary regarding poverty and inequality in the United States in 2000:

> The average U.S. citizen enjoys a standard of living among the highest on the globe. Nonetheless, many millions of Americans live in poverty. Many more millions of workers struggle to make ends meet. The gap between rich and poor is much greater than in most advanced industrial countries and has grown wider in recent years.
>
> Some amount of inequality is no doubt necessary in order to motivate people and allocate resources efficiently. But we will see that the extremely high levels of poverty and inequality in the United States are *not* required for economic efficiency, they do *not* simply reflect people's work effort and productivity, and they are *not* beyond our control. Countries as rich as our own have achieved prosperity with far less poverty and inequality. We have a choice.[51]

Indeed, policy makers in the United States do have a choice. There are a number of public policy reforms that could have the cumulative net effect of reducing poverty and inequality in the United States. The reform proposals in question will be presented in chapter 5.

The framers of the early republic in the late 18th century did not envision, nor did they endorse, the kind of inequality and poverty that are the norm today. In *Plutocracy in America*, Ronald Formisano contended:

> Some of the gentlemen who formed the governing class in the early republic privately modeled themselves (at least to a certain degree) on the European grandees they publically scorned. Jefferson treasured books and learning and enjoyed fine French wine, as well as the comforts dozens of African American slaves provided on his Virginia plantation. Other founders, northerners as well as southerners, also benefited from slave labor. But many of those who framed the Constitution believed that the survival of a republican form of government depended on a very general "equality of condition" that prevailed in society among white males. Enfranchising women and people of color did not cross their minds, and they had reservations about "the lower orders" of white males participating in the body politick. They envisioned no measures to redistribute property, much less a classless utopia, but they did see America as a land of opportunity absent the extremes of wealth and privilege of Old Europe.
>
> That ideal of the founders has been forgotten—if not discarded—by contemporary plutocrats and their enablers, forming a political class that has turned government and society into entities very much resembling an

aristocracy. A republic of opportunity has been submerged by a government of the extremely wealthy who now isolate and remove themselves from contact with ordinary citizens by a withdrawal into gated neighborhoods, private jets, chauffeured limousines, and helicopters and by disdain for mingling in common, public spaces. This plutocracy continues to enjoy the fruits of years of government policy directed toward maintaining their inordinate political influence that, in turn, enables the upper caste's continued accumulation of wealth at the expense of everyone else.[52]

A strange reality pervades the United States, which purports to be the land of opportunity. The gap between rich and poor is currently at a historic level, the middle class is shrinking, and poor people are particularly disadvantaged, and even punished, by public policies created by members of Congress and the president. It is difficult to sustain the argument that a vast superpower, such as the United States, can sustain its global leadership role and any sense of moral authority with regard to other nation-states when such inequities perpetuate in the contemporary United States.[53] This current situation was not part of the historical tradition of this country tracing back to its founding. The entire notion of a landed aristocracy was repudiated precisely because it stifled an essential component of a republic—equality of opportunity. Having such a comparatively high level of class stratification is not a sign of a healthy democracy; fortunately, there are ways to reverse this situation.

President Abraham Lincoln issued one of the greatest statements of national purpose in U.S. history on November 19, 1863, when he presented the Gettysburg Address during the Civil War. He ended this brief speech during the nation's most difficult internal crisis:

> It is rather for us to be here dedicated to the great task remaining before us—that from these honored dead we take increased devotion to that cause for which they gave the last full measure of devotion—that we here highly resolve that these dead shall not have died in vain, that this nation under God shall have a new birth of freedom, and that government of the people, by the people, for the people shall not perish from the earth.[54]

Leaders who serve in the national government must serve everyone. This is the essence of republicanism. A fundamental understanding of representative democracy is that it is incumbent upon policy makers to heed the plight of a diverse array of people in society when crafting public policies. Lincoln demonstrated steadfast and principled leadership during his tenure in office (1861–1865). His example of moral leadership under duress is a testimony to the premise that though there are some significant challenges in American society today, they can be addressed directly with appropriate leadership and resolve.

Notes

1. Lester J. Cappon (ed.), *The Adams-Jefferson Letters: The Complete Correspondence between Thomas Jefferson and Abigail and John Adams* (Chapel Hill: University of North Carolina Press, 1959), Volume II, 388.

2. Cappon (ed.), *The Adams-Jefferson Letters: The Complete Correspondence Between Thomas Jefferson and Abigail and John Adams*, Volume II, 391.

3. Gabriel Kolko, *Wealth and Power in America: An Analysis of Social Class and Income Distribution* (New York: Praeger, 1962).

4. Kolko, *Wealth and Power in America: An Analysis of Social Class and Income*, 3.

5. Kolko, *Wealth and Power in America: An Analysis of Social Class and Income*, 6–7.

6. Bernadette D. Proctor, Jessica L. Semega, and Melissa A. Kollar, *Income and Poverty in the United States: 2015* (Washington, DC: U.S. Census Bureau, September 2016), https://www.census.gov/content/dam/Census/library/publications/2016/demo/p60-256.pdf (accessed May 2, 2017).

7. Robert I. Lerman and Shlomo Yitzhaki, "A Note on the Calculation and Interpretation of the Gini Index," *Economics Letters* 15, no. 3-4 (1984): 363–68.

8. Branko Milanovic and Shlomo Yitzhaki, "Decomposing World Income Distribution: Does the World Have a Middle Class?" *Review of Income and Wealth* 48, no. 2 (2002): 175; and Robert A. Isaak, *The Globalization Gap: How the Rich Get Richer and the Poor Get Left Further Behind* (Upper Saddle River, NJ: Prentice Hall Financial Times, 2005).

9. Paul Krugman, "Economic Inequality Has Accelerated," in *Is the Gap Between Rich and Poor Growing?*, ed. Robert Sims (Detroit, MI: Greenhaven Press, 2006), 12–3.

10. Mark Twain and Charles Dudley Warner, *The Gilded Age: A Tale of Today* (Seattle: University of Washington Press, 1968).

11. Twain and Warner, *The Gilded Age: A Tale of Today*, xiv–xv.

12. Twain and Warner, *The Gilded Age: A Tale of Today*, ix–x.

13. Uri Dadush, Kemal Derviş, Sarah Puritz Milsom, and Bennett Stancil, *Inequality in America: Facts, Trends, and International Perspectives* (Washington, DC: Brookings Institution Press, 2012), 1–2.

14. Estelle Sommeiller, Mark Price, and Ellis Wazeter, *Income Inequality in the U.S. by State, Metropolitan Area, and County* (Washington, DC: Economic Policy Institute, June 16, 2016), 1, http://www.epi.org/files/pdf/107100.pdf (accessed May 15, 2017).

15. Chad Stone, Danilo Trisi, Arloc Sherman, and Emily Horton, *A Guide to Statistics on Historical Trends in Income Inequality* (Washington, DC: Center on Budget and Policy Priorities, October 11, 2017), https://www.cbpp.org/research/poverty-and-inequality/a-guide-to-statistics-on-historical-trends-in-income-inequality (accessed January 7, 2018).

16. History.com, "The Roaring Twenties," http://www.history.com/topics/roaring-twenties/ (accessed May 20, 2017).

17. Stone, Trisi, Sherman, and Horton, *A Guide to Statistics on Historical Trends in Income Inequality.*

18. Lane Kenworthy and Timothy Smeeding, *Growing Inequalities and Their Impacts in the United States: Country Report for the United States* (Stockholm: GINI, January 2013), 96.

19. Kenworthy and Smeeding, *Growing Inequalities and Their Impacts in the United States: Country Report for the United States*, 97.

20. U.S. Bureau of Labor Statistics, Office of Occupational Statistics and Employment Projections, "Employment Projections: Unemployment Rates and Earnings by Educational Attainment," https://www.bls.gov/emp/ep_chart_001 .htm (accessed May 22, 2017).

21. University of California, Berkeley, Goldman School of Public Policy, "Robert Reich," https://gspp.berkeley.edu/directories/faculty/robert-reich (accessed May 24, 2017).

22. Robert B. Reich, *The Work of Nations: Preparing Ourselves for 21st-Century Capitalism* (New York: Vintage Books, 1992).

23. Reich, *The Work of Nations: Preparing Ourselves for 21st-Century Capitalism*, 198–99.

24. Robert B. Reich, *Supercapitalism: The Transformation of Business, Democracy, and Everyday Life* (New York: Alfred A. Knopf, 2007), 4–5.

25. Stephen Haseler, *The Super-Rich: The Unjust New World of Global Capitalism* (New York: St. Martin's Press, 2000), 43; and Global Policy Institute, "Professor Stephen Haseler," http://www.gpilondon.com/people/professor-stephen-haseler/ (accessed May 24, 2017).

26. Haseler, *The Super-Rich: The Unjust New World of Global Capitalism*, 1–2.

27. See Chernow, *Titan: The Life of John D. Rockefeller, Sr.*; Nasaw, *Andrew Carnegie*; and Steven Watts, *The People's Tycoon: Henry Ford and the American Century* (New York: Alfred A. Knopf, 2005).

28. Jonathan Kozol, *Savage Inequalities: Children in America's Schools* (New York: Crown Publishers, 1991), 233.

29. Fife, *Old School Still Matters: Lessons from History to Reform Public Education in America*, 1–41.

30. Lee Rainwater, *What Money Buys: Inequality and the Social Meanings of Income* (New York: Basic Books, 1974), 1.

31. Peter Edelman, *So Rich, So Poor: Why It's So Hard to End Poverty in America* (New York: The New Press, 2012), 141–42.

32. *New York Times*, "Two Clinton Aides Resign to Protest New Welfare Law," September 12, 1996, http://www.nytimes.com/1996/09/12/us/two-clinton-aides -resign-to-protest-new-welfare-law.html (accessed May 26, 2017).

33. Denny Braun, *The Rich Get Richer: The Rise of Income Inequality in the United States and the World* (Chicago: Nelson-Hall Publishers, 1997).

34. Braun, *The Rich Get Richer: The Rise of Income Inequality in the United States and the World*, 1–2.

35. Braun, *The Rich Get Richer: The Rise of Income Inequality in the United States and the World*, 415–16.

36. There are numerous biographies on Louis Brandeis: Melvin I. Urofsky, *Louis D. Brandeis: A Life* (New York: Pantheon Books, 2009); Philippa Strum (ed.), *Brandeis on Democracy* (Lawrence: University Press of Kansas, 1995); Lewis J. Paper, *Brandeis: An Intimate Biography of One of America's Truly Great Supreme Court Justices* (Englewood Cliffs, NJ: Prentice-Hall, 1983); Philippa Strum, *Brandeis: Beyond Progressivism* (Lawrence: University Press of Kansas, 1993); Jeffrey Rosen, *Louis D. Brandeis: American Prophet* (New Haven, CT: Yale University Press, 2016); David C. Gross, *A Justice for All the People: Louis D. Brandeis* (New York: E. P. Dutton, 1987); and Alfred Lief, *The Social and Economic Views of Mr. Justice Brandeis* (New York: Vanguard Press, 1930).

37. Urofsky, *Louis D. Brandeis: A Life*, 670–71.

38. Lief, *The Social and Economic Views of Mr. Justice Brandeis*, xix.

39. Urofsky, *Louis D. Brandeis: A Life*, 253.

40. McGerr, *A Fierce Discontent: The Rise and Fall of the Progressive Movement in America*, 118.

41. McGerr, *A Fierce Discontent: The Rise and Fall of the Progressive Movement in America*, 119–20.

42. Thomas Piketty and Emmanuel Saez, "Income Inequality in the United States, 1913–1998," *The Quarterly Journal of Economics* 117, no. 1 (2003): 1–39.

43. Piketty and Saez, "Income Inequality in the United States, 1913–1998," 37.

44. Emily Horton, "The Legacy of the 2001 and 2003 'Bush' Tax Cuts," http://www.cbpp.org/research/federal-tax/the-legacy-of-the-2001-and-2003-bush-tax-cuts (accessed May 28, 2017).

45. Miles Corak, "Income Inequality, Equality of Opportunity, and Intergenerational Mobility," *Journal of Economic Perspectives* 27, no. 3 (2013): 79–102.

46. Corak, "Income Inequality, Equality of Opportunity, and Intergenerational Mobility," 97–9.

47. Arthur M. Okun, *Equality and Efficiency: The Big Tradeoff* (Washington, DC: Brookings Institution Press), 1.

48. Harvard University, John F. Kennedy School of Government, "Lawrence H. Summers," https://www.hks.harvard.edu/about/faculty-staff-directory/lawrence-summers (accessed May 30, 2017).

49. Okun, *Equality and Efficiency: The Big Tradeoff*, x–xii.

50. N. Gregory Mankiw, "Defending the One Percent," *Journal of Economic Perspectives* 27, no. 3 (2013): 33.

51. Benjamin I. Page and James R. Simmons, *What Government Can Do: Dealing with Poverty and Inequality* (Chicago: University of Chicago Press, 2000), 11.

52. Ronald P. Formisano, *Plutocracy in America: How Increasing Inequality Destroys the Middle Class and Exploits the Poor* (Baltimore, MD: Johns Hopkins University Press, 2015), 10–1.

53. There are numerous other works on the subject of income equality: Richard Wilkinson and Kate Pickett, *The Spirit Level: Why Greater Equality Makes Societies Stronger* (New York: Bloomsbury Press, 2009); David Cay Johnston (ed.), *Divided: The Perils of Our Growing Inequality* (New York: The New Press, 2014); Chuck Collins, *Born on Third Base: A One Percenter Makes the Case for Tackling*

Inequality, Bringing Wealth Home, and Committing to the Common Good (White River Junction, VT: Chelsea Green Publishing, 2016); Branko Milanovic, *The Haves and the Have Nots: A Brief and Idiosyncratic History of Global Inequality* (New York: Basic Books, 2011); and Robert S. Rycroft, *The Economics of Inequality, Discrimination, Poverty, and Mobility* (Armonk, NY: M. E. Sharpe, 2009).

54. Yale University Law School, Avalon Project: Documents in Law, History and Diplomacy, "Gettysburg Address," http://avalon.law.yale.edu/19th_century /gettyb.asp (accessed on June 4, 2017).

CHAPTER FOUR

Liberal versus Conservative Beliefs about Poverty in an Individualist Capitalist System

Contemporary liberals tend to believe that most poor people are victims of external forces that have largely determined their plight. Such structural forces as globalization and outsourcing, coupled with the decline of labor unions, have limited a poor person's ability to escape poverty. To liberals, there are too many jobs in the U.S. economy that do not pay a living wage, and the result of this systemic reality is that many citizens, especially women and people of color, fall further and further behind their more affluent counterparts. To liberals, there are many opportunities for people in a capitalist society, but some do not flourish even though they have a sufficient work ethic and are making reasonably prudent choices in their lives. This is why liberals generally endorse government intervention in the form of programs to assist the needy. The basic premise on the part of contemporary liberals in the United States is that capitalism works well for most, but certainly not all, citizens. To them, this is justification for policies such as an increase in the minimum wage, federally subsidized job training, public assistance, and a wide array of public assistance programs for children in particular.

Contemporary conservatives tend to view the poor with disdain, in that many envision ample opportunities in the capitalist economy and view the poor as being lazy, as making poor choices, such as having children out of wedlock, perhaps succumbing to the scourge of drug and alcohol abuse, and seeking immediate gratification in lieu of going to school and obtaining a degree or multiple degrees. Within conservative circles, the critique of the poor has often encompassed a moral condemnation as well. In addition, conservatives have generally viewed the welfare system as creating a culture of dependency and making the poverty problem worse as a result. In short, conservatives generally believe there are ample opportunities in a capitalist economy, and it is incumbent upon the individual to maximize them. Too much intervention in the marketplace, to them, is therefore unwarranted and unjustified.

To illustrate these aforementioned beliefs, pollsters at the Pew Research Center conducted an illuminating poll in 2017 concerning partisanship, ideology, and public policy. Those surveyed were asked to respond to two questions; the first question was "In your opinion, which generally has more to do with why a person is rich?"[1] Two choices were offered: worked harder and had advantages in life. According to 66 percent of Republicans and those who lean Republican, people are rich because they work harder, while only 21 percent responded that rich people had advantages in life. Conversely, only 29 percent of Democrats and those who lean Democratic believe that people are rich because they worked harder, while 60 percent responded that rich people had advantages in life.[2]

The second question was "In your opinion, which generally has more to do with why a person is poor?"[3] The two choices offered were lack of effort and circumstances beyond control. Fifty-six percent of Republicans and those who lean Republican responded that people are poor due to lack of effort, while 32 percent determined that people are poor due to circumstances beyond their control.[4] Only 19 percent of Democrats or those who lean Democratic responded that being poor is due to lack of effort, while 71 percent said poor people experienced their plight due to circumstances beyond their control.[5] The Pew survey was conclusive in that most Republicans link a person's financial standing to their own diligence, while Democrats attribute being rich or poor to circumstances beyond the control of the affluent and less affluent alike.[6]

Democrats represent the more liberal creed in the contemporary United States, while Republicans represent contemporary conservatism, particularly in the post-Reagan era. Clearly, on the poverty issue, the parties and corresponding ideologies that dominate both mainstream parties have a definitive vision when it comes to the poor. It is important to highlight these differences, as the pragmatic reality of American politics is that a diverse citizenry makes constant and often contradictory demands on policy makers. Yet liberals and conservatives do share a few important things in common. First, both embrace capitalism as the optimum economic system, although obviously there are stark differences of opinion when it comes to regulatory matters in particular. Second, representatives from both camps share the same political culture. Americans generally revere the notion of rugged individualism, or the general perception that individuals, free of too much government interference, can accomplish great things and achieve the American Dream.

Many sociologists contend that the individualist creed in this country was first recognized and documented in detail by Alexis de Tocqueville (1805–1859). Tocqueville was a French philosopher and sociologist who traveled in the United States extensively in the early 19th century and wrote a two-volume (1835 and 1840) account of his travels and observations entitled *Democracy in America*. His book on the United States was very influential in the 19th century, a time when many European elites were pondering why democracy under the federal Constitution had not yet failed in the United States as it had under the Articles of Confederation.[7] As Harvey Mansfield and Delba Winthrop noted:

> *Democracy in America* is at once the best book ever written on democracy and the best book ever written on America. Tocqueville connects the two subjects in his Introduction, and in his title, by observing that America is the land of democracy. It is the country where democracy is least hindered and most perfected, where democracy is at its most characteristic and at its best. Today that claim might be contested, but it is at least arguable. If the twentieth century has been an American century, it is because the work of America—not altogether unsuccessful—has been to keep democracy strong where it is alive and to promote it where it is weak or nonexistent. Somehow, after 165 years, democracy is still in America.[8]

As policy makers and citizens alike ponder how to address the ongoing challenge of poverty in the United States, much can be learned and extracted from de Tocqueville's analysis and prophesy regarding individualism in the United States. This is how he defined individualism during his travails in the United States:

> I have brought out how, in centuries of equality, each man seeks his beliefs in himself; I want to show how, in the same centuries, he turns all his sentiments toward himself alone. *Individualism* is a recent expression arising from a new idea. Our fathers knew only selfishness. Selfishness is a passionate and exaggerated love of self that brings man to relate everything to himself alone and to prefer himself to everything. Individualism is a reflective and peaceable sentiment that disposes each citizen to isolate himself from the mass of those like him and to withdraw to one side with his family and his friends, so that after having thus created a little society for his own use, he willingly abandons society at large to itself. Selfishness is born of a blind instinct; individualism proceeds from an erroneous judgment rather than a depraved sentiment. . . . As conditions are equalized, one finds a great number of individuals who, not being wealthy enough or powerful enough to exert a great influence over the fates of those like them, have nevertheless acquired or preserved enough enlightenment and goods to be able to be self-sufficient. These owe nothing to anyone, they expect so to speak nothing from anyone; they are in the habit of always

considering themselves in isolation, and they willingly fancy that their whole destiny is in their hands. Thus not only does democracy make each man forget his ancestors, but it hides his descendants from him and separates him from his contemporaries; it constantly leads him back toward himself alone and threatens finally to confine him wholly in the solitude of his own heart.[9]

Individualism taken to an extreme can cause people to be inward in their outlook. This can be dangerous to the goal of promoting the greater common good, as those who succumb to this approach view public policy issues only in terms of what is perceived to be in their self-interest, as opposed to creating policies that are beneficial to greater society. In the estimation of a number of social scientists, American individualism in the contemporary era has shifted away from individualism toward egoism, which suggests that Americans are self-absorbed and inward in their world view.

Daniel Elazar maintained that Tocqueville was instructive about the cultural basis of American democracy during the early era of Jacksonian democracy:

> The third bridge Tocqueville builds is between ideas, culture, institutions, and behavior. It is to be found in his contrast between (American) individualism and (French) egoism. In making that distinction, he emphasizes the way in which American individualism combines the spirit of religion with the spirit of liberty and leads to the establishment of free associations to provide a corrective to the kind of individualism that knows no bonds, which Tocqueville refers to as "egoism." It is especially useful for contemporaries to examine this third bridge. Following Tocqueville, the change in American individualism as a result of the revolutionary events of the 1960s is its shift to egoism, namely to individualism strictly as self-concern, with a concomitant erosion of American institutions and all that this erosion means for the future of American democracy.[10]

Tocqueville's vision of democracy, as he articulated originally during President Andrew Jackson's tenure (1829–1837), was that individualism was basically a positive characteristic in a democracy as long as citizens had faith and trust in institutions and as long as citizens possessed and maintained civic virtue. As pollsters at Gallup report, Americans' confidence in institutions remains historically low. In particular, Americans have a fairly low level of confidence in the following entities: churches, the medical system, the presidency, the U.S. Supreme Court, public schools, banks, organized labor, the criminal justice system, television news, newspapers, big business, and Congress.[11] Without faith and trust in institutions, combined with a decline in civic virtue perhaps measurable in terms of voter turnout, individualism is adversely affected, in Tocqueville's view. In the modern era, cynicism is joined with low levels of citizen participation, a combination that runs quite counter to the vision Tocqueville articulated about nine generations ago, particularly considering the popular opinion of Congress, the institution that has the most obvious link between citizens and their national government in this representative democracy.[12]

Individualism in the Modern Era

In the mid-1980s, Robert Bellah and his colleagues communicated their understanding of Tocqueville's vision regarding individualism in the contemporary era:

> Tocqueville saw the isolation to which Americans are prone as ominous for the future of our freedom. It is just such isolation that is always encouraged by despotism. And so Tocqueville is particularly interested in all those countervailing tendencies that pull people back from their isolation into social communion. Immersion in private economic pursuits undermines the person as   citizen. On the other hand, involvement in public affairs is the best antidote to the pernicious effects of individualistic isolation: "Citizens who are bound to take part in public affairs must turn from the private interests and occasionally take a look at something other than themselves." It is precisely in these respects that mores become important. The habits and practices of religion and democratic participation educate the citizen to a larger view than his purely private world would allow. These habits and practices rely to some extent on self-interest in their educational work, but it is only when self-interest has to some degree been transcended that they succeed. In ways that Jefferson would have understood, Tocqueville argues that a variety of active civic organizations are the key to American democracy. Through active involvement in common concerns, the citizen can overcome the sense of relative isolation and powerlessness that results from the insecurity of life in an increasingly commercial society. Associations, along with decentralized, local administration, mediate between the individual and the centralized state, providing forums in which opinion can be publicly and intelligently shaped and the subtle habits of public initiative and responsibility learned and passed on. Associational life, in Tocqueville's thinking, is the best bulwark against the condition he feared most: the mass society of mutually antagonistic individuals, easy prey to despotism.[13]

As Bellah and colleagues contended, "American citizenship was anchored in the ethos and institutions of the face-to-face community of the town."[14] The United States is no longer a country of small towns where citizens interact on a regular and consistent basis. In fact, according to demographers, 62.7 percent of all Americans live in cities, though the cities in question only account for 3.5 percent of the land area in this country.[15] In short, the 19th-century United States is gone, and it has been replaced with a more densely populated citizenry where people are more isolated and empathy for fellow citizens is being challenged accordingly. The tangible result is most unfortunate, for individualism has gone awry in the manner in which Tocqueville envisioned it.

The spirit of public service that pervaded this country during the early decades of the republic, the Progressive Era, the Great Depression, and the 1960s has largely disappeared.[16] Some prominent leaders, such as President Ronald Reagan, are part of the reason why so many tend to espouse individualism and self-interest as relative virtues in American society:

> From the time he accepted his party's nomination as a candidate for the presidency in 1980, Reagan has eloquently defined his mission as one of building "a new consensus with all those across the land who share a community of values embedded in these words: family, work, neighborhood, peace and freedom." In Reagan's rhetoric, however, such words, charged with moral resonance, are evocations of private, rather than public, virtues. Work is an economic activity pursued by self-reliant individuals in the interests of themselves and their families. In his inaugural address, Reagan said that "we the people" are "a special interest group" that is "made up of men and women who raise our food, patrol our streets, man our mines and factories, teach our children, keep our homes and heal us when we're sick." By defining us by our occupations, Reagan sees us not as a polity but as an economy, in which the population is an all-inclusive "interest group," chiefly concerned with "a healthy, vigorous, growing economy that provides equal opportunity for all Americans."[17]

To some, the notion of citizenship has been supplanted by individualism. The sheer premise that citizens are somehow akin to special interest groups consisting of individuals pursuing their own economic self-interest is antithetical to the democratic ethos articulated by Tocqueville and other advocates of democracy. In fact, it is dangerous in the extreme.

In *Bowling Alone: The Collapse and Revival of American Community* (2000), Robert Putnam examined trends in political participation in the United States and concluded:

> Organizational records suggest that for the first two-thirds of the twentieth century Americans' involvement in civic associations of all sorts rose steadily, except for the parenthesis of the Great Depression. In the last third of the century, by contrast, only mailing list membership has continued to expand, with the creation of an entirely new species of "tertiary" association whose members never actually meet. At the same time, active involvement in face-to-face organizations has plummeted, whether we

consider organizational records, survey reports, time diaries, or consumer expenditures. We could surely find individual exceptions—specific organizations that successfully sailed against the prevailing winds and tides— but the broad picture is one of declining membership in community organizations. During the last third of the twentieth century formal membership in organizations in general has edged downward by perhaps 10–20 percent. More important, active involvement in clubs and other voluntary associations has collapsed at an astonishing rate, more than halving most indexes of participation within barely a few decades.[18]

The case that individualism in the United States promotes democracy can no longer be sustained. On January 20, 1961, President John F. Kennedy eloquently stated, "And so, my fellow Americans: ask not what your country can do for you—ask what you can do for your country."[19] Individualism in the United States is the result of growing isolation, wherein many Americans do not support fundamental institutions in society. Instead, more and more people have become withdrawn from their neighbors and communities, and a growing libertarian ethos, arguably established when Ronald Reagan was first elected president in 1980, has taken root. As William Hudson explained:

> Eventually politicians would integrate libertarian-based policy proposals into their campaign platform. Conservative Republican presidential candidate Barry Goldwater translated his personal libertarian outlook into major themes in his 1964 campaign. Although Goldwater endured a massive repudiation at the polls, the conservative activists he inspired and other politicians, such as Ronald Reagan, carried forward the conservative dream and the libertarian ideas that formed a part of it. By the 1970s, libertarian proposals were taken seriously in political debate and well represented in policy discussions in Washington. At this time, policy think tanks like the Cato Institute and the Heritage Foundation were founded to promote these policy ideas. The world of academic scholarship took more respectful regard for libertarian ideas when Harvard political philosopher Robert Nozick formulated a systematic justification of libertarianism in *Anarchy, State, and Utopia*, published in 1974. So when Ronald Reagan took the presidential oath in 198[1], libertarianism was no longer an obscure doctrine of eccentric émigré thinkers but a coherent and influential set of ideas that would guide one side of the public policy debate into the next century.[20]

The libertarian and communitarian creeds will be discussed later in this chapter. In another book, Hudson contends that Americans have succumbed to radical individualism:[21]

> Americans have always associated individualism with the chance to get ahead based on one's own efforts, free of cultural, social, and political

constraints. Americans also associate individualism with freedom to express their individuality. They value the chance to define for themselves their own ideas of what is good for them. This freedom is claimed for nearly all aspects of life: Americans expect to say, believe, live, eat, and wear whatever they like based on individual choice. Attempts to regulate individual behavior on behalf of the broader good—such as requiring the wearing of seat belts or motorcycle helmets—always meet opposition. As long as they regard such behavior as harmless to others, Americans are quick to demand the right to do whatever they want. Many Americans would easily agree with one of the respondents to a recent survey of American young people who, when asked what was special about the United States, replied, "Individualism, and the fact that it is a democracy and you can do whatever you please."[22]

Hudson reflected on Tocqueville's 19th-century vision of the United States:

> Is what Tocqueville observed in the 1830s still true of the United States today? Do Americans still possess "habits of the heart" conducive to a civic-minded outlook? I believe that we have reason to worry about the balance between individualism and civic virtue in the United States today. American "habits of the heart" have evolved in the direction of less understanding of the social ties that bind us together in a common democratic society and a more selfish preoccupation with our individual selves. Individualism seems to have become excessive—to the point that Tocqueville, visiting the United States today, would probably have grave concern that our healthy democratic individualism was degenerating into the radical form he called "egoism."[23]

Admittedly, it is very difficult to measure, in an empirical manner, the extent to which Americans have succumbed to excessive individualism. However, a cross-national comparison on the subject of individualism is most illuminating.

Pollsters from the Pew Research Center surveyed people in 44 countries including the United States. Fifty-seven percent of Americans disagreed with the statement "Success in life is pretty much determined by forces outside our control"; this was far above the global median of 38 percent. Seventy-three percent of Americans responded that it was very important to work hard to get ahead in life; the global median was 50 percent. Thus, Americans recorded more individualistic responses than their counterparts in 43 other nations.[24] In fact, scholars at the Pew Research Center have concluded that in addition to individualism, Americans differ from their fellow citizens in European democracies when it comes to the role of government in society, freedom of expression, and religion and morality.[25]

The implications of individualism taken to an unhealthy level are sobering and will hinder efforts to help the indigent in American society. A primary challenge of people who are prone to looking inward in public policy debates is that they may render cause-and-effect conclusions that are not based on reality. If people are poor because they are lazy or guilty of making counterproductive choices, it becomes easier to blame the poor for their own plight. In other words, a smaller number of people may be willing to at least try to empathize with the less fortunate, because they have already determined that, to a considerable extent, poor people are to blame for their situation in life. A sense of community is lost when poverty is individualized, and it allows the more affluent to be far less attentive to their poverty-stricken fellow citizens. Hudson identified the implications of "radical individualism":

> American radical individualism challenges democracy in several ways. Most fundamentally, it erodes the habits of the heart that tie democratic citizens to one another and promote civic virtue. The relationship between radical individualism and civic-minded habits is circular. The more individuals see themselves as isolated and the more they are preoccupied with their own individual goals, the less they participate in public affairs or support the public sphere. As participation declines and the public sphere atrophies, individual isolation grows and individuals understand less about their interdependence with others. In short order, the society becomes merely an aggregation of isolated individuals whose limited perspective cannot encompass a larger society outside themselves. In this infertile ground, as Tocqueville understood, democracy is in peril.[26]

Indeed, democracy is under considerable assault if we the people refuse to participate in public affairs and policy and only focus inward when it comes to political and policy debates. Certainly voter turnout is a significant concern as the world's oldest democracy struggles to get more than half of adults to vote in presidential elections when most democracies have a much higher voter participation rate.

Included in table 4.1 is voter turnout in the United States from 1932 to 2016. Voter turnout is measured as the percentage of all those 18 and older who voted.[27] Turnout in presidential election years is always higher than in nonpresidential election years, which are commonly referred to as midterm elections. The highest voter turnout in the modern era in a presidential election year was 62.8 percent in the contest between John F. Kennedy and Richard Nixon in 1960. Bear in mind that 18–20-year-olds could not vote in presidential elections until 1972. Turnout in a presidential election year has not exceeded 60 percent since 1968. The highest turnout in a midterm election in the modern era is 45.4 percent (in 1962 and 1966). Using past

Table 4.1   Voter Turnout in U.S. Federal Elections, 1932–2016 (Percentage of Voting Age Population that Voted)

Election Year	Voter Turnout
1932	52.6
1934	42.1
1936	56.9
1938	Not available
1940	58.8
1942	32.5
1944	56.1
1946	37.1
1948	51.1
1950	41.2
1952	61.6
1954	41.7
1956	59.3
1958	43.0
1960	62.8
1962	45.4
1964	61.4
1966	45.4
1968	60.7
1970	43.6
1972	55.1
1974	35.7
1976	53.6
1978	34.5
1980	52.8
1982	37.7
1984	53.3
1986	33.6
1988	50.3
1990	33.6
1992	55.2
1994	36.5

Table 4.1   (*Continued*)

Election Year	Voter Turnout
1996	49.0
1998	33.1
2000	50.3
2002	34.8
2004	55.7
2006	36.1
2008	57.1
2010	37.0
2012	53.6
2014	33.2
2016	54.7

Sources: (1932–2010): U.S. Census Bureau. 2012. *Statistical Abstract of the United States: 2012.* Section 7: Elections. Accessed June 22, 2017, from https://www.census.gov/prod/2011pubs/12statab /election.pdf; and (2012–2016): U.S. Elections Project. 2017. Voter Turnout. Accessed June 22, 2017, from http://www.electproject .org/home/voter-turnout/voter-turnout-data.

elections and history as a guide, turnout is currently projected to be between 50 and 55 percent in a presidential election year and about 33 to 38 percent in a midterm election. Voter turnout in the rest of the free world in an analogous election is typically in the 60th to 80th percentile.[28] In a midterm election in the United States, more than 6 in 10 adults will not participate.

Clearly, some of the lower voter turnout in the United States can be attributed to fairly stringent voting laws (e.g., voter identification requirements, registration in advance of voting requirements, and laws governing felons and the franchise), as well as being a two-party state without proportional representation in the national legislature. Nevertheless, it is clear that the United States lags behind most of the free world in electoral participation.[29] It is very difficult to counter the contention that low voter turnout and a disenchanted citizenry that has little trust and faith in basic institutions are dangerous to democracy. Americans are increasingly isolated and frustrated. It is no wonder why the libertarian ethos is surging in the post-Reagan era as Hudson highlighted.

The Libertarian Philosophy

According to the Cato Institute, a libertarian think tank founded in 1974 by Ed Crane, Murray Rothbard, and Charles Koch, and now headquartered in

Washington, DC, a number of key libertarian concepts are rooted in the philosophy of John Locke, David Hume, Adam Smith, Thomas Jefferson, and Thomas Paine in the 17th and 18th centuries:

Individualism: libertarians see the individual as the basic unit of social analysis. Only individuals make choices and are responsible for their actions.

Individual rights: because individuals are moral agents, they have a right to be secure in their life, liberty, and property. These rights are not granted by government or by society; they are inherent in the nature of human beings.

Spontaneous order: a great degree of order in society is necessary for individuals to survive and flourish. It's easy to assume that order must be imposed by a central authority, the way we impose order on a stamp collection or a football team. The great insight of libertarian social analysis is that order in society arises spontaneously, out of the actions of thousands or millions of individuals who coordinate their actions with those of others in order to achieve their purposes.

The rule of law: libertarianism proposes a society of liberty under law, in which individuals are free to pursue their own lives so long as they respect the equal rights of others.

Limited government: to protect rights, individuals form governments. But government is a dangerous institution. Libertarians have great antipathy to concentrated power . . .

Free markets: to survive and to flourish, individuals need to engage in economic activity. The right to property entails the right to exchange property by mutual agreement. Free markets are the economic system of free individuals, and they are necessary to create wealth. Libertarians believe that people will be both freer and more prosperous if government intervention in people's economic choices is minimized.

The virtue of production: modern libertarians defend the right of productive people to keep what they earn, against a new class of politicians and bureaucrats who would seize their earnings to transfer them to non-producers.

Natural harmony of interests: libertarians believe that there is a natural harmony of interests among peaceful, productive people in a just society. One person's individual plans—which may involve getting a job, starting a business, buying a house, and so on—may conflict with the plans of others, so the market makes many of us change our plans. But we all prosper from the operation of the free market, and there are no necessary conflicts between farmers and merchants, manufacturers and importers.

Peace: libertarians have always battled the age-old scourge of war. They understand that war brought death and destruction on a grand scale, disrupted family and economic life, and put more power in the hands of the ruling class—which may explain why the rulers did not always share the popular sentiment for peace.[30]

The core concepts of the contemporary libertarian movement are apparent in the preamble of the 2016 platform of the Libertarian Party:

> As Libertarians, we seek a world of liberty; a world in which all individuals are sovereign over their own lives and no one is forced to sacrifice his or her values for the benefit of others. We believe that respect for individual rights is the essential precondition for a free and prosperous world, that force and fraud must be banished from human relationships, and that only through freedom can peace and prosperity be realized. Consequently, we defend each person's right to engage in any activity that is peaceful and honest, and welcome the diversity that freedom brings. The world we seek to build is one where individuals are free to follow their own dreams in their own ways, without interference from government or any authoritarian power.[31]

The ultimate focus for libertarians is the individual, and the philosophy is based on a dubious assumption that what is good for the individual in the free market is subsequently good for society. As Hudson noted in his refutation of the libertarian philosophy:

> The Libertarian Party offers a pristine form of libertarianism that encompasses both economic and social liberties. The Libertarian Party advocates dismantling nearly all government programs; the decriminalization of all drugs, prostitution, and pornography; the elimination of nearly all business regulation; and reducing the size of the military. Although few libertarians belong to, or subscribe to all the tenets of, the Libertarian Party, they take seriously the central premise of libertarianism: A truly democratic society is precisely one in which individuals have maximum freedom to pursue their own goals, independent of others in society. . . . I argue that this libertarian view of society is flawed. It fails to take into account the many ways in which individuals are inevitably connected to and dependent on one another and on society as a whole. A society in which people concern themselves only with pursuing their individual goals and do not take responsibility for the whole community could not survive. Because we live in society, we cannot avoid being concerned with others and with the good of the collectivity.[32]

In Hudson's book entitled *The Libertarian Illusion: Ideology, Public Policy, and the Assault on the Common Good*, he articulates his view that libertarianism has intuitive but superficial appeal; if one examines the implications of libertarianism, it is clear that it would be downright dangerous if this ethos and theory were put into practice through the implementation of public policy.

Americans tend to decry "big government," at least when asked by pollsters. In the abstract, it is easy to criticize "the government." However, what is the government, and why do we have it? Our ancestors created a republic so that the people could indirectly rule through their elected leaders. We have the opportunity, though many do not exercise their right to vote, to elect 100 U.S. senators and 435 members of the U.S. House of Representatives. We should have the right to directly elect the president as well in the world's oldest democracy.[33] Many laws require unelected technocrats (public administrators) to create regulations through the rule-making process in order to implement the laws in question.[34] What people tend to ignore is that there are reasons why laws and regulations exist. This does not mean that the laws or regulations that were created are perfect. They may be flawed in some way. Nevertheless, the point to consider is that history suggests that policy makers and administrators alike believed, in their professional opinions, that some form of intervention was necessary in order to address a societal reality at the time.

But how nice would it be to live in a country where freedom was almost absolute and people could do as they please? Libertarians advocate less or no government in many instances, and many Americans find this appealing. History, however, is full of examples where government intervention was justified in order to promote the greater common good. Think of the many laws and regulations that affect the daily lives of American citizens. Why are all aspects of the economy regulated? Consider the lessons of history on this matter, and the fundamental flaws inherent in libertarianism become quite apparent.

Regulations and laws have been created since the republic began under the current Constitution in 1789. Yet why did regulatory activity, in particular, increase dramatically in the modern era? Consider the licensing of health care professionals and the development of prescription drugs. Why not allow people to do what they so desire, free of government interference? After all, libertarians contend that individuals making choices in the free market is the optimum scenario. The reality of the health care industry is that more regulation has protected citizens to a much greater extent from fraud than during previous eras in U.S. history. Why are polluters regulated? Libertarians believe that the unimpeded marketplace is preferable to government interference. Yet this defies the environmental history of the United States. Some polluters were permitted to maximize profits without governmental intervention; regulations and laws forced many polluters to conform to new standards when they would have kept polluting because it was profitable to do so.

Why is food safer for consumption? Why are children safer from unscrupulous manufacturers? Why are virtually all modes of transportation safer than in the past? Government intervention has provided many citizens with a healthier way of life. Interestingly, the intervention in question was typically a response to either public opinion in that citizens demanded that government officials intervene in a given issue in order to protect them from externalities, or, as Teddy Roosevelt explained, because it was perceived to promote the greater common good:

> By the time I became President I had grown to feel with deep intensity of conviction that governmental agencies must find their justification largely in the way in which they are used for the practical betterment of living and working conditions among the mass of the people. I felt that the fight was really for the abolition of privilege; and one of the first stages in the battle was necessarily to fight for the rights of the workingman. For this reason I felt most strongly that all that the government could do in the interest of labor should be done. The Federal Government can rarely act with the directness that the State governments act. It can, however, do a good deal. My purpose was to make the National Government itself a model employer of labor, the effort being to make the per diem employee just as much as the Cabinet officer regard himself as one of the partners employed in the service of the public, proud of his work, eager to do it in the best possible manner, and confident of just treatment.[35]

Many aspects of life in the United States can be traced back to historical periods when the people collectively demanded more effective public policies from their elected leaders, or strong leadership resulted in public policies that had a significant impact on society as a whole. Older Americans have retirement income and Medicare due to government intervention. The environment is cleaner because many laws were passed, especially at the federal level. Civil and voting rights were extended in the aftermath of lengthy conflicts.

Contemporary libertarian thought can be traced to some very influential conservative political thinkers in the 20th century, including Friedrich Hayek, Leo Strauss, and Milton Friedman. The impact of their work on the Republican Party in the United States has been quite pronounced since the initial election of Ronald Reagan.[36]

Friedrich Hayek (1899–1992)

According to officials at the Mises Institute, Hayek is the most influential modern Austrian economist; he was also a founding board member of the Mises Institute.[37] In Hayek's seminal book, *The Road to Serfdom*, published in 1944, he argued that well-intended government intervention had led to socialist or fascist oppression and tyranny; the result of too much government intrusion in the marketplace was serfdom for the individual citizen.[38] Hayek's vision of government intervention was apparent in this work:

> The choice open to us is not between a system in which everybody will get what he deserves according to some absolute and universal standard of

right, and one where the individual shares are determined partly by acci-
dent or good or ill chance, but between a system where it is the will of a
few persons that decides who is to get what, and one where it depends at
least partly on the ability and enterprise of the people concerned and
partly on unforeseeable circumstances. This is no less relevant because in
a system of free enterprise chances are not equal, since such a system is
necessarily based on private property and (though perhaps not with the
same necessity) on inheritance, with the differences in opportunity which
these create. There is, indeed, a strong case for reducing this inequality of
opportunity as far as congenital differences permit and as it is possible to
do so without destroying the impersonal character of the process by which
everybody has to take his chance and no person's view about what is right
and desirable overrules that of others.[39]

In the context of World War II, Hayek concluded that Western progressives
had succumbed to a false and misleading notion that more government
intervention could remedy the social and economic ills in society. To Hayek,
socialistic policies would result in governmental oppression of the people
where individual freedom, the key tenet of libertarianism, would be greatly
diminished.[40]

Hayek was a fervent believer in the 19th-century liberal creed that prevailed in both Western Europe and the United States. The pursuit of the
good society could only come through limited government intervention:

If we are to build a better world, we must have the courage to make a new
start—even if that means some *reculer pour mieux sauter* [back up in order
to better jump forward]. It is not those who believe in inevitable tendencies
who show this courage, not those who preach a "New Order" which is no
more than a projection of the tendencies of the last forty years, and who
can think of nothing better than to imitate Hitler. It is, indeed, those who
cry loudest for the New Order who are most completely under the sway of
the ideas which have created this war and most of the evils from which we
suffer. The young are right if they have little confidence in the ideas which
rule most of their elders. But they are mistaken or misled when they believe
that these are still the liberal ideas of the nineteenth century, which, in
fact, the younger generation hardly knows. Though we neither can wish
nor possess the power to go back to the reality of the nineteenth century,
we have the opportunity to realize its ideals—and they were not mean. We
have little right to feel in this respect superior to our grandfathers; and we
should never forget that it is we, the twentieth century, and not they, who
have made a mess of things. If they had not yet fully learned what was
necessary to create the world they wanted, the experience we have since
gained ought to have equipped us better for the task. If in the first attempt
to create a world of free men we have failed, we must try again. The

guiding principle that a policy of freedom for the individual is the only true progressive policy remains as true today as it was in the nineteenth century.[41]

Hayek envisioned a definitive link between increased government intervention in the economy and society and individual oppression. The optimum manner in which to pursue individual freedom was through the laissez-faire vision articulated by Adam Smith in 1776.[42]

In 1960, in the aftermath of a plethora of post–World War II activities, Hayek published *The Constitution of Liberty*.[43] The progressive tradition of the 20th century had a profoundly negative impact on individual freedom from his libertarian perspective:

> It has been a long time since that ideal of freedom which inspired modern Western civilization and whose partial realization made possible the achievements of that civilization was effectively restated. In fact, for almost a century the basic principles on which this civilization was built have been falling into increasing disregard and oblivion. Men have sought for alternative social orders more often than they have tried to improve their understanding or use of the underlying principles of our civilization. It is only since we were confronted with an altogether different system that we have discovered that we have lost any clear conception of our aims and possess no firm principles which we can hold up against the dogmatic ideology of our antagonists.[44]

Hayek's conclusions about government intervention and the negative consequences associated with it had a profound influence on President Ronald Reagan, not only with regard to Reagan's views about tax cuts and government regulation but also his social welfare policies. To Reagan, the rise of the welfare state of the New Deal and Great Society, along with the evolution of the modern administrative state, resulted in a loss of individual freedom in the United States and across Western democracies.[45]

Hayek did not dispute a role for government in the economy and society. He envisioned a very modest role based on his libertarian philosophy:

> All these activities of government are part of its effort to provide a favorable framework for individual decisions; they supply means which individuals can use for their own purposes. Many other services of a more material kind fall into the same category. Though government must not use its power of coercion to reserve for itself activities which have nothing to do with the enforcement of the general rules of law, there is no violation of principle in its engaging in all sorts of activities on the same terms as the citizens. If in the majority of fields there is no good reason why it should

do so, there are fields in which the desirability of government action can hardly be questioned.[46]

Hayek very much embraced the values and tenets of 19th-century classical liberalism. His ideals led him to perceive government intervention as typically doing more harm than good, for the intervention itself resulted in the curtailing of individual freedom from the perspective of that libertarian stalwart.[47]

Leo Strauss (1899–1973)

Leo Strauss spent most of his professional career at the University of Chicago and is considered to be one of the most influential political philosophers of the 20th century. The Leo Strauss Center at the University of Chicago exists in order to document and delineate Straussian political theory for future generations.[48] Strauss published *Natural Right and History* in 1953,[49] and he said this about political philosophy:

> The historicist contention can be reduced to the assertion that natural right is impossible because philosophy in the full sense of the term is impossible. Philosophy is possible only if there is an absolute horizon or a natural horizon in contradistinction to the historically changing horizons or the caves. In other words, philosophy is possible only if man, while incapable of acquiring wisdom or full understanding of the whole, is capable of knowing what he does not know, that is to say, of grasping the fundamental problems and therewith the fundamental alternatives, which are, in principle, coeval with human thought. But the possibility of philosophy is only the necessary and not the sufficient condition of natural right. The possibility of philosophy does not require more than that the fundamental problems always be the same; but there cannot be natural right if the fundamental problem of political philosophy cannot be solved in a final manner.[50]

In this work, Strauss articulated his adherence to classical political philosophy. He yearned for a genuine social science through this theoretical approach.[51] In a later work, Strauss reflected on the tyrannical regimes of Adolf Hitler and Joseph Stalin:

> A social science that cannot speak of tyranny with the same confidence with which medicine speaks, for example, of cancer, cannot understand social phenomena as what they are. It is therefore not scientific. Present-day social science finds itself in this condition. If it is true that present-day social science is the inevitable result of modern social science and of

modern philosophy, one is forced to think of the restoration of classical social science. Once we have learned again from the classics what tyranny is, we shall be enabled and compelled to diagnose as tyrannies a number of contemporary regimes which appear in the guise of dictatorships. This diagnosis can only be the first step toward an exact analysis of present-day tyranny, for present-day tyranny is fundamentally different from the tyranny analyzed by the classics.[52]

The Straussian belief that a return to classical political philosophy in the modern world resulted in a great deal of criticism from the American left. Shadia Drury, for example, accused Strauss of advocating the use of political deception, religion, and excessive nationalism in order to pursue his conservative and libertarian agendas. She provided the following capsule summary of Strauss's impact on American politics and public affairs:

> Strauss's impact on academic life in North America has been something of a phenomenon; historian Gordon S. Wood described it as the largest academic movement in the twentieth century. Nor is this influence confined to political philosophy. It extends into religious studies, literary criticism, intellectual history, classics, American history, and American constitutional law. In 1987, the year of the two-hundredth anniversary of the US Constitution, Wood observed that the Straussians, as they are known in the academy, dominated the conferences; they were well-organized and well-funded. And even though most of them were political scientists by training, they outnumbered historians when it came to giving papers and organizing conferences on the American founding, which is a topic of great *political* [italics in original] and not just historical significance for the Straussians.[53]

The impact of Strauss's neoconservative movement in the 20th century has been substantial, particularly with Reagan's ascendancy into the White House following the 1980 presidential election. The Republican Party (Grand Old Party, GOP) has been dominated by the conservative wing ever since Reagan was elected. The liberals in the GOP are basically extinct; and the moderate wing is in the minority. The conservatives have controlled the party for the last two generations. Drury offered the following summary observation:

> In short, neoconservatism is the legacy of Leo Strauss. It echoes all the dominant features of his philosophy—the political importance of religion, the necessity of nationalism, the language of nihilism, the sense of crisis, the friend/foe mentality, the hostility toward women, the rejection of modernity, the nostalgia of the past, and the abhorrence of liberalism. And

having established itself as the dominant ideology of the Republican party, it threatens to remake America in its own image.[54]

While labels such as conservatism, neoconservatism, and libertarianism can be debated, it is clear that the Republican Party of the post-1980 era is far more conservative than it was in the past and that the GOP members have embraced many libertarian ideas as mainstream in the contemporary era. Individualism has gone awry in the United States because there is too much emphasis on the individual under the guise of liberty. People should have the freedom to do as they please. School choice, for example, sounds appealing to many who do not consider the implications of choice. If choice results in diminished funding for public education, the use of taxpayer money for parochial education, the resegregation of the races, and less accountability, is it worth it? Do we dismantle Horace Mann's vision for public education that is more than 150 years old for a libertarian ethos that could exacerbate social, economic, and political strife in the United States? Do we keep cutting taxes for the wealthy in spite of our knowledge that the gap between rich and poor is widening and trickle-down economics only makes the rich more affluent and the poor more destitute?

Milton Friedman (1912–2006)

Friedman was considered by many to be the most prominent advocate of free markets, a key libertarian ideal, in the 20th century.[55] He was influential on Reagan and served on his Economic Advisory Board.[56] During the 1970s, a time of comparatively high inflation, unemployment, interest rates, and budget deficits, Keynesian economic theory, which had been prominent since the New Deal, came under heavy criticism from the right. Leaders such as Reagan were very attracted to the laissez-faire ideology, and Paul Krugman gave Friedman much of the credit for Reagan's public policy platform:

> The odds are that the great swing back toward *laissez-faire* policies that took place around the world beginning in the 1970s would have happened even if there had been no Milton Friedman. But his tireless and brilliantly effective campaign on behalf of free markets surely helped accelerate the process, both in the United States and around the world. By any measure— protectionism versus free trade; regulation versus deregulation; wages set by collective bargaining and government minimum wages versus wages set by the market—the world has moved a long way in Friedman's direction. And even more striking than his achievement in terms of actual policy changes has been the transformation of the conventional wisdom: most influential people have been so converted to the Friedman way of thinking that it is simply taken as a given that the change in economic policies he promoted has been a force for good.[57]

Friedman's free-market philosophy was delineated in *Capitalism and Freedom* in 1962.[58] In this book, Friedman presented a spirited defense of laissez-faire capitalism. He began by criticizing the vision that President John Kennedy articulated in his aforementioned inaugural address in early 1961:

> In a much quoted passage in his inaugural address, President Kennedy said, "Ask not what your country can do for you—ask what you can do for your country." It is a striking sign of the temper of our times that the controversy about this passage centered on its origin and not on its content. Neither half of the statement expresses a relation between the citizen and his government that is worthy of the ideals of free men in a free society. The paternalistic "what your country can do for you" implies that government is the patron, the citizen the ward, a view that is at odds with the free man's belief in his own responsibility for his own destiny. The organismic, "what you can do for your country" implies that government is the master or the deity, the citizen, the servant or the votary. To the free man, the country is the collection of individuals who compose it, not something over and above him. He is proud of a common heritage and loyal to common traditions. But he regards government as a means, an instrumentality, neither a grantor of favors and gifts, nor a master or god to be blindly worshipped and served. He recognizes no national goal except as it is the consensus of the goals that the citizens severally serve. He recognizes no national purpose except as it is the consensus of the purposes for which the citizens severally strive.[59]

Friedman articulated the classic libertarian ethos; the United States is a nation of over 300 million individual citizens who should strive to promote their own self-interest. In so doing, libertarians contend that individual freedom will be enhanced and the United States will come closer to the vision of limited government promulgated by the framers of the Constitution in the late 18th century. The reality, however, is that the decision making of a few can affect the many in a profound manner. To suggest that it is advantageous for all people to pursue their own self-interest ignores the reality that, in doing so, some people will make choices that are harmful to greater society. Under the guise of individual freedom, do people have the right to engage in behavior that has profoundly negative implications for the greater common good?

Friedman's defense of laissez-faire capitalism is apparent in his vision of government intervention. He determined that government has two primary functions:

> First, the scope of government must be limited. Its major function must be to protect our freedom both from the enemies outside our gates and from our fellow-citizens: to preserve law and order, to enforce private contracts,

to foster competitive markets. Beyond this major function, government may enable us at times to accomplish jointly what we would find it more difficult or expensive to accomplish severally. However, any such use of government is fraught with danger. We should not and cannot avoid using government in this way. But there should be a clear and large balance of advantages before we do. By relying primarily on voluntary co-operation and private enterprise, in both economic and other activities, we can insure that the private sector is a check on the powers of the governmental sector and an effective protection of freedom of speech, of religion, and of thought. The second broad principle is that government power must be dispersed. If government is to exercise power, better in the county than in the state, better in the state than in Washington. If I do not like what my local community does, be it in sewage disposal, or zoning, or schools, I can move to another local community, and though few may take this step, the mere possibility acts as a check. If I do not like what my state does, I can move to another. If I do not like what Washington imposes, I have few alternatives in this world of jealous nations.[60]

Friedman's ideal vision of classical economic philosophy as manifested in the contemporary era simply ignores the reality that though Americans decry "big government" in the abstract, they expect the very same government to provide an array of services and protections that are very costly. When something goes wrong, the very people who yearn for less government nevertheless expect officials serving in the national government to respond to economic and security crises in a regular and consistent manner.

Both Milton and Rose Friedman exalted the virtues of free marketplace capitalism in 1980 in another book:

The two ideas of human freedom and economic freedom working together came to their greatest fruition in the United States. Those ideas are still very much with us. We are all of us imbued with them. They are part of the very fabric of our being. But we have been straying from them. We have been forgetting the basic truth that the greatest threat to human freedom is the concentration of power, whether in the hands of government or anyone else. We have persuaded ourselves that it is safe to grant power, provided it is for good purposes. Fortunately, we are waking up. We are again recognizing the dangers of an overgoverned society, coming to understand that good objectives can be perverted by bad means, that reliance on the freedom of people to control their own lives in accordance with their own values is the surest way to achieve the full potential of a great society. Fortunately, also, we are as a people still free to choose which way we should go—whether to continue along the road we have been following to ever bigger government, or to call a halt and change direction.[61]

The Friedmans associate the growth in size and scope of the federal government with a corresponding loss of individual freedom. Yet it is important to fully consider historical context when making such causal conclusions. The size and scope of government increased because the public demanded that it do so. There was a high level of popular support for more government intervention during the Progressive Era, the Great Depression and ensuing New Deal, the Great Society, the women's movement, the civil rights movement, the environmental movement, and the consumer rights movement. A candid appraisal of history is that Americans have typically demanded more government intervention to help alleviate some of the excesses of capitalism.[62]

The Communitarian Philosophy

Amitai Etzioni is currently a professor of sociology at George Washington University; he served as senior advisor to the White House during Jimmy Carter's administration and was the editor of *The Responsive Community: Rights and Responsibilities*, a communitarian quarterly, that was published from 1990 to 2004. He is considered by many to be the founder of the modern communitarian movement.[63]

Etzioni articulated his vision of communitarianism in *The Encyclopedia of Political Thought*:

Communitarianism is a social philosophy that, in contrast to theories that emphasize the centrality of the individual, emphasizes the importance of society in articulating the good. Communitarianism is often contrasted with liberalism, a theory which holds that each individual should formulate the good on his or her own. Communitarians examine the ways shared conceptions of the good are formed, transmitted, justified, and enforced. Hence, their interest in communities (and moral dialogues within them), the historical transmission of values and mores, and the societal units that transmit and enforce values—such as the family, schools, and voluntary associations (including places of worship), which are all part of communities. Although the term "communitarian" was coined only in the mid-nineteenth century, ideas that are communitarian in nature can be found in the Old and New Testaments, Catholic theology (e.g., emphasis on the church as community, and more recently on subsidiarity), Fabian and socialist doctrine (e.g., writings about the early commune and about workers' solidarity), and the writings of Edmund Burke. In recent decades, there have been two major waves of communitarianism: the academic communitarianism of the 1980s, and the responsive communitarianism of the 1990s. The academic communitarians of the 1980s were a small group of political theorists concerned with outlining the "social dimension" of the person. Responsive communitarians, also called political or neocommunitarians, were a group of scholars and policy-makers who, in the 1990s, stressed that societies cannot be based on one normative principle, and that both individual rights and the common good are major sources of normativity, without either one being a priori privileged.[64]

As Hudson explained, the key tenets of communitarianism are community, the common good, regulated markets, moral government, and civil society.[65] Whereas the core value for libertarians is individual liberty, the central communitarian value is the notion of community:

> Communitarians emphasize the responsibilities and obligations that go with community membership, along with its rights and benefits. This is not merely a limited contractual relationship or the sort of voluntary exchanges that sum up societal ties for most libertarians. Individual ties to the community are deeper, more diffuse, and more open-ended than implied in a contract. They may require individuals to sacrifice for the good of the community, including other individual members, without any obvious individual, direct, return compensation. Soldiers who sacrifice their lives for the good of the national political community are a dramatic example. Because human beings are socially embedded creatures, human history is replete with examples of individuals willing to sacrifice for the good of their communities and fellow citizens.[66]

Public K–12 education is a classic example of individuals sacrificing for the good of their communities. Not all people have children who attend public schools, but they pay taxes in order to help educate children so that they may become contributing members of society in their adult years.

To libertarians, promoting the greater common good is anathema because individuals should be free to promote their own agenda. While communitarians believe that individual choices should be respected, they nevertheless maintain that the common good often requires individuals to subjugate their own desires in order to promote the interests of society as a whole. Libertarians are typically in opposition to government regulation; communitarians advocate monitoring market outcomes to make sure that the common good is not impinged. Accordingly, they tend to support more government regulation, especially to promote the needs of the disadvantaged in society. Libertarians view government intervention as a wholly negative force that should be avoided as much as possible. Communitarians believe in positive government and believe it is incumbent upon government officials to create public policies that will help society as a whole. As such, communitarians believe that a moral government is one that promotes social justice for its citizens. Both libertarians and communitarians believe in the value and importance of a vibrant civil society. To libertarians, civil society is all about individuals making voluntary choices through voluntary relationships. To communitarians, individuals organize to meet the needs of the community. People learn to work together and coexist in a democratic society in order to meet the needs of the community. To libertarians, the lack of laws and regulations creates a vibrant civil society. Communitarians believe in the opposite. Civil society to them requires good and moral laws and regulations in order to nurture it and provide for the greater common good.[67]

Etzioni delineated his vision of communitarianism in 1993 with the publication of *The Spirit of Community: Rights, Responsibilities, and the Communitarian Agenda*.[68] In it, he offered his "communitarian thesis":

> The Communitarian assertions rest upon a single core thesis: Americans—who have long been concerned with the deterioration of private and public morality, the decline of the family, high crime rates, and the swelling of corruption in government—can now act without fear. We can act without fear that attempts to shore up our values, responsibilities, institutions, and communities will cause us to charge into a dark tunnel of moralism and authoritarianism that leads to a church-dominated state or a right-wing world.[69]

It is important to note that communitarians do not envision themselves yielding morality matters to the conservative right or to liberals on the left. As Etzioni explained:

> Liberal friends, who read a draft version of this book, expressed concern about the use of the term *moral*. Americans don't like to be told about morals, said one, and it sounds like preaching. Another suggested that the term reminds him of the Moral Majority. I do not mean to preach, but to share a concern and perhaps an agenda. I am sorry if I remind people of the Moral Majority, because I believe that although they raised the right questions they provided the wrong, largely authoritarian and dogmatic, answers. However, one of the purposes of this book is to retrieve the realm of democratic discourse good, basic terms that we have allowed to become the political slogans of archconservatives and the right wing. Just because a Pat Robertson talked about family values, community, and morality when he tried to keep social conservatives in the Bush camp during election campaigns should not mean that the rest of us should shy away from applying these pivotal social concepts. And just because some abuse these terms to foment divisiveness and hate, and to attack all intellectuals or liberals as if they were one "cultural elite," hostile to all that is good in America, should not lead us implicitly to accept this notion. Just as we should not give up on patriotism because some politicians wrap

themselves with the flag when it suits their narrow purposes, so should we not give up on morality because some abuse it to skewer their fellow community members.[70]

Indeed, no one has an exclusive domain on morality, and there are diverse opinions about what is moral and what is not depending on values, belief systems, views of history, ideology, and the proper role of government in society.

Communitarians also emphasize responsibility in their philosophy. Etzioni explained the difference in views between libertarians and communitarians:

It has been argued by libertarians that responsibilities are a personal matter, that individuals are to judge which responsibilities they accept as theirs. As we see it, responsibilities are anchored in community. Reflecting the diverse moral voices of their citizens, responsive communities define what is expected of people; they educate their members to accept these values; and they praise them when they do and frown upon them when they do not. While the ultimate foundation of morality may be commitments of individual conscience, it is communities that help introduce and sustain these commitments.[71]

Etzioni is critical of excessive individualism, but it is important to note that he does not refute the existence or positive features of individualism in American history. In his presidential address to the American Sociological Association in 1995, Etzioni touted a balance between individualism and the need to be responsive to the greater community. As Tocqueville discussed a long time ago, individualism itself does not necessarily run counter to democracy unless people allow it to happen:

Take, for example, the argument that individualism is a basic feature of American society, and hence, criticisms of individualism constitute attacks on the core value of the American society, versus the notion that individualism is a form of societal malaise. If one views such arguments as misleadingly dichotomous and applies the concept of inverting symbiosis, both claims are off the mark: The American tradition is a mixture of the two formations and of a quest for "corrections" when one formation becomes too strong. The fact that both individualization and communal bonds are part of the American experience is well reflected in our founding documents. The Declaration of Independence and the U.S. Constitution contain statements such as "[W]e mutually pledge to each other our Lives, our Fortunes and our sacred trust"; "We have appealed to their [the British] native justice and magnanimity, and we have conjured them by the ties of our common kindred to disavow these usurpations"; and "We the people of the United States, in order to form a more perfect union, . . . promote the general welfare . . . "

However, when prescriptions for more individualism are applied to contemporary and highly individualistic Western societies, especially the United States, they have the opposite effect: Such prescriptions move society deeper into the antagonistic zone.

In the same vein, recent statements by communitarians pointing to the need for increased emphasis on community in the United States have been misconstrued as antithetical to individuation. To the extent that these statements are made in a context seen as excessively individualistic, they point to a need to move from the antagonistic zone toward the mutually enhancing one, one in which order and autonomy sustain one another, and both are well served.[72]

A standard of reasonableness can be applied to the debate between Hudson's notion of radical individualism and the repudiation of the individualistic creed. Individualism has run amuck in the United States in the contemporary period; this does not mean that all tenets of individualism are necessarily bad or even harmful. It simply means that Tocqueville's concern about individualism evolving to egoism has been realized, and the baneful effects of excessive individualism are quite apparent in this country and can certainly be categorized as "antagonistic," as Etzioni highlighted over 20 years ago.

Contemporary Individualism and the Republican Party

Most Americans consider the Libertarian Party to be extreme and radical, and candidates seeking office under that party label tend to do poorly. But the impact of the libertarian philosophy on contemporary politics is quite significant, nevertheless. This is due to the reality that contemporary members of the Republican Party have absorbed libertarian ideas, and they have become mainstream Republican policies. Recent presidents such as Reagan and George W. Bush have promoted the libertarian economic agenda under the banner of the GOP.[73]

Republican Barry Goldwater lost a landslide election to incumbent Lyndon Johnson in 1964.[74] Goldwater was a firm believer in the libertarian economic policies of the Austrian economists such as Hayek. Yet his defeat would be vindicated by conservatives 16 years later when Reagan was first elected. The laissez-faire beliefs of Hayek, Strauss, and Friedman, among others, were embraced in the modern GOP and have been ever since. Ideas that were once perceived to be too extreme and radical are now commonplace in contemporary politics. Libertarian ideas are quite apparent and visible in the GOP today. Tax cuts for the wealthy, deregulation of virtually all policy sectors, cutting the social welfare state, education vouchers, school choice, charter schools, eliminating the minimum wage, and a flat personal income tax rate at the federal level are all libertarian policies associated with contemporary conservatism.

Though opinions vary about the plausibility of the policies of the Reagan era, there can be little doubt that he was a transformational leader. As the historian David Farber reported:

> Ronald Reagan ended his presidency on a wave of popularity equaled in the twentieth century only by his former idol, Franklin Roosevelt. A leading expert on the American presidency, Stephen Skowronek, places Reagan in the rich company of the presidents who transformed the United States. Thomas Jefferson, Andrew Jackson, Abraham Lincoln, and Franklin Roosevelt . . . Reagan took the dreams and ideas of the conservative movement that had been in the works for decades and made them, in many cases, the law of the land—and, just as telling, conventional wisdom. By no means did all Americans accept his conservative plan for the United States. At the end of his presidency, Reagan's social policies remained enormously divisive, and in many cases a majority rejected his attempts to rollback the government-assisted struggles for racial justice, gender equity, and equal opportunity in American life. Liberals believed his indifference to the plight of the poor and to growing economic inequality in the United States were terrible wounds in the body politic, and they vowed to heal them. Reagan transformed American politics, but he also contributed to the growing polarization of the American people. When he left office, just as when he gained it, liberals despised him. But conservatives, even more, loved him for what he had accomplished. Reagan's electoral coattails remained long. Reagan's vice president, George H.W. Bush, who once scorned Reaganomics as "voodoo economics," had refashioned himself as a Reagan acolyte and won the 1988 election. Much of what Reagan had created would be continued.[75]

Republican presidential candidates that followed Reagan have mostly pledged their homage to Reagan and his legacy; the libertarian ideals deeply rooted in Reaganomics are firmly entrenched in the folklore of the Republican Party. This reality was well documented by Hudson:

> When Kennedy became president, the ideas of Friedman and those who agreed with him existed on the margins of American political life, a fact that Friedman himself acknowledges in his book. In the decade following that cold January morning, Americans would be called to numerous common endeavors for the common good, from sending a man to the moon to fighting a war on poverty. Americans mobilized to fight racial injustice and guarantee civil rights for all. They also were called to a disastrous war in

southeast Asia . . . Sentiments like Friedman's have gained currency, and by the 1980s many of his specific policy recommendations were being adopted. Today, libertarian solutions are invariably major contenders when any policy problem reaches the public agenda, and many have been implemented, transforming profoundly the character of American life. No matter what the issue, proponents of providing individuals with freedom of choice on the matter—an ability to determine for themselves what they want free from governmental interference—will make themselves heard.[76]

Libertarians often package their ideas in terms of freedom of choice. In terms of marketing, it is a savvy technique. The impact of the libertarian ethos on the United States is devastating to the country, for individualism has been taken to an extreme. Too many Americans focus only on themselves with fairly callous disregard for the other citizens in this republic. Unfortunately, many politicians promote individual liberty without considering, at least outwardly certainly in political campaigns, its impact on society. It is a deceitful and cunning practice, indeed, for it makes egoism appear to be reasonable when the cultural and social fabric of the country is being cast aside with a recklessness that would not have been condoned in key periods of American history. Democracy and republicanism are better served with a proactive citizenry who put the needs of the country ahead of their own individual agendas.[77]

The contemporary fixation on freedom of choice is analogous to the debate about the doctrine of states' rights in the past. When people focus exclusively on their understanding and perception of rights, without considering the implications of the exercise of the alleged rights in question, tyranny is the likely outcome. Consider the words shared by "A Veteran Observer" in 1863:

> Though many have read this, probably few have ever read the strong language on State Rights. In the debates on the Constitution, MADISON said:
>
> "Some contend that States are sovereign when, in fact, they are only political societies. There is a gradation of power in all societies, from the lowest corporation to the highest sovereign. The States never possessed the essential rights of sovereignty. The State of Maryland voted by counties; did this make the counties sovereign? The States at present are only great corporations, having the power of making by-laws; and those are effectual only if they are not contradictory to the General Confederation. The States ought to be placed under the control of the General Government—at least so much as they were formerly under the King and British Parliament."
>
> Thus MADISON hooted at the idea of State sovereignty. That idea, and secession, and the perpetuity of Slavery—which were its legitimate consequence—were the inventions of modern demagogues, who have no

pretence of authority, save a loose expression, in one of the amendments to the Constitution. But I shall not argue a point which is submitted to the arbitration of arms, nor discuss a doctrine which is rapidly, I am thankful to say, passing to the tomb of perished follies with its twin sister, Slavery. Others may expect to revive them, but they will be mistaken. No more will the American nation suffer curses like these to put this noble Government in danger. No more will the infinite folly, conserving slave property, and defending freedom by State Constitutions, impose upon the intelligent intellect of the American people. We are passing through this dreadful ordeal of war and convulsion to establish a nationality which is strong enough to survive the follies of its friends, as well as the hostility of its enemies. I think I may congratulate all patriot hearts on the victory of freedom and the stability of Government. The storm is passing and the battle raging, but the silver lining is on the cloud. Soon the fields will grow verdant, and every plant give fruit.[78]

The libertarian ethos of today does not have to persevere into the future. The United States is a nation of interdependent citizens, and the needs of the greater community will have to be carefully balanced with the preservation of individual civil liberties. This balance will result in conflict, and it will not be easy to implement. Said balance, however, must be achieved and preserved into the future because the benchmark of a great nation is when people put the needs of the nation ahead of their own individual self-interest. If Americans will ever succeed in the quest to eradicate poverty as it currently exists, the cultural ethos of libertarianism must be cast aside. Extreme individualism will have to yield to civic virtue, empathy, and the yearning for a better society. Indeed, the challenge confronting contemporary Americans is clear. Are citizens willing to pursue a more perfect union, where all Americans can hope to experience the dream of passing a better way of life to their successors than the one they may have experienced? Victory in the War on Poverty will not be achieved without reassessing cultural values and attitudes toward the poor. Only then can public policies be created, adjusted, modified, or eliminated in order to win the crusade.

Notes

1. Pew Research Center, "Why People Are Rich and Poor: Republicans and Democrats Have Very Different Views," May 2, 2017, http://www.pewresearch.org/fact-tank/2017/05/02/why-people-are-rich-and-poor-republicans-and-democrats-have-very-different-views/ (accessed September 12, 2017).

2. Pew Research Center, "Why People Are Rich and Poor: Republicans and Democrats Have Very Different Views," May 2, 2017.

3. Pew Research Center, "Why People Are Rich and Poor: Republicans and Democrats Have Very Different Views," May 2, 2017.

4. Pew Research Center, "Why People Are Rich and Poor: Republicans and Democrats Have Very Different Views," May 2, 2017.

5. Pew Research Center, "Why People Are Rich and Poor: Republicans and Democrats Have Very Different Views," May 2, 2017.

6. Pew Research Center, "Why People Are Rich and Poor: Republicans and Democrats Have Very Different Views," May 2, 2017.

7. History.com, "Alexis de Tocqueville," http://www.history.com/topics /alexis-de-tocqueville (accessed June 11, 2017).

8. Alexis de Tocqueville, *Democracy in America* (Chicago: University of Chicago Press, 2000), xvii.

9. Tocqueville, *Democracy in America*, 482–84.

10. Daniel J. Elazar, "Tocqueville and the Cultural Basis of American Democracy," *PS: Political Science and Politics* 32, no. 2 (1999): 208.

11. Gallup Poll, "Americans' Confidence in Institutions Stays Low," June 13, 2016, http://www.gallup.com/poll/192581/americans-confidence-institutions-stays -low.aspx (accessed June 13, 2017). In June 2016, the percentage of Americans who indicated that they had "a great deal" or "quite a bit" of confidence in churches = 41 percent; medical system = 39 percent; presidency = 36 percent; U.S. Supreme Court = 36 percent; public schools = 30 percent; banks = 27 percent; organized labor = 23 percent; criminal justice system = 23 percent; television news = 21 percent; newspapers = 20 percent; big business = 18 percent; and Congress = 9 percent.

12. Gallup Poll, "Congress and the Public," http://www.gallup.com/poll/1600 /congress-public.aspx (accessed July 13, 2017). Most of the time Gallup pollsters survey the American public about Congress it has a low approval rating, at least compared to U.S. presidents. A significant crisis, such as the September 11, 2001, terrorist attacks, resulted in a Gallup record approval for President George W. Bush and Congress.

13. Robert N. Bellah, Richard Madsen, William M. Sullivan, Ann Swidler, and Steven M. Tipton, *Habits of the Heart: Individualism and Commitment in American Life* (Berkeley, CA: University of California Press, 1985), 37–8.

14. Bellah et al., *Habits of the Heart: Individualism and Commitment in American Life*, 39.

15. U.S. Census Bureau, "U.S. Cities Are Home to 62.7 Percent of the U.S. Population, but Comprise Just 3.5 Percent of Land Area: March 4, 2015," https:// www.census.gov/newsroom/press-releases/2015/cb15-33.html (accessed June 19, 2017).

16. Louis C. Gawthrop, *Public Service and Democracy: Ethical Imperatives for the 21st Century* (New York: Chatham House Publishers, 1998).

17. Bellah et al., *Habits of the Heart: Individualism and Commitment in American Life*, 262–63.

18. Robert D. Putnam, *Bowling Alone: The Collapse and Revival of American Community* (New York: Simon & Schuster, 2000), 63. See also Robert D. Putnam, "Bowling Alone: America's Declining Social Capital," *Journal of Democracy* 6, no. 1 (1995): 65–78.

19. American Presidency Project, "John F. Kennedy: Inaugural Address, January 20, 1961," http://www.presidency.ucsb.edu/ws/index.php?pid=8032& (accessed June 20, 2017).

20. William E. Hudson, *The Libertarian Illusion: Ideology, Public Policy, and the Assault on the Common Good* (Washington, DC: CQ Press, 2008), 23.

21. William E. Hudson, *American Democracy in Peril: Eight Challenges to America's Future,* 8th ed. (Thousand Oaks, CA: CQ Press, 2017).

22. Hudson, *American Democracy in Peril: Eight Challenges to America's Future,* 8th ed., 107.

23. Hudson, *American Democracy in Peril: Eight Challenges to America's Future,* 8th ed., 109.

24. Pew Research Center, "How Do Americans Stand Out from the Rest of the World?" March 12, 2015, http://www.pewresearch.org/fact-tank/2015/03/12/how-do-americans-stand-out-from-the-rest-of-the-world/ (accessed September 12, 2017).

25. Pew Research Center, "5 Ways Americans and Europeans Are Different," April 19, 2016, http://www.pewresearch.org/fact-tank/2016/04/19/5-ways-americans-and-europeans-are-different/ (accessed September 12, 2017).

26. Hudson, *American Democracy in Peril: Eight Challenges to America's Future,* 8th ed., 132–33.

27. See Walter Dean Burnham, "Those High Nineteenth-Century American Voting Turnouts: Fact or Fiction?," *Journal of Interdisciplinary History* 16, no. 4 (1986): 613–44; and Brian L. Fife, *Reforming the Electoral Process in America: Toward More Democracy in the 21st Century* (Santa Barbara, CA: Praeger, 2010).

28. Fife, *Reforming the Electoral Process in America: Toward More Democracy in the 21st Century,* 64–5.

29. Fife, *Reforming the Electoral Process in America: Toward More Democracy in the 21st Century,* 31–49.

30. Cato Institute, "Key Concepts of Libertarianism," https://www.cato.org/publications/commentary/key-concepts-libertarianism (accessed July 3, 2017). More information about libertarianism can be secured from David Boaz (ed.), *The Libertarian Reader: Classic and Contemporary Readings from Lao-tzu to Milton Friedman* (New York: The Free Press, 1997).

31. Libertarian Party, "2016 Platform," https://www.lp.org/platform (accessed July 3, 2017).

32. Hudson, *American Democracy in Peril: Eight Challenges to America's Future,* 8th ed., 115.

33. Fife, *Reforming the Electoral Process in America: Toward More Democracy in the 21st Century.*

34. Warren, *Administrative Law in the Political System,* 5th ed.; and Cornelius M. Kerwin and Scott R. Furlong, *Rulemaking: How Government Agencies Write Law and Make Policy,* 4th ed. (Washington, DC: CQ Press, 2011).

35. Theodore Roosevelt, *Theodore Roosevelt: An Autobiography* (New York: Macmillan, 1914), 476.

36. Hudson, *The Libertarian Illusion: Ideology, Public Policy, and the Assault on the Common Good,* 1–28; and Fife, *Old School Still Matters: Lessons from History to Reform Public Education in America,* 63–77.

37. Mises Institute, "Profiles: Friedrich Hayek," https://mises.org/profile/fried rich-hayek (accessed July 8, 2017).

38. Friedrich Hayek, *The Road to* Serfdom (Chicago: University of Chicago Press, 1944); and Fife, *Old School Still Matters: Lessons from History to Reform Public Education in America*, 45–8.

39. Hayek, *The Road to* Serfdom, 101–02.

40. Fife, *Old School Still Matters: Lessons from History to Reform Public Education in America*, 46.

41. Hayek, *The Road to* Serfdom, 241; and Fife, *Old School Still Matters: Lessons from History to Reform Public Education in America*, 47.

42. Fife, *Old School Still Matters: Lessons from History to Reform Public Education in America*, 47; and Adam Smith, *The Wealth of Nations*, 2 vols. (New York: E. P. Dutton, 1910).

43. Friedrich Hayek, *The Constitution of Liberty* (Chicago: University of Chicago Press, 1960).

44. Hayek, *The Constitution of Liberty*, 1–2.

45. Fife, *Old School Still Matters: Lessons from History to Reform Public Education in America*, 47–8.

46. Hayek, *The Constitution of Liberty*, 223; and Fife, *Old School Still Matters: Lessons from History to Reform Public Education in America*, 48.

47. Fife, *Old School Still Matters: Lessons from History to Reform Public Education in America*, 48.

48. University of Chicago, "The Leo Strauss Center," https://leostrausscenter .uchicago.edu/ (accessed July 8, 2017).

49. Leo Strauss, *Natural Right and History* (Chicago: University of Chicago Press, 1953). See also Leo Strauss, "Natural Right and the Historical Approach," *The Review of Politics* 12, no. 4 (1950): 422–42.

50. Strauss, *Natural Right and History*, 35.

51. Fife, *Old School Still Matters: Lessons from History to Reform Public Education in America*, 50.

52. Leo Strauss, *On Tyranny* (New York: Free Press of Glencoe, 1963), 189; and Fife, *Old School Still Matters: Lessons from History to Reform Public Education in America*, 50.

53. Shadia B. Drury, *Leo Strauss and the American Right* (New York: St. Martin's Press, 1997), 2; and Fife, *Old School Still Matters: Lessons from History to Reform Public Education in America*, 51.

54. Drury, *Leo Strauss and the American Right*, 178; and Fife, *Old School Still Matters: Lessons from History to Reform Public Education in America*, 52.

55. Library of Economics and Liberty, "Milton Friedman (1912–2006)," http://www .econlib.org/library/Enc/bios/Friedman.html (accessed July 9, 2017).

56. Cato Institute, "Milton Friedman: Biography," https://www.cato.org/special /friedman/friedman/index.html (accessed July 9, 2017).

57. Paul Krugman, "Who Was Milton Friedman?" *New York Review of Books*, February 15, 2007, http://www.nybooks.com/articles/archives/2007/feb/15/who -was-Milton-Friedman (accessed July 9, 2017); and Fife, *Old School Still Matters: Lessons from History to Reform Public Education in America*, 60–1.

58. Milton Friedman, *Capitalism and Freedom* (Chicago: University of Chicago Press, 1962).

59. Friedman, *Capitalism and Freedom*, 1–2; and Fife, *Old School Still Matters: Lessons from History to Reform Public Education in America*, 61.

60. Friedman, *Capitalism and Freedom*, 2–3; and Fife, *Old School Still Matters: Lessons from History to Reform Public Education in America*, 61.

61. Milton Friedman and Rose Friedman, *Free to Choose: A Personal Statement* (New York: Harcourt Brace Jovanovich, 1980), 309–10; and Fife, *Old School Still Matters: Lessons from History to Reform Public Education in America*, 62.

62. Fife, *Old School Still Matters: Lessons from History to Reform Public Education in America*, 62–3.

63. George Washington University, "Amitai Etzioni," https://sociology.columbian .gwu.edu/amitai-etzioni (accessed July 10, 2017).

64. Amitai Etzioni, "Communitarianism," https://icps.gwu.edu/sites/icps.gwu .edu/files/downloads/Communitarianism.Etzioni.pdf (accessed July 6, 2017). For more information about communitarianism, see Amitai Etzioni (ed.), *The Essential Communitarian Reader* (Lanham, MD: Rowman & Littlefield, 1998).

65. Hudson, *The Libertarian Illusion: Ideology, Public Policy, and the Assault on the Common Good*, 14–21.

66. Hudson, *The Libertarian Illusion: Ideology, Public Policy, and the Assault on the Common Good*, 15.

67. Hudson, *The Libertarian Illusion: Ideology, Public Policy, and the Assault on the Common Good*, 14–21.

68. Amitai Etzioni, *The Spirit of Community: Rights, Responsibilities, and the Communitarian Agenda* (New York: Crown Publishers, 1993).

69. Etzioni, *The Spirit of Community: Rights, Responsibilities, and the Communitarian Agenda*, 2.

70. Etzioni, *The Spirit of Community: Rights, Responsibilities, and the Communitarian Agenda*, 13.

71. Etzioni, *The Spirit of Community: Rights, Responsibilities, and the Communitarian Agenda*, 266–67.

72. Amitai Etzioni, "The Responsive Community: A Communitarian Perspective," *American Sociological Review* 61, (February 1996): 7–8.

73. Fife, *Old School Still Matters: Lessons from History to Reform Public Education in America*, 65.

74. See Barry Goldwater, *The Conscience of a Conservative* (New York: Hillman Books, 1960).

75. David Farber, *The Rise and Fall of Modern Conservatism: A Short History* (Princeton, NJ: Princeton University Press, 2010), 207–08; and Fife, *Old School Still Matters: Lessons from History to Reform Public Education in America*, 68–9.

76. Hudson, *The Libertarian Illusion: Ideology, Public Policy, and the Assault on the Common Good*, 3.

77. See Michael Schudson, *The Good Citizen: A History of American Civic Life* (New York: The Free Press, 1998).

78. *The New York Times*, "The Doctrine of State Rights; Exploded Ideas Revived the True Power of the Rebellion False Political Doctrines Their Danger, and the Necessity of Their Destruction," May 15, 1863, http://www.nytimes.com/1863 /05/15/news/doctrine-state-rights-exploded-ideas-revived-true-power-rebellion -false.html?pagewanted=all (accessed July 14, 2017).

CHAPTER FIVE

The Path to Welfare Reform: An 18-Point Plan

Winning the War on Poverty will not be easy, and there is no singular simple solution to this vexing problem. History is replete on the subject. I offer a systemic vision of how poverty can be minimized in the United States. Since we do not live in a utopian world, and human beings are imperfect by definition, poverty will continue to be a challenge for Americans into the future. As the world's wealthiest nation, the level of poverty in this country is not acceptable, and accusing most people who live in poverty of laziness, bad choices, and the like is not productive and will not help them, or society in general, for that matter. The reform proposals will be difficult to implement in a political sense. They will require changes in law, public policy, cultural nuances, and even value systems. No one entity can prevail in this noble war; all citizens must participate, and we cannot expect government officials alone to address this moral reality in the United States. Nor can we simply expect poor people to work harder to get themselves out of their current situation. This assumes that all poor people are lazy and are not working diligently already; this is simply not the case. We cannot expect that a capitalist economy provides ample opportunities for all citizens. Clearly, the affluent are doing quite well in the contemporary era, and the middle and working classes are struggling.

Inherent in the reform proposals is a core value—democracy. The world's oldest democracy has expanded opportunities for its citizens during its history. The natural progression of this historical context is to afford citizens more democracy and not less. I also reject the notion that certain things are not possible because the votes cannot be mustered, either in Congress, the White House, or the Supreme Court. Anything is possible if we the people have the political will, perseverance, and acumen to keep advocating for what we believe. The abolitionists were rebuffed for decades, as were the suffragists. Civil rights advocates historically have met with defeat after defeat, but reformers did not abdicate their cause in spite of initial setbacks. They did not quit; nor shall those of us who really desire to alleviate poverty in the land of plenty.

The Goal of Winning the War on Poverty

The pursuit of alleviating poverty is nothing new in human history. If it were a simple phenomenon, then presumably the goal would have been achieved some time ago. Progress toward this goal must be achieved. Failure to make inroads in the minimization of poverty in the United States literally sentences millions of people to live without hope. As Michael Harrington, the author of *The Other America: Poverty in the United States*, indicated in an updated version of his classic 1962 book:

> In the Seventies the poor may become invisible again. And even if that tragedy does occur, there will still be tens of millions living in the other America when the country celebrates its two hundredth anniversary in 1976. This prediction should be improbable. Lyndon B. Johnson declared an "unconditional war" on poverty in 1964, Congress agreed, and for the next four years the White House recited awesome statistics on the billions that were being spent on social purposes. And the Sixties were a time of marches and militancy, of students and churches committing themselves to abolish want, and of documentary presentations of the nation's domestic shame by all the mass media. Indeed the impression of frenetic Government activity was so widespread that Richard Nixon campaigned in 1968 with a promise to slow down the pace of innovation. So how, then, argue that poverty will persist in the Seventies and perhaps once again drop out of the society's conscience and consciousness? As usual, the Government has carefully assembled the figures to debunk the former President's optimism and the current President's quietism. In every crucial area—food, housing, education and other social responsibilities—the United States provides its worst-off citizens only a percentage of what they desperately need. And since half of the poor are young people destined to enter a sophisticated economy at enormous disadvantage, unless countermeasures are taken the children of this generation's impoverished will become the parents of an even larger generation of the other America.[1]

What we need in the United States is a much smaller version of the other America. Continuance of the same policies and trends will not reduce the poverty problem in the United States; it will only make it exponentially larger.

Reflecting on the challenge of poverty over 50 years ago, Harrington offered this prophesy:

> So the Seventies need planned, long-range social investments to provide a decent home for every citizen and to guarantee either a living income or a good job for all. But as the decade begins, the nation, including its Chief Executive, believes in myths which keep us from even defining the problem as it is. They think we tried too much when actually we did so little. And the official thinkers and statisticians are even winning paper victories over poverty and making the poor invisible. Therefore there is reason for pessimism. But if these menacing trends are to be reversed, then America must understand one crucial proposition: that it is in the interest of the entire society to end the outrage of the other America. The poor are the most sorely tried and dramatic victims of economic and social tendencies which threaten the entire nation. They suffer most grievously from unplanned, chaotic urbanization, but millions of the affluent are affected too. They are the first to experience technological progress as a curse which destroys the old muscle-power jobs that previous generations used as a means to fight their way out of poverty. . . . If, in other words, the cities sprawl and technology revolutionizes the land in a casual, thoughtless way, polluting the very fundamentals of human existence, like air and water, it is the poor who will be the most cruelly used but the entire nation will experience a kind of decadence. In morality and in justice every citizen should be committed to abolishing the other America, for it is intolerable that the richest nation in human history should allow such needless suffering.[2]

The reader must be thinking, and rightfully so, what has changed in 50 years? Indeed, nothing has changed, and the vision and promise of the 1960s have not had the results that Harrington had earnestly hoped to achieve and witness during his lifetime. Almost 30 years have lapsed since his passing; it is not too late to realize his vision, but the work must begin in earnest without any further delay.[3]

A Vision for Winning the War on Poverty

David Easton expressed the importance of theory in the social sciences in a 1953 book:

> All mature scientific knowledge is theoretical. Obviously this does not mean that facts are immaterial. At the present highly empirical stage in the development of the social sciences, there is little need to insist that scientific knowledge must be well-grounded in facts. What does need emphasis, however, is that in and of themselves facts do not enable us to explain

or understand an event. Facts must be ordered in some way so that we can see their connections. The higher the level of generality in ordering such facts and clarifying their relations, the broader will be the range of explanation and understanding. A set of generalizations that orders all the kinds of facts we call political would obviously be more useful for purposes of understanding political activity than a single generalization that related only two such facts. It is for this reason . . . that the search for reliable knowledge about empirical political phenomena requires ultimately the construction of systematic theory, the name for the highest order of generalization.[4]

Differential paradigms regarding poverty are undoubtedly as old as the human experience on this planet. Upton Sinclair offered an interesting vision of how to end poverty in California during the Great Depression. In 1926 and 1930, he was the Socialist nominee for governor of California and received about 4 percent of the popular vote in each election. In 1934, however, he was the Democratic nominee and received 37.8 percent of the vote; the Republican, Frank Merriam, won the election with 48.9 percent of the vote.[5] Sinclair ran on an EPIC (End Poverty in California) platform. His theoretical framework is encompassed in "The Twelve Principles of EPIC":

1. God created the natural wealth of the earth for the use of all men, not of a few.
2. God created men to seek their own welfare, not that of masters.
3. Private ownership of tools, a basis of freedom when tools are simple, becomes a basis of enslavement when tools are complex.
4. Autocracy in industry cannot exist alongside democracy in government.
5. When some men live without working, other men are working without living.
6. The existence of luxury in the presence of poverty and destitution is contrary to good morals and sound public policy.
7. The present depression is one of abundance, not of scarcity.
8. The cause of the trouble is that a small class has the wealth, while the rest have the debts.
9. It is contrary to common sense that men should starve because they have raised too much food.
10. The destruction of food or other wealth, or the limitation of production, is economic insanity.
11. The remedy is to give the workers access to the means of production, and let them produce for themselves, not for others.
12. This change can be brought about by action of a majority of the people, and that is the American way.[6]

Sinclair's intent in 1934 was to use the Democratic Party as a reasonable mechanism for change, as running as a Socialist proved to be cumbersome at least in terms of garnering votes. This intriguing state election was described by one researcher in this manner:

> American political history has produced many fascinating stories. Few, however, can match the 1934 California gubernatorial campaign in both substance and style. Substantively, the campaign served as a watershed by confirming liberal-leftist ideology as a significant force in California politics—especially in the Democratic party—behind the candidacy of Upton B. Sinclair and his End Poverty in California (EPIC) League. Sinclair lost the election, but EPIC captured and helped revive the state Democratic party, elected two of its three state senate candidates and twenty-four of its thirty-nine assembly nominees, and compelled Sinclair's victorious opponent, Republican Governor Frank F. Merriam, to support New Deal policies in the state. In addition, peripheral parts of the EPIC program were eventually enacted, including a state income tax, the repeal of sales tax on essential goods, and pensions for the elderly and the blind. Sinclair's campaign—and the harsh conservative reaction to it—also energized California's left wing, especially in Hollywood, helping to lead to the state's reputation as a center of progressive politics. Finally, the ambivalent reaction to Sinclair's radical EPIC campaign by Democratic leaders, including President Franklin D. Roosevelt, illustrated tensions and contradictions within Democratic and New Deal political philosophy.[7]

Not surprisingly given other progressive causes in U.S. history, the EPIC movement was largely orchestrated by white, middle-aged, and middle-class individuals.[8] In addition to highlighting progressive causes (such as ending poverty), the 1934 gubernatorial campaign in California ushered in a new era for political campaigns, including the use of film, radio, and direct mail.[9]

The prominent 20th-century sociologist John Gillin offered a stark account of the challenges of poverty almost a century ago:

> Every year gives fresh emphasis to the importance of the problems of poverty and dependency. Definite knowledge of the amounts which the public relief authorities have to expend for dependents has shocked those who had been unaware of the burden thus imposed on the taxpayers. Recent studies by the Bureau of Labor Statistics of the United States have shown an unexpected amount of poverty. We have been so obsessed by the belief that in rich America there is little poverty, except that of the inefficient, that it was startling to learn that a growing number of fairly capable, industrious and frugal people have been pushed into the quagmire. The War with its disturbance of price levels and its psychological effects has quickened our perception of such problems. The draft revealed to us the

scandalous volume of physical and mental deficiency in our population. As with a magnifying glass the situation growing out of the War has shown us conditions menacing our prosperity and welfare, the maladjustments in our machinery for managing employment, stabilizing industry, caring for the dependent and preventing the propagation of the inefficient.[10]

World War I illuminated a plethora of societal challenges in the United States, including poverty. The fact that it still persists in this society suggests that this pattern will be replicated without a series of interventions designed to create and institutionalize systemic reform. Before the onset of World War II, James and Katherine Morrow Ford expressed their views about minimizing poverty in the United States:

The vastness of the problem and the multifariousness of its aspects should not be a deterrent to action for the banishment of human misery. It should be realized that such an ambitious program cannot be carried out and completed in one year or even a generation. It is bound to be slow and at times will seem impossible of achievement. Mistakes will be made. There will be setbacks. But obstructions are to be found in the execution of the best of human plans. To take a simple analogy—a flight around the globe has been for a full generation a goal of aviation. It has taken years to develop each step toward that goal. It has required prodigious research, experimentation, trial and error. Obstructions have appeared to be insuperable. But as a result of informed persistent effort world-wide aviation is becoming an actuality.[11]

So many technological advances have been made since the publication of their book in 1937. The great accomplishments in science, technology, engineering, and public health highlight the omnipresent reality that winning the War on Poverty will not be easy, and it will take a sustained, concerted, longitudinal effort where the results will not always be apparent to the citizen and policy maker alike.

George L. Record's *How to Abolish Poverty* was published three years after his death.[12] As James G. Blauvelt described Record:

Political parties and shibboleths meant little to Record. He believed in a government of ideas and that both the old parties had sunk to the low level of patronage and graft machines. At first a Democrat, he bolted Bryanism and went over to the Republican Party on the "sound money" issue. He was one of the organizers and leaders of the Progressive Party in 1912, when the Republican National convention refused to accept Theodore Roosevelt's "social justice" program. He supported Robert LaFollette in his independent candidacy for the presidency in 1924. Defeat—the loss of an election—meant nothing to him. He believed in the common people and their fundamental honesty and sense of justice as did Abraham Lincoln, who was his great exemplar, and whom, in many traits, he resembled.[13]

Record was a leader in the "New Idea" movement in New Jersey in the early 20th century, which was later embraced by Woodrow Wilson when he became governor and then later president of the United States.[14] Record believed that the key to abolishing poverty was to fundamentally address the gap between rich and poor:

> The principle, therefore, which underlies the solution of these problems, is the abolition of privilege. Privilege is due to the exclusive possession by a few of advantages which are either natural or artificial. The artificial privileges grow out of the private operation of the service of the transportation of passengers, freight and intelligence, and this service should be operated by the government. The natural privileges grow out of the ownership by a few of the greater part of such natural advantages as water powers, mineral deposits, oil wells and vast timber tracts, and the tendency to accumulate city and farming lands in a few hands.[15]

In the context of his time in history, he challenged the plausibility of a relatively small number of people controlling the means of production in certain sectors of the economy as a small number of people benefited greatly (e.g., John D. Rockefeller and Andrew Carnegie) at the direct expense of the masses of society.

There are numerous works from varying disciplines where researchers and authors offer their visions of reducing poverty in the United States.[16] Like those who came before me, my vision has been affected by my own experiences, interpretation of history, values, policy priorities, and a plethora of other variables.

Winning the War on Poverty in a Generation or Two

Included in table 5.1 is an 18-point plan to win the War on Poverty in the United States. By winning the war, I am not suggesting that all poverty afflicting all individuals will be eliminated; I earnestly believe that poverty as we know it today can be greatly and proportionately reduced by proactively enacting and implementing a series of reform measures. The reform proposals are embodied in the 18-point plan. The plan is comprehensive in nature and does not lend itself to simplicity. Like it or not, poverty is a very complicated multivariate issue by definition. A simple solution has not been enacted because poverty is quite a complicated phenomenon that does not just affect a singular portion of the general population. Complex problems require in-depth, sophisticated responses,

Table 5.1   Winning the War on Poverty

Reform Proposal	Substantive Premise of the Reform Proposal
1	Use two poverty measures
2	One-stop community centers to assist the impoverished
3	Universal health insurance coverage
4	Progressive tax structure and elimination of some deductions
5	Enhanced educational opportunities
6	Reinvigorate the social safety net (especially SNAP) and repeal TANF
7	Invest in new meaningful infrastructure jobs
8	*E Pluribus Unum*—embrace the communitarian philosophy
9	Enhance the culture of citizenship and individual responsibility
10	Decent and affordable housing for all citizens
11	Raise the federal minimum wage and index it for inflation
12	Address the challenge of climate change
13	Reform the machinery of voting
14	Public financing of all federal campaigns
15	Revitalize political parties and labor unions
16	Reject the doctrine of states' rights and revitalize the spirit of cooperative federalism
17	Utilize science and data analysis to make informed judgments about the impoverished
18	Do right by children at all times

or treatments. The following presentation is my vision for a United States where officials at all levels of government can be better equipped to manage the existence of poverty in the world's oldest democracy.

Point 1: U.S. Officials Should Routinely Use Two Measures of Poverty

As measuring poverty is the focus of chapter 1, not much more by way of background needs to be included in the general discussion. Mollie Orshansky made a significant contribution by devising an absolute definition of poverty in the United States; it had never been done before her. I reiterate my respect for her contributions to what we have known about poverty over the last half century and more. Yet Victor Fuchs's research can be vindicated now. Why not use his relative measure as well, as Gilbert contended in 2008? While the reduction of poverty using Orshansky's measure remains a primary objective of current poverty-relief efforts, one day more progress with regard to poverty will be achieved in the United States. A new goal could be to further enhance efforts to alleviate the existence of poverty in society by increasing the standard. The United States can and must do better when it comes to identifying, and then rectifying, the extent to which poverty exists here. Thus, the continuation of the Orshansky measure should ensue in perpetuity as a baseline of absolute poverty in the United States. The Fuchs measure of relative poverty could be employed as a visionary statement of where citizens collectively wish to evolve in the pursuit of a more perfect union when it comes to curtailing poverty in this country well into the future.

Point 2: One-Stop Community Centers to Assist the Impoverished

With regard to the implementation of poverty-relief programs, David Shipler has offered an idea with profound implications for the indigent.[17] Poverty, as he describes it, effectively amounts to the absence of choices in life. Those afflicted with poverty may have substantial debt and an insufficient amount of resources. Such individuals are commonly challenged with regard to access to transportation, poor nutrition, high levels of stress, poor health, lack of decent and affordable housing, and a substandard education. In other words, the poor have to contend with many vexing issues simultaneously with no immediate apparent relief. They also have to contend with societal condemnation, as depicted by Shipler:

> A society's myths are often valuable, as is this one about the American Dream. It is useful because it sets a high standard, a lofty goal to which we aspire. And the gap between the goal and the reality is a gap that most Americans yearn to close. That is the noble yearning. The myth has a judgmental side, however, for if it is true that anyone who works hard can prosper in America, then it must also be true that anyone who does not prosper does not work hard. So this myth is a coin with two sides: one an ideal, one a condemnation.[18]

To Shipler, part of the solution to the poverty challenge is to provide "gateways" for the poor. The key to the gateways vision is to understand that the poor typically require extensive assistance:

> Those who work with the poor, including teachers and social workers, probation officers and job trainers, recognize that people who come to an agency with one problem invariably suffer from an array of problems. Yet

few agencies are equipped to tackle any issue other than the one presented. Teachers who take granola bars to school to toss to pupils with the glazed look of hunger in their eyes know that hungry children cannot concentrate and cannot learn. Yet most schools offer teachers no tools to help families get food stamps or housing subsidies or other benefits to which they may be entitled. Probation officers who see the violent homes and low skills of those they supervise know that their parolees will be back in prison without a systemic change in their lives. Yet most jurisdictions provide officers with little or no capacity to get their charges into services and programs that could help them and perhaps save them. If schools, probation departments, job-training centers, medical clinics, and other institutions were broadened into gateways through which needy families could pass into multiple services for their multiple problems, a great deal of good could be done. . . . Would this cost money? Yes, but some of the expense would ultimately be saved. The more we invest in children, the less we will have to invest later in prisons. The more we invest in health insurance and preventive care, the more productive our workforce will be. The lower the dropout rate from high school, the lower the associated costs in later life, and these savings can be substantial.[19]

Our social welfare system is very fragmented. There has to be a better way to coordinate services to families in need who are working diligently and following programmatic rules. If we have "one-stop" shopping centers, such as Walmart, why not have a one-stop social service delivery system at the local level?

Given that the poor have varied needs (e.g., public assistance, nutrition, transportation, housing, health care, criminal justice, psychology and counseling, family intervention, education, and energy) across this vast, diverse country, it would be beneficial to the family if social welfare needs could be largely addressed in one physical location. The needs of the indigent could be better addressed in a more efficient and compassionate manner if there was more coordination between and among governmental, nonprofit, church, and private organizations.

A national poverty summit needs to be commissioned by the members of Congress. In so doing, our federal leaders could create state-level organizations in the 50 states and the District of Columbia. State and local officials could literally devise a mechanism to implement the vision of one-stop community centers in their respective states. Undoubtedly, no singular mechanism will be applicable or relevant in all areas of the country. What may work in a high-density state, such as New Jersey, may not be feasible in Montana. With all the school closings over the past few decades, there are likely tangible facilities that could, with perhaps minor modifications, be used as community centers all across the country, particularly in urban centers. Many vacant schools, which have not been condemned but have been closed due to decreasing enrollments, shifting demographics, and racial balance considerations, could be suitable venues for the "gateway" phenomenon. As Shipler noted, implementing this concept will require money. The only entity with sufficient resources is the federal government, if policy makers make it a priority and agree to allocate the resources necessary. Obviously, it would take state officials some time to devise tangible plans, and it would be incumbent upon the members of Congress, in consultation with relevant experts in the field, to not only fund the proposition but to establish reasonable guidelines that would provide sufficient clarity to state and local officials involved in this collective effort. Representatives from the federal, state, and local governments would be participants, along with applicable church, nonprofit, and private officials. The secretary of Health and Human Services would have to be an instrumental political player in this process as well.

Point 3: Universal Health Insurance Coverage

When Theodore Roosevelt was the Progressive candidate for president in 1912, he embraced his party's stance on health insurance coverage:

> We favor the union of all the existing agencies of the Federal Government dealing with the public health into a single national health service without discrimination against or for any one set of therapeutic methods, school of medicine, or school of healing with such additional powers as may be necessary to enable it to perform efficiently such duties in the protection of the public from preventable diseases as may be properly undertaken by the Federal authorities, including the executing of existing laws regarding pure food, quarantine and cognate subjects, the promotion of vital statistics and the extension of the registration area of such statistics, and co-operation with the health activities of the various States and cities of the Nation.[20]

Roosevelt basically advocated health insurance coverage for all citizens provided through the national government presumably funded through tax revenue. Many would label his vision, in today's terms, as universal health coverage (UHC). According to the World Health Organization, UHC embodies three related objectives:

1. Equity in access to health services—everyone who needs services should get them, not only those who can pay for them.
2. The quality of health services should be good enough to improve the health of those receiving services.
3. People should be protected against financial risk, ensuring that the cost of using services does not put people at risk of financial harm.[21]

To date, the United States has not been part of the universe of UHC nations, typically defined as those countries that provide more than 90 percent of their population with health insurance.[22] When the Affordable Care Act was passed, it was projected to cover 94 percent of the population following full implementation in 2014.[23] To date, this goal has not been achieved. According to the Gallup Poll, the highest rate of coverage achieved under the act since it began tracking insurance coverage in 2008 is 89.1 percent, just under the UHC threshold.[24] However, since Obama left office, the ACA has been under siege by the Republicans, and the percentage of uninsured has increased.[25] What may happen to it politically is unknown, but there may be a more stable and plausible option for health insurance for the American people. It is time for the Roosevelt vision of 1912 to be realized, and this entails the creation of a single-payer system. The advocacy group Physicians for a National Health Program define "single-payer insurance":

> Single-payer national health insurance, also known as "Medicare for all," is a system in which a single public or quasi-public agency organizes health care financing, but the delivery of care remains largely in private hands. Under a single-payer system, all residents of the U.S. would be covered for all medically necessary services, including doctor, hospital, preventive, long-term care, mental health, reproductive health care, dental, vision, prescription drug and medical supply costs. The program would be funded by the savings obtained from replacing today's inefficient, profit-oriented, multiple insurance payers with a single streamlined, nonprofit, public payer, and by modest new taxes based on ability to pay. Premiums would disappear; 95 percent of all households would save money. Patients would no longer face financial barriers to care such as co-pays and deductibles, and would regain free choice of doctor and hospital. Doctors would regain autonomy over patient care. The Expanded and Improved Medicare for All Act, H.R. 676, based on PNHP's AJPH-published Physicians' Proposal, would establish an American single-payer health insurance system.[26]

Representative John Conyers sponsored this bill in the 115th session of Congress with 116 cosponsors.[27] It is an issue that Bernie Sanders attempted to champion during his quest for the Democratic nomination for the presidency in 2016. According to Sanders:

> It has been the goal of Democrats since Franklin D. Roosevelt to create a universal health care system guaranteeing health care to all people. Every other major industrialized nation has done so. It is time for this country to join them and fulfill the legacy of Franklin D. Roosevelt, Harry Truman, Lyndon B. Johnson and other great Democrats. The Affordable Care Act was a critically important step towards the goal of universal health care. Thanks to the ACA, more than 17 million Americans have gained health

insurance. Millions of low-income Americans have coverage through expanded eligibility for Medicaid that now exists in 31 states. Young adults can stay on their parents' health plans until they're 26. All Americans can benefit from increased protections against lifetime coverage limits and exclusion from coverage because of pre-existing conditions. . . . But as we move forward, we must build on the success of the ACA to achieve the goal of universal health care. Twenty-nine million Americans today still do not have health insurance and millions more are underinsured and cannot afford the high copayments and deductibles charged by private health insurance companies that put profits before people. The U.S. spends more on health care per person, and as a percentage of gross domestic product, than any other advanced nation in the world, including Australia, Canada, Denmark, France, Germany, Japan, New Zealand and the United Kingdom. But all that money has not made Americans healthier than the rest of the world. Quite simply, in our high-priced health care system that leaves millions overlooked, we spend more yet end up with less. Other industrialized nations are making the morally principled and financially responsible decision to provide universal health care to all of their people—and they do so while saving money by keeping people healthier. Those who say this goal is unachievable are selling the American people short.[28]

Medicare was created over 50 years ago to provide health insurance for all Americans 65 and older; it is a single-payer system, and it has worked fairly effectively and is commonly well regarded among the general public, typically right behind Social Security as the most popular entitlement programs.[29] What has worked for decades for retirees can work for all other citizens as well. It is time to heed Teddy Roosevelt's counsel and fully join the UHC community of nations. Health insurance should be considered a public good, and it should be guaranteed to all citizens.[30] National health insurance is a moral issue. All countries similar to the United States in industrialized status have UHC. Americans spend more than peers everywhere else, and we still do not provide coverage to all citizens. Continuing the status quo is not an option. The ACA has clearly been helpful with regard to access to health care. It would be immoral to repeal the ACA with no plan for UHC for the populace. Over 100 years have passed since the Progressive platform was issued; clearly, in spite of a barrage of criticism, the Republicans have no plan or even vision for UHC. Repealing the ACA and returning to the marketplace means that at least 15 percent of the population will not have coverage on any given day. This will hinder efforts to address the poverty challenge in the United States in a serious and unacceptable manner. Members of Congress may wish to consider a single-payer plan offered by the Physicians for a National Health Program.[31] No citizen in this country should be confronted with a situation of compromising her or his health in order to save money. Money has been a primary driving force in the American health care system for far too long, and the time to join the rest of the world committed to UHC is way past due.

Point 4: Maintain Progressive Tax Structure and Eliminate Some Deductions

While there are a plethora of different perspectives about taxation in the United States, there appears to be a clear consensus that the American system of taxation is very complicated. Debates regarding how to simplify it render a diversity of reform visions. Another reality is that many Americans perceive themselves to be taxed too much.[32] In addition, Americans tend to believe that they are taxed more than citizens in other democracies, when by comparison, the United States is actually a low-tax country.[33] A progressive tax is one that levies a larger percentage of income from high-income groups. Conversely, a regressive tax takes a larger percentage of income from low-income groups than from high-income groups. A proportional tax is one that takes the same percentage of income from all income groups.[34] Teddy Roosevelt is often credited with being the early leading advocate of progressive taxation. In a speech delivered on April 14, 1906, he said:

> As a matter of personal conviction, and without pretending to discuss the details or formulate the system, I feel that we shall ultimately have to consider the adoption of some such scheme as that of a progressive tax on all fortunes, beyond a certain amount, either given in life or devised or bequeathed upon death to any individual—a tax so framed as to put it out of the power of the owner of one of these enormous fortunes to hand on more than a certain amount to any one individual; the tax of course, to be imposed by the national and not the state government. Such taxation should, of course, be aimed merely at the inheritance or transmission in their entirety of those fortunes swollen beyond all healthy limits. Again, the national government must in some form exercise supervision over corporations engaged in interstate business—and all large corporations engaged in interstate business—whether by license or otherwise, so as to permit us to deal with the far reaching evils of overcapitalization.[35]

Bear in mind that contextually, the 16th Amendment, which gave Congress the authority to tax personal income, did not get ratified until 1913. Thus, it should be understood that Roosevelt's focus on a progressive tax structure for inheritances is a product of its times, but the analytical framework can be used and made applicable to personal income.

Later, Teddy Roosevelt's fifth cousin, Franklin Roosevelt, would articulate his reapplication of his cousin's premise about inheritances:

> With the enactment of the Income Tax Law of 1913, the Federal Government began to apply effectively the widely accepted principle that taxes

should be levied in proportion to ability to pay and in proportion to the benefits received. Income was wisely chosen as the measure of benefits and of ability to pay. This was, and still is, a wholesome guide for public policy. It should be retained as the governing principle of Federal taxation. The use of other forms of taxes is often justifiable, particularly for temporary periods; but taxation according to income is the most effective instrument yet devised to obtain just contribution from those best able to bear it and to avoid placing onerous burdens upon the mass of our people. The movement toward progressive taxation of wealth and of income has accompanied the growing diversification and interrelation of effort which marks our industrial society. Wealth in the modern world does not come merely from individual effort; it results from a combination of individual effort and of the manifold uses to which the community puts that effort. The individual does not create the product of his industry with his own hands; he utilizes the many processes and forces of mass production to meet the demands of a national and international market.[36]

As of 2017, the current federal tax structure is progressive, but there are a myriad of deductions that are available to citizens, especially the affluent. Included in table 5.2 is a compendium of the current income tax brackets at the federal level.

Table 5.2   Single Taxable Income Brackets and Rates (2017)

Rate	Taxable Income Bracket	Tax Owed
10%	$0-$9,325	10% of taxable income
15%	$9,325-$$37,950	$932.50 plus 15% of the excess over $9,325
25%	$37,950-$91,900	$5,226.25 plus 25% of the excess over $$37,950
28%	$91,900-$191,650	$18,713.75 plus 28% of the excess over $91,900
33%	$191,650-$416,700	$46,643.75 plus 33% of the excess over $191,650
35%	$416,700-$418,400	$120,910.25 plus 35% of the excess over $416,700
39.6%	$418,400+	$121,505.25 plus 39.6% of the excess over $418,400

Source: Adapted from Tax Foundation. 2017. 2017 Tax Brackets. Accessed August 16, 2017, from https://taxfoundation.org/2017-tax-brackets/.

While the federal tax structure is progressive, some noteworthy federal taxes are regressive. The current Medicare tax is 2.9 percent of all wages (split evenly between the employer and employee). Married tax filers over $250,000 and single tax filers over $200,000 are taxed an additional 0.9 percent, for a total of 3.8 percent tax on total income.[37] Social Security is a tax that is levied on the first $127,200 of total income (in 2017; it can change every year).[38] Social insurance payroll taxes are regressive because people with lower incomes pay a higher percentage of their incomes in payroll taxes than more affluent people. However, when evaluated by the impact of the benefits that are collected by recipients, Social Security and Medicare in particular can be viewed as progressive in terms of programmatic objectives and their strategic impact on general society.[39]

Part of the inherent complexity with the tax system is that numerous deductions can be made. Some of the more costly deductions to the federal treasury include the following: employer-paid health care; lower tax rates on dividends and long-term capital gains; deferral of active income of controlled foreign corporations; contributions to and earnings of defined-contribution retirement plans; mortgage interest deduction; Earned-Income Tax Credit; deductibility of state and local income, sales, and personal property taxes; contributions to and earnings of defined-benefit pension plans; credit for children under age 17; and subsidies for insurance purchased through health benefit exchanges.[40] Eliminating or decreasing some of them could presumably save revenue, which may be advantageous since the federal budget continues to be in deficit mode by more than half a trillion dollars annually over the last several years. Some deductions tend to benefit the more affluent to a greater extent than the less affluent. This is particularly the case with the home mortgage interest deduction:

> 77 percent of the benefits from the mortgage interest deduction went to homeowners with incomes above $250,000; taxpayers in this income group who claimed the deduction received an average subsidy of about $5,000 . . . Close to half of homeowners with mortgages—receive no benefit from the mortgage interest deduction. Some of these households do not owe federal income taxes, even though they typically pay substantial federal payroll taxes and/or state and local taxes. Owners claim the standard deduction rather than itemize deductions . . . The deduction's value depends on a household's marginal tax rate, so households in higher tax brackets benefit more. To see why, consider this example of two households. An investment banker making $675,000 who has a $1 million mortgage who pays $40,000 in mortgage interest each year receives a housing subsidy of about $14,000 annually from the mortgage interest deduction. The banker pays about 65 cents per dollar of mortgage interest, and the taxpayers pick up the remaining 35 cents. By contrast, a

schoolteacher making $45,000 and paying $10,000 a year in mortgage interest on a more modest home receives a housing subsidy worth $1,500 annually. Here, the family pays 85 cents of every dollar of mortgage interest and taxpayers pick up 15 cents. The banker's subsidy is not only larger than the teacher's in dollar terms, but also represents a greater share of the banker's mortgage interest expenses.[41]

If it was the goal of members of Congress and presidents to balance the federal budget and strive to be fiscally responsible, then the elimination or reduction of certain tax breaks that disproportionately benefit the rich over the poor would be a good place to start. Another net advantage of this approach to fiscal policy would be to slow the growth rate of the total national debt, which approaches $20 trillion as of this writing.[42]

Point 5: Enhanced Educational Opportunities

It is imperative that education be considered a public good if Americans are going to seriously address the challenges of poverty. This means that education investment at the K–12 level must be on traditional public education, not with vouchers, charter schools, or virtual schools.[43] The common school ideology articulated by Horace Mann must be preserved; bringing children from diverse backgrounds together in the same classroom to teach them about citizenship and civility where differences of opinion can be shared freely and in a nonviolent manner is of crucial importance in order to perpetuate this democracy. Horace Mann (1796–1859) was not the first person to articulate the common school vision, for Benjamin Rush, Thomas Jefferson, Noah Webster, and several others already embraced the vision of all children attending schools together paid by all citizens through taxation.[44]

Yet the common school ideal is under assault, particularly by conservatives and libertarians who tout school choice as the key to education reform. Consider the implications of school choice. To those with a free-market philosophy, vouchers would be a mechanism to compete for countless billions of dollars spent on public education nationally and remove education from the realm of democratic control and therefore democratic accountability. To libertarians such as Milton Friedman, vouchers would promote the cause of individual freedom, because schools would have to compete, and parents would choose the right school for their children. But imagine the societal implications of school choice, whether it be vouchers, charter schools, or virtual education. Should public taxpayers' money be used to promote parochial education? Recall that it was Thomas Jefferson who espoused a wall of separation in his famous Letter to the Danbury

Baptists on January 1, 1802. Jefferson, who was very spiritual in his convictions, declared:

> Believing with you that religion is a matter which lies solely between man & his god, that he owes account to none other for his faith or his worship, that the legitimate powers of government reach actions only and not opinions, I contemplate with sovereign reverence that act of the whole American people which declared that their legislature should "make no law respecting an establishment of religion, or prohibiting the free exercise thereof;" thus building a wall of eternal separation between Church & State.[45]

The framers of the Constitution did not wish to establish a theocracy in the United States, and that is why the Constitution does not create an official religion in this republic. The wall of separation described so brilliantly by Jefferson needs to be maintained; this separation ensures that children are educated but not indoctrinated into a specific view, ideology, or ethos. Children can use the knowledge gained in public schools as they see fit and on their own terms.

Mass privatization of education would come at an extremely high cost to the democratic experiment known as the United States of America. Imagine leaving issues of accessibility, education quality, legal mandates, student safety, environmental safeguards, and many other matters entirely up to private-sector officials working for private companies whose primary motivation is profit. The United States would be in danger of becoming a theocracy, and concrete science may give way to ideology. It is possible to reform traditional public education without replacing it with a reckless and rigid ideology that would prove harmful to children, the entire learning process, and the progress that has already been witnessed with regard to racially balancing U.S. public schools. In short, reducing poverty and strengthening public K–12 education are joint ventures and must be treated accordingly in the spirit and tradition of Horace Mann.[46] Another reality at the K–12 level is that education financing is still skewed to the more affluent suburbs due, in part, to the use of property taxes to partly finance our nation's public schools.[47]

With regard to higher education, Barack Obama presented an idea in 2015 that has profound implications for the cause of expanding educational opportunities in the United States. On January 8, 2015, he announced a proposal, which unfortunately did not get enacted by Congress, to make two years of community college free for eligible students, which would allow them to earn half of a bachelor's degree at no cost and gain professional skills that could help them in the workforce. As Obama explained it:

In our growing global economy, Americans need to have more knowledge and more skills to compete—by 2020, an estimated 35 percent of job openings will require at least a bachelor's degree, and 30 percent will require some college or an associate's degree. Students should be able to get the knowledge and the skills they need without taking on decades' worth of student debt.[48]

It is estimated that 44 million Americans collectively owe more than $1.4 trillion as of the summer of 2017.[49] In order to expand opportunities in higher education, college costs have to be reasonable for working- and middle-class Americans. Obviously, we have many students in this country who find it necessary to pay for their education through borrowing. Under Obama's plan, students would have to attend at least half time and maintain a 2.50 grade point average. Seventy-five percent of the funding for this program would come from the federal government. State officials that opted to participate would pay the remaining 25 percent.[50]

During his tenure, President Bill Clinton offered Congress and the American public some concrete ideas regarding education reform. These proposals were not enacted into law, but they would be helpful in improving education quality, which could enhance the educational experience for all, particularly during the critical formative years. In 1999, he recommended the hiring of 100,000 public school teachers to reduce class sizes nationally, especially in grades K–3, and the building or modernizing of 5,000 public schools.[51] This kind of national investment in public education needs to be facilitated by federal officials, because state officials across the country are struggling to maintain the status quo with public education funding, both at the K–12 and higher education levels. The sustained resource support has the potential to yield impressive results for student success.

Point 6: Reinvigorate the Social Safety Net (Especially SNAP) and Repeal TANF

Another key to winning the War on Poverty is to reestablish trust in government. Franklin Roosevelt understood this keenly. In a democracy, it is essential for the people to trust their leaders in government. The very essence of democracy was fully appreciated by the 32nd president:

The final word belongs to no man; yet we can still believe in change and in progress. Democracy, as a dear old friend of mine in Indiana, Meredith Nicholson, has called it, is a quest, a never-ending seeking for better things, and in the seeking for these things and the striving for them, there are many roads to follow. But, if we map the course of these roads, we find that there are only two directions.[52]

During the 1932 campaign in his quest to defeat Herbert Hoover for the White House, Roosevelt explained his views on social contract theory:

> The Declaration of Independence discusses the problem of Government in terms of a contract. Government is a relation of give and take, a contract, perforce, if we would follow the thinking out of which it grew. Under such a contract rulers were accorded power, and the people consented to that power on consideration that they be accorded certain rights. The task of statesmanship has always been the re-definition of these rights in terms of a changing and growing social order. New conditions impose new requirements upon Government and those who conduct Government . . . The terms of that contract are as old as the Republic, and as new as the new economic order. Every man has a right to life; and this means that he has also a right to make a comfortable living. He may by sloth or crime decline to exercise that right; but it may not be denied him. We have no actual famine or dearth; our industrial and agricultural mechanism can produce enough and to spare. Our Government formal and informal, political and economic, owes to everyone an avenue to possess himself of a portion of that plenty sufficient for his needs, through his own work.[53]

Assuming that the citizen in question was able-bodied and willing to work, it was incumbent upon federal officials to ensure that citizen was able to secure meaningful employment. To Roosevelt, during times of extreme duress, such as the Great Depression, federal officials were obligated to provide public assistance to eligible citizens because gainful employment was not available in many areas all across the country. The key point is the lack of jobs during this time was not the fault of most Americans, but to Roosevelt, officials at the federal level had a responsibility to assist citizens in need. This was based on trust, and it was a social contract. As indicated earlier in this book, this trust has been broken with Temporary Assistance for Needy Families (TANF). If able-bodied citizens are in need of assistance now, and their eligibility has expired due to the legislative restrictions in TANF, they will receive nothing from the federal government by way of assistance in spite of their willingness to work if jobs were available to them.

Roosevelt concluded the aforementioned campaign speech by declaring:

> Faith in America, faith in our tradition of personal responsibility, faith in our institutions, faith in ourselves demand that we recognize the new terms of the old social contract. We shall fulfill them, as we fulfilled the obligation of the apparent Utopia which Jefferson imagined for us in 1776, and which Jefferson, Roosevelt and Wilson sought to bring to realization. We must do so, lest a rising tide of misery, engendered by our common failure, engulf us all. But failure is not an American habit; and in the strength of great hope we must all shoulder our common load.[54]

A social contract is a sacred covenant between the people and their national leaders, most visibly through the presidency. When Clinton signed so-called welfare reform in 1996, he effectively terminated the social contract that Roosevelt established with the members of Congress at the time. This was unwise, for history suggests that an economic calamity is always possible, even when it has not been witnessed during an extended period of time.

I am not advocating public assistance for those who refuse to work or make unfortunate choices in their lives. My point is that recessions and depressions have occurred every century since this republic began. They will undoubtedly occur again. For people who are responsible, and actually desire to be employed, public assistance should remain on open-ended possibility just in case it is absolutely needed by citizens. It is essential that in this land of vast abundance, we maintain a public commitment to those with insufficient food. SNAP should be considered a sacred program that should not be cut so long as there is a definitive need for it. Cutting food and nutrition for the needy, especially vulnerable children, is downright immoral and not reflective of a compassionate value system.

Point 7: Invest in New Meaningful Infrastructure Jobs

Donald Trump promised to bring more manufacturing jobs back to the United States in the 2016 presidential campaign. Whether this is either possible or plausible is debatable. The reality is that foreign competitors did not steal American jobs; many industry leaders chose to move factories overseas. This practice resulted in increasing profits for the company in question and reducing the price for that company's products for the American consumer. Bringing back jobs would likely have the implication of higher prices. While some people tell pollsters that they would pay higher prices for products made in the United States, the question remains how much more would people be willing to pay for the same product if it were made in this country? Another reality that tends to get ignored is that many jobs that have been lost in the United States were not due to foreign competition, especially from China, but to automation. In other words, human workers were replaced by machines.[55] The amount of labor costs that are incorporated into a price for a product is another issue. As one analyst described it: "The quest for cheap labor has led manufacturers from New England to North Carolina, then Brazil and Taiwan, China and Vietnam, then Indonesia, Bangladesh and maybe next Ethiopia."[56]

But there is a model to create meaningful jobs in the United States, and it was accomplished, perhaps in a different way and a unique circumstance, during the Great Depression. Many people were put to work in the Civil Conservation Corps (CCC). In fact, it is estimated that about 3 million men took part in the CCC in its existence from 1933 to 1942. Congress ended the program at the beginning of American involvement in World War II to divert funds to the war effort. More than 3.5 billion trees were planted on land that was barren due to fire, soil erosion, or lumbering. The CCC was responsible for over half the reforestation (public and private) in U.S. history.[57]

Why not borrow from this historical model to meet the United States' current infrastructure needs? Since 1988, the American Society of Civil Engineers (ASCE) has issued a report card on the United States' infrastructure. ASCE was founded in 1852 and is the oldest national engineering organization. Using traditional letter grades, the ASCE ranked the nation in aviation (D), dams (D), energy (D+), inland waterways (D), ports (C+), rail (B), schools (D+), and solid waste (C+). The country received an overall infrastructure grade of a D+ in 2017.[58] Clearly, our nation's trained experts are recommending fundamental change in the national infrastructure. The changes recommended will not be cheap as the improvement costs are estimated to be $4.59 trillion, though a combination of public and private funding would be needed.[59]

Using 2015 as the year of analysis, the ASCE officials determined that there were over 8.7 million flights; there are 7,000 aircraft in the air at any given time; and 2.25 million people travel by air every day. Investing in advances in technology could result in enhanced public safety, less fuel consumption, better on-time efficiency, and fewer delays for the traveling public.

There are over 90,000 dams in the United States, and their average age as of 2016 is 56 years. Over 15,000 of them (17 percent) are classified as high hazard potential. By 2025, 70 percent of all dams in the country will be over 50 years old.

With regard to energy, much of the system used in this country predates the 20th century. Most electric transmission and distribution lines in the United States were constructed in the 1950s and 1960s; they have a 50-year life expectancy. Without investing in updating equipment, Americans will experience longer, more frequent, and more costly power outages.

The United States has over 25,000 miles of inland waterways and 239 locks, which are operated and maintained by the Army Corps of Engineers. Most locks and dams in the system are well beyond their 50-year design life.

There are 926 ports in the United States, and they are essential in the global economy. Almost all overseas trade passes through the ports, which accounts for about one-fourth of the total U.S. economy. More investments in the ports are needed to remain competitive, particularly connections to the ports in question (roads, rail, inland waterways, and navigation channels).

The rail system in the United States received the highest grade. Today, rail carries about one-third of U.S. exports and delivers 5 million tons of freight and 85,000 passengers every day. There are over 140,000 miles of track and over 100,000 bridges in the country. Investments in technology can enhance public safety, as 237 people were killed and 991 injured in rail accidents in 2015.[60]

Almost 50 million K–12 children attend school every day in the United States in almost 100,000 public school buildings occupying 2 million acres of land. Twenty-four percent of all public school buildings were rated by the ASCE as fair or poor, and 53 percent of all schools need improvements to reach the good condition category. The experts estimate that the country underinvests in its public schools to the tune of a $38 billion gap annually.

With regard to solid waste, Americans generate 258 million tons of municipal solid waste annually. Fifty-three percent of the solid waste is deposited in landfills. Almost 35 percent is recycled, and 13 percent is combusted for energy production. There is a discernible need for citizens to recognize that what people discard can, in fact, be a reusable resource. There are a number of critical concerns with solid waste management, including public health, impact on groundwater, and overall environmental degradation in areas near landfills and other waste facilities.[61]

Improving the nation's infrastructure could provide meaningful jobs that would create a solid foundation for the United States' economic growth for generations into the future and help to alleviate poverty simultaneously. With regard to transportation needs specifically, and this will obviously overlap with another point regarding climate change, a high-speed rail system in the United States could do much to reduce traffic on the nation's highways, reduce air pollution, and provide opportunities for all Americans, including the impoverished, to travel in a fast, safe, and cleaner mode of transportation. In 1992, Bill Clinton touted high-speed rail as a means to boost American productivity and jobs, conserve energy, and provide an opportunity to avoid airport expansion.[62] Of the recent presidents, he made the pursuance of high-speed rail service a higher priority, but members of Congress have not come to a consensus on high-speed rail, certainly in budgetary terms, to date. In fact, many countries, including Japan, China, France, Spain, Italy, and Germany are far ahead of the United States in the investment and implementation of high-speed rail.[63] Some state officials (e.g., California and Texas) are attempting to find ways to implement this mode of transportation through public and private investment.[64]

Point 8: *E Pluribus Unum*—Embrace the Communitarian Philosophy

Another important step in the alleviation of poverty is to develop a culture and awareness that individual decisions have a profound impact on the broader society. The libertarian philosophy will do little to alleviate poverty in the United States because it is a societal phenomenon by definition. This country of 50 states and well over 300 million people is interconnected whether citizens choose to accept the premise or not. We cannot simply accept the notion that poor people make bad decisions and that is why they are poor. We cannot accept stereotypes as the norm. In 2017, the secretary of housing and urban development and former GOP presidential candidate in 2016, Ben Carson, referred to poverty as a "state of mind."[65] This assumes that the poor are poor because they desire to be so. That is a counterintuitive contention, to put it mildly.

During the 1976 presidential campaign, Ronald Reagan often referred to the "welfare queen."[66] As Reagan himself indicated at the time:

> There's a woman in Chicago . . . She has 80 names, 30 addresses, 12 Social Security cards and is collecting veterans' benefits on four nonexisting deceased husbands. And she's collecting Social Security on her cards. She's got Medicaid, getting food stamps and she is collecting welfare under each of her names. Her tax-free cash income alone is over $150,000.[67]

While the facts involved in the case of Linda Taylor were complicated and convoluted, it is clear that Reagan was engaging in hyperbole. His message resonated with many Americans: welfare fraud was rampant, social spending was too high, and lazy and unscrupulous people were taking advantage of the welfare system. He made it sound that welfare fraud was widespread in the United States, and not the vast exception to the norm. Citizens should always ask how policy ideas and proposals affect society first and foremost. Our first instinct should be the promotion of the greater common good ahead of individual self-interest. We have opted for this route at various times in history, particularly in the midst of a crisis. Doing so again would assist in the crusade against poverty.

A societal problem such as poverty will not magically go away without a sustained effort by all citizens. We must understand that whether we live in Maine, Indiana, South Dakota, or California, collectively we are the people of the United States of America. Embracing a communitarian philosophy will assist the indigent because we will reject the politics of isolationism and instead accept the premise that a societal problem requires a societal solution.

On June 20, 1782, the Confederate Congress in the United States adopted the Great Seal of the United States after debating the matter for six years. *E Pluribus Unum* is Latin for out of many, one. The Great Seal is a depiction of the 13 states coming together as one.[68] A common purpose and sense of a shared mission prompted officials from the states to join in a larger alliance and structural arrangement beyond themselves as isolated entities. A strong commitment is needed to alleviate poverty in the land of relative affluence. It can only be accomplished by subjugating individual self-interest for the greater public good. Since 1956, the official motto of the United States has been "In God We Trust."[69] Some consider it a replacement of the unofficial motto created by the Great Seal; others consider it simply an alternative.

Point 9: Enhance the Culture of Citizenship and Individual Responsibility

One indicator of a healthy democracy is the extent to which people accept their duties and responsibilities as citizens.[70] According to U.S. Citizenship and Immigration Services, citizenship comes with many rights (freedom of expression, freedom to worship, right to a trial by jury, right to vote in elections, right to apply for federal employment requiring U.S. citizenship, right to run for elected office, and freedom to pursue life, liberty, and happiness) as well as responsibilities (support and defend the Constitution; stay informed of the issues affecting the community; participate in the democratic process; respect and obey all laws; respect the rights, beliefs, and opinions of others; participate in the local community; pay all income taxes in an honest manner; serve on a jury if called upon; and defend the country if the need should arise).[71] Many Americans are aware of their rights but seemingly not their responsibilities in a republic. Americans of all social classes could stand to become more engaged citizens in this democracy. An engaged citizenry is resistant to political manipulation and would undoubtedly seek to assist those who are less fortunate than them to a greater extent. Simply being aware of the present while heeding the lessons from history would assist in winning the War on Poverty. Political campaigns tend to be divisive, where the various sides are pitted against one another. Addressing the needs of the poor in this nation does not mean that other groups will have something to lose. I would make the opposite argument—winning the War on Poverty will be positive for all Americans, and our society will be greatly enhanced. Less poverty will make for a more vibrant society with fewer social problems and less crime.

All Americans should be expected to be responsible for their individual actions, including the impoverished. The essence of good citizenship, in part, is abiding by existing laws and being willing to make contributions in the community. Obviously the opportunity costs for the affluent are far less than for the poor when it pertains to issues of community engagement. This is precisely why the eradication of poverty establishes the conditions for a more robust democracy where millions escape the vicissitudes of poverty and are better positioned to give back to their respective communities.

Point 10: Decent and Affordable Housing for All Citizens

President Harry Truman signed the Housing Act of 1949 into law on July 15 of that year.[72] On that day, he shared his vision of this particular law:

> The Housing Act of 1949 also establishes as a national objective the achievement as soon as feasible of a decent home and a suitable living environment for every American family, and sets forth the policies to be

followed in advancing toward that goal. These policies are thoroughly consistent with American ideals and traditions. They recognize and preserve local responsibility, and the primary role of private enterprise, in meeting the Nation's housing needs. But they also recognize clearly the necessity for appropriate Federal aid to supplement the resources of communities and private enterprise.[73]

Truman's vision is as pertinent today as it was almost 70 years ago. Too many Americans do not have a decent home, or are homeless altogether, and are frankly not in a "suitable living environment." According to officials at the National Alliance to End Homelessness, on a given night in January 2015, there were 564,708 homeless people in the United States.[74] In New York City alone, there are 62,000 men, women, and children sleeping in shelters each night.[75] It is very difficult to count the homeless, and some people may be homeless at some point in a given year but perhaps secure housing at another point. Since counting the homeless is a daunting challenge, the full extent of homelessness is undoubtedly unknown. Most studies are somewhat limited by practical realities, such as counting the number of people in shelters or that can be physically viewed on the streets.[76]

According to officials at the Center for American Progress, homes are central to the lives of Americans as people in this country spend 70 percent of their time inside their residence.[77] The reality in the United States is that one's health and life expectancy is likely to be determined more by the applicable zip code than any genetic code. People who live in poor neighborhoods are much more likely to experience higher levels of segregation, unemployment, a single-parent family, and exposure to neighborhood violence. Citizens who live in such environments also tend to have more health challenges. Race is a very significant variable in that African American, American Indian, and Latino American children are six to nine times more likely to live in poverty than white children.[78]

Many might find it surprising that of the 135 million homes in the United States, 30 million have serious health and safety hazards (e.g., gas leaks, damaged plumbing, and poor heating), and this is without further degradation caused by natural disasters. Six million homes have structural problems, while another 6 million are still afflicted by toxic lead paint.[79] There are approximately 43.3 million rental households in the United States, housing more than 80 million adults and over 30 million children. The renter share of U.S. households is the highest it has been in 50 years (37 percent).[80] In terms of affordability, almost half of all renter households are cost-burdened, meaning that more than 30 percent of their income is spent on rent alone.[81] This is a particular burden on the poor, and it makes purchasing other necessities, including food, clothing, transportation, medical care, and insurance very challenging.

Truman's vision can be pursued in earnest and achieved with a combination of public and private funds. However, what he articulated in 1949 is still true today. Federal officials have to play a leading role and make decent and affordable housing a priority. According to Center on Budget and Policy Priorities officials, $190 billion was spent on housing in 2015 in order for Americans to buy or rent homes, but little of these funds were actually allocated to Americans who struggle the most to afford housing. Federal housing expenditures are currently imbalanced in two ways: they target a disproportionate share of subsidies on higher-income households, and they favor home ownership over renting. While federal assistance is effective at helping low-income renters, rental assistance programs are vastly underfunded and only reach about 25 percent of eligible households.[82] While the level of funding for housing assistance can certainly be debated, one thing is clear. The current laws and rules regarding housing could be redirected to assist the needy if the political will existed to do so. Our leaders need to revisit the premise that people who can afford a house should receive a disproportionate subsidy compared to people who cannot afford a home purchase and are thus required to rent housing. This is particularly salient as the surge in rental demand across the country has reached an unprecedented level.[83]

Point 11: Raise the Federal Minimum Wage and Index It for Inflation

One of the most disconcerting debates in the United States involves the federal minimum wage. When Franklin Roosevelt signed the Fair Labor Standards Act of 1938, among other things, a federal minimum wage was established for the first time in U.S. history,[84] despite strong opposition that still exists today. The first minimum wage was set at 25 cents an hour. Included in table 5.3 is a compendium of minimum wage increases since it was originally established. It has been $7.25 since 2009. Progressives and liberals, in the tradition of Franklin Roosevelt, typically support a higher minimum wage and contend that its low level is not a living wage and is not sufficient to combat poverty in the United States. Conservatives generally opposed the creation of a federal minimum wage and have typically opposed efforts to increase it since its original inauguration. To many on the right, the federal minimum wage is an unwarranted intrusion into the marketplace that does more harm than good as it is generally argued that increasing the minimum wage increases the cost of goods and services and results in a net job reduction in order to accommodate the higher labor costs.

In a speech to a joint session of Congress on May 24, 1937, Roosevelt offered four reasons why opponents to the creation of a federal minimum wage were flawed in their analytical framework:

Table 5.3 History of Changes in the Federal Minimum Wage, 1938–2017

Implementation Date	Minimum Wage Rate
October 24, 1938	$0.25
October 24, 1939	$0.30
October 24, 1945	$0.40
January 25, 1950	$0.75
March 1, 1956	$1.00
September 3, 1961	$1.15
September 3, 1963	$1.25
February 1, 1967	$1.40
February 1, 1968	$1.60
May 1, 1974	$2.00
January 1, 1975	$2.10
January 1, 1976	$2.30
January 1, 1978	$2.65
January 1, 1979	$2.90
January 1, 1980	$3.10
January 1, 1981	$3.35
April 1, 1990	$3.80
April 1, 1991	$4.25
October 1, 1996	$4.75
September 1, 1997	$5.15
July 24, 2007	$5.85
July 24, 2008	$6.55
July 24, 2009	$7.25

Source: U.S. Department of Labor, Wage and Hour Division. 2017. History of Federal Minimum Wage Rates Under the Fair Labor Standards Act, 1938–2009. Accessed August 24, 2017, from https://www.dol.gov/whd/minwage/chart.htm.

The truth of the matter, of course, is that the exponents of the theory of private initiative as the cure for deep-seated national ills want in most cases to improve the lot of mankind. But, well intentioned as they may be, they fail for four evident reasons—first, they see the problem from the point of view of their own business; second, they see the problem from the point of view of their own locality or region; third, they cannot act unanimously because they have no machinery for agreeing among themselves; and, finally, they have no power to bind the inevitable minority of chiselers within their own ranks.[85]

It is simple to oppose the minimum wage on the grounds that it is an unwarranted intrusion into the marketplace, but if all business owners provided a reasonable wage, there would be no need for the federal intervention in the first place. The reality is that some unscrupulous owners have not been reasonable with their workers, and that is precisely why Roosevelt articulated his belief in a living wage, a societal statement that all workers have to at least be compensated at some level that would be determined by the collective wisdom of the members of Congress.

On February 12, 2014, President Obama signed Executive Order 13658, which established a minimum wage of $10.10 for all workers on federal construction and service contracts.[86] This policy was enacted shortly after more than 600 economists across the nation urged congressional leaders to increase the federal minimum wage to $10.10 by 2016.[87] In their statement, the economists highlighted that full-time minimum wage workers would get a salary increase from about $15,000 to $21,000 per year. The increase would affect almost 17 million workers in the United States immediately, while another 11 million workers might experience a spillover effect because their wages are just above the minimum wage and might be adjusted by their employers.[88] Members of Congress did not heed the counsel at the time.

In 2015, Senator Bernie Sanders (I-Vermont) introduced a bill to raise the federal minimum wage to $15 per hour in five steps by 2020. At the time, he had five Democratic cosponsors in the Senate: Sherrod Brown (Ohio), Richard Durbin (Illinois), Kirsten Gillibrand (New York), Ed Markey (Massachusetts), and Elizabeth Warren (Massachusetts).[89] In 2017, Sanders introduced a bill that would immediately raise the minimum wage to $9.25 and then established annual raises until 2024, when it would become $15. This time, he had 30 Democratic cosponsors in the Senate: Brown, Durbin, Gillibrand, Markey, and Warren, as well as Tammy Baldwin (Wisconsin), Richard Blumenthal (Connecticut), Cory Booker (New Jersey), Maria Cantwell (Washington), Ben Cardin (Maryland), Tammy Duckworth (Illinois), Dianne Feinstein (California), Al Franken (Minnesota), Kamala Harris (California), Mazie Hirono (Hawaii), Tim Kaine (Virginia), Amy Klobuchar (Minnesota), Patrick Leahy (Vermont), Jeff Merkley (Oregon), Chris Murphy (Connecticut), Patty Murray (Washington), Bill Nelson (Florida), Gary Peters (Michigan), Jack Reed (Rhode Island), Brian Schatz (Hawaii), Chuck Schumer (New York), Debbie Stabenow (Michigan), Chris Van Hollen (Maryland), Sheldon Whitehouse (Rhode Island), and Ron Wyden (Oregon).[90] As of this writing, the members of Congress have not increased the minimum wage.

History has been clear on the issue of the minimum wage: increases over the years have not had the adverse effect on jobs and the economy that opponents have contended. As the aforementioned letter by the economists duly noted:

In recent years there have been important developments in the academic literature on the effect of increases in the minimum wage on employment, with the weight of the evidence now showing the increases in the minimum wage have had little or no negative effect on the employment of minimum-wage workers, even during times of weakness in the labor market. Research suggests that a minimum-wage increase could have a small stimulative effect on the economy as low-wage workers spend their additional earnings, raising demand and job growth, and providing some help on the jobs front.[91]

We can debate the appropriate figure, whether it be $10.10, $15.00, or some other amount. Across the country, $7.25 is not a livable wage, and there should be a national statement in the spirit and tradition of Roosevelt that establishes a moral commitment to minimum-wage workers, and it should be indexed to inflation thereafter so that workers who are directly affected by the wage do not have to wait possibly years for a raise in salary.

Point 12: Address the Challenge of Climate Change

Climate change is a serious issue affecting the entire world in a profound manner. According to the Union of Concerned Scientists:

Global warming is happening now. The planet's temperature is rising. The trend is clear and unmistakable. Every one of the past 40 years has been warmer than the 20th century average. 2016 was the hottest year on record. The 12 warmest years on record have all occurred since 1998. Globally, the average surface temperature has increased more than one degree Fahrenheit since the late 1800s. Most of that increase has occurred over just the past three decades. We are the cause. We are overloading our atmosphere with carbon dioxide, which traps heat and steadily drives up the planet's temperature. Where does all this carbon come from? The fossil fuels we burn for energy—coal, natural gas, and oil—plus the loss of forests due to deforestation, especially in the tropics. The scientific evidence is clear. Within the scientific community, there is no debate. An overwhelming majority of climate scientists agree that global warming is happening and that human activity is the primary cause.[92]

The implications of a planet that is warming at an accelerated level are somber.[93] Recently, researchers have examined the impact of climate change on the affluent versus the impoverished. Perhaps not surprisingly, a significant study recently found that climate change will aggravate economic inequality in the United States.[94] The gap between the rich and poor is destined to widen due to climate change.[95] According to Solomon Hsiang and his associates, the U.S. economy will lose about 0.7 percent of its gross domestic product for each degree Fahrenheit increase in global temperatures, but the financial suffering will be disproportionately felt by the poor and not the affluent, especially for the poorest third of counties in the country. Many of the counties in question are in the South and lower Midwest; affected regions could sustain economic losses that would be comparable to the Great Depression in the 20th century.[96] At the current pace of global warming, scientists project that world temperatures will increase by about 4°C by the end of this century, further exacerbating the gap between the haves and the have-nots.[97]

Most of the world's leaders are joining forces to combat the problem of climate change. On December 12, 2015, the Paris Agreement was adopted at the 21st session of the Conference of the Parties to the United Nations Framework Convention on Climate Change.[98] Under the terms of the agreement, leaders from the nations of the world had from April 22, 2016, until April 21, 2017, to sign the accord. By the latter date, leaders from 195 nations had signed the agreement.[99] However, on June 1, 2017, President Trump announced the U.S. withdrawal from the agreement. At a news conference, Trump indicated that he was putting American workers first by withdrawing. He perceived that the agreement would result in a loss of wealth and a loss of jobs in the United States. Under the terms of the agreement, however, Trump cannot actually withdraw the commitment already made by Obama until November 2020.[100] Trump's announcement led to a global condemnation of the decision.

The United States is the second leading producer of carbon dioxide emissions on earth (behind China).[101] The Paris Agreement relies on voluntary cuts in emissions by participating nations and establishes a global target to keep the increase in the average temperature of the world to no higher than 2°C above preindustrial levels. It requires about $100 billion a year in funding from developed countries to assist developing countries in the creation of green energy sources. Only two countries have completely rejected the deal (Syria and Nicaragua). Leaders from several dozen nations have signed but not approved the agreement; these include Iran, Turkey, and Russia, which ranks as the third-largest emitter of carbon dioxide in the world.[102]

U.S. leadership on climate change is sorely needed. Since climate change is a global phenomenon, it requires a global solution. The Paris Agreement was a diplomatic achievement; many environmentalists believed that the goals were too incremental, but at least they were a hopeful sign for the future on this ever-contentious issue. According to the agreement:

Acknowledging that climate change is a common concern of humankind, Parties should, when taking action to address climate change, respect, promote and consider their respective obligations on human rights, the right of health, the rights of indigenous peoples, local communities, migrants, children, persons with disabilities and people in vulnerable situations and the right to development, as well as gender equality, empowerment of women and intergenerational equity.[103]

Combatting poverty requires an environment capable of sustaining humans, animals, and plants alike. It is incumbent upon leaders from all industrialized nations, especially the United States, to play a facilitative role in the cause of environmental protection. Ignoring the science of climate change is reckless; the harm done to the poor, and society in general, will be devastating in ways that many citizens cannot even imagine. The time is ripe to invest in and produce forms of energy that do not pollute the environment. As a nation, we must curtail the use of fossil fuels and accelerate investment in clean and renewable sources of energy without delay. This absolutely must happen whether the Democrats or Republicans control the White House or both chambers of Congress.

Point 13: Reform the Machinery of Voting

One way that Americans, including the poor and those who may be poor but not qualify under the existing definition of poverty, could advance their issues and interests is to participate in the electoral process.[104] As discussed in chapter 4, voter turnout in the United States is quite low compared to the rest of the free world. Why not hold our leaders accountable by increasing the pool of participants in American elections? We already know that the more income and formal education a person has in this country, the more likely she or he will vote in elections. We have to remember that this is our democracy in a collective sense, as the people are the ultimate sovereigns in the United States, not our elected leaders. If we do not approve of the job performance of our senators and representatives, we should hold them accountable via elections. This can be done with a surge of citizen interest corresponding with an end to the many barriers that, I would argue, are intended to keep voter turnout down.

A number of structural changes are required to make conditions more amenable to electoral participation. First, it is way past time for Americans to elect their own president directly. The framers limited direct election to the U.S. House of Representatives in the original Constitution; the people could not directly elect their own U.S. senators. That was changed when the 17th Amendment was added to the Constitution in 1913. It has been more than a century since democracy was extended in this manner; it needs to happen again with the presidency. We have had a number of "wrong winners" in U.S. history, where the people's choice did not get the job due to the electoral college.[105] This happened in 1824, 1876, 1888, 2000, and 2016. It has happened twice in the modern era (2000 and 2016). Al Gore won the popular vote in 2000 over George W. Bush by about 540,000 votes; Hillary Clinton prevailed in the popular tally in 2016 by almost 3 million votes.[106] But the presidency is awarded by garnering 270 out of 538 votes in the electoral college (a simple majority) due to the requirements established by the framers in Article II of the Constitution. To some Americans, the electoral college is sacred because the framers of the Constitution created it. But many in this country do not realize that the framers of the Constitution debated numerous options for presidential selection. They were not enamored with the notion of an electoral college, but it was a compromise measure that ultimately prevailed on the matter. Professor Robert Dahl provided a succinct explanation:

> Every solution seemed worse than the rest. The arrangement they finally cobbled together at the last minute was adopted more out of desperation, perhaps, than out of any great confidence in its success. So why did the delegates finally give their approval to the electoral college? Probably the best answer to our question would be: the Framers settled on an electoral college because they had run out of alternatives.[107]

Today, many Republicans embrace the electoral college because it is an advantage to their party. The electoral college provides disproportionate political power, in the form of votes, to sparsely populated, rural states. Throughout the Plains states and the western states, Republican candidates have a significant advantage over their Democratic counterparts. This advantage helped George W. Bush in 2000 and Trump in 2016 become president, in spite of losing the national popular vote. This is not a political advantage that Republicans will cede any time soon, unless the public demands a constitutional amendment requiring direct election.[108]

Impediments to voting in the 21st century should be eliminated. Structural barriers with the intent to diminish voter turnout by specific groups in the population should all be an artifact of the past. Yet this is not the case today. Many state officials have devised cunning plans under the guise of eliminating "fraud" in elections in order to implement their political agenda. Officials at New York University School of Law determined:

> The Brennan Center's seminal report on this issue, *The Truth About Voter Fraud*, found that most reported incidents of voter fraud are actually traceable to other sources, such as clerical errors or bad data matching practices. The report reviewed elections that had been meticulously studied for voter fraud, and found incident rates between 0.0003 percent and 0.0025 percent. Given this tiny incident rate for voter impersonation fraud, it is more likely, the report noted, that an American "will be struck by lightning than he will impersonate another voter at the polls.[109]

One example of a state intervention in order to presumably prevent "fraud" is a photo identification requirement. This was designed to keep poor people, especially African Americans, Latino Americans, and Native Americans, from voting. Some state officials are purging voter registration lists if voters have not voted since a specific date. The objective is clear in that it will have a disparate impact on the poor and non-Caucasians. Voter registration deadlines are absolutely in need of change. The Supreme Court justices determined in 1972 that states could have up to a 30-day registration in advance of election day requirement, based, in part, on the computer technology of 1972.[110] Has computer technology changed since the early 1970s? Americans can get thousands of dollars in credit literally in minutes, but in a given state, a person cannot vote on election day if she or he did not register about a month before the election. Such laws are truly transparent, for they do not protect us from fraud but simply diminish voter turnout. A majority of the states have registration deadlines 21–30 days before election day. North Dakota is the only state where citizens do not have to register themselves. State officials automatically register eligible residents.[111] Currently, 15 states and the District of Columbia offer same-day registration. Residents in this instance can register first and then vote on the day of the election.[112] Across the country, voting needs to be made more facilitative by state legislators; if state lawmakers do not encourage more citizens to participate by passing less-restrictive voting laws, members of Congress are encouraged to intervene. In the past, through very long struggles and a great deal of human suffering, amendments were added to the federal Constitution to expand democracy, not restrict it (e.g., 15th, 17th, 19th, 23rd, 24th, and 26th Amendments). The purging of registration lists, photo identification requirements, lengthy requirements to register in advance of election day, the curtailing of early voting or its cessation altogether, as well as trying to prevent people with past convictions from voting all need to stop now. All political parties should present their platforms through their candidates and let the people make a choice accordingly. Trying to prevent certain people from voting, particularly based on the perception that they may vote for candidates in a rival political party, is completely unacceptable and downright immoral. It is also illegal. In recent years, GOP officials at the national and state levels have been accused of such activities.[113] If such allegations are tangible, corrective measures need to be implemented without delay.

With the low rate of voter participation in the United States, I cannot help but think our leaders would reorder their public policy priorities if they were compelled to do so by millions of citizens who started voting at higher rates. A change in the status quo with regard to existing voting patterns could lead to significant public policy changes that could ameliorate the plight of the poor in the United States.

Point 14: Public Financing of All Federal Campaigns

Most democracies on earth use some semblance of publicly financed campaigns for national offices. The United States is the stark exception. Historically, President Theodore Roosevelt was the first president to ask members of Congress to pass a law establishing publicly financed campaigns, where the nominees from the major parties would be allocated the same exact budget and rules governing the campaign and would not be allowed to solicit or accept contributions from individuals and corporations alike. This is what Roosevelt said in his 1907 State of the Union address:

> Under our form of government voting is not merely a right but a duty, and, moreover, a fundamental and necessary duty if a man is to be a good citizen. It is well to provide that corporations shall not contribute to Presidential or National campaigns, and furthermore to provide for the publication of both contributions and expenditures. There is, however, always danger in laws of this kind, which from their very nature are difficult of enforcement; the danger being lest they be obeyed only by the honest, and disobeyed by the unscrupulous, so as to act only as a penalty upon honest men. Moreover, no such law would hamper an unscrupulous man of unlimited means from buying his own way into office. There is a very radical measure which would, I believe, work a substantial improvement in our system of conducting a campaign, although I am well aware that it will take some time for people so to familiarize themselves with such a proposal as to be willing to consider its adoption. The need for collecting large campaign funds would vanish if Congress provided an appropriation for the proper and legitimate expenses of each of the great national parties, an appropriation ample enough to meet the necessity for thorough organization and machinery, which requires a large expenditure of money. Then the stipulation should be made that no party receiving campaign funds from the Treasury should accept more than a fixed amount from any individual subscriber or donor; and the necessary publicity for receipts and expenditures could without difficulty be provided.[114]

Currently, 11 states (Arizona, Connecticut, Florida, Hawaii, Maine, Maryland, Massachusetts, Michigan, Minnesota, Rhode Island, and Vermont) have some version of public financing for elections for governor and lieutenant governor, and five states have it for state legislative offices (Arizona, Connecticut, Hawaii, Maine, and Minnesota).[115]

An important reality in politics is that perceptions matter. The people perceive that their national leaders are far more attentive to the rich and the powerful than average Americans. For example, in a 2015 poll, Americans were asked, "Thinking about United States elections, do you think all Americans have an equal chance to influence the elections process, or do you think wealthy Americans have more of a chance to influence the elections process than other Americans?" According to 66 percent of respondents, the wealthy have more influence compared to 31 percent who believe that there is equal influence. Furthermore, citizens were asked, "Thinking about the role of money in American political campaigns today, do you think money has too much influence, too little influence or is it just about right?" Eighty-four percent of respondents believe that money has too much influence, compared to 5 percent who feel that it is too little, and 10 percent who said it was about right.[116]

Americans are clearly uncomfortable with the role of money in contemporary campaigns. While difficult to measure, this may be a contributing factor in the habitual low levels of voter turnout, especially among the less affluent. In the 2016 federal elections, 22 individuals in this country contributed more than $10 million each; the highest contributor exceeded $91 million. The total combined contributions for these 22 people exceeded $580 million.[117] It is no wonder that people who cannot afford to contribute to a campaign, or can only contribute a modest amount, do not feel that they are equally represented in Washington, DC. It is time to take Roosevelt's advice from 1907.[118]

The perception that our national leaders are attentive to the rich and powerful but not most people must be eliminated in the oldest democracy in the world. It is no wonder that Congress has had an abysmal approval rating the last several years (typically less than 20 percent).[119] It is debatable whether pluralism is alive and well in the United States today, but if people believe that it is not, this raises an obvious and perplexing problem in a nation with substantial diversity. Public campaign financing would be a positive change in this regard and perhaps cause federal leaders to empathize more with the impoverished than is presently the case.

Point 15: Revitalize Political Parties and Labor Unions

Two current realities are not advantageous to the goal of winning the War on Poverty. The first pertains to the state of the United States' two major political parties today. In 1942, Professor E. E. Schattschneider shared his vision of political parties in a democracy:

The rise of political parties is indubitably one of the principal distinguishing marks of modern government. The parties, in fact, have played a major role as *makers* of governments, more especially they have been the makers of democratic government. It should be stated flatly at the outset that this volume is devoted to the thesis that the political parties created democracy and that modern democracy is unthinkable save in terms of the parties. As a matter of fact, the condition of the parties is the best possible evidence of the nature of any regime. The most important distinction in modern political philosophy, the distinction between democracy and dictatorship, can be made best in terms of party politics. The parties are not therefore merely appendages of modern government; they are in the center of it and play a determinative and creative role in it.[120]

Though many Americans have disdainful views toward both the Democratic and Republican parties, Schattschneider's contention about parties has profound implications for democracy in general but also specifically for the plight of the poor. In a democracy, strong (not corrupt) political parties perform a vital function in elections and in terms of public policy. Party leaders can present the electorate with a slate of ideas and corresponding platforms to educate people about how their ideas can be implemented in a tangible manner. Parties also present a slate of candidates for the voters. Strong parties therefore link people with their government in a republic. To Schattschneider and other political scientists in a later work, strong parties would therefore have a serious responsibility to the electorate:

> Party responsibility means the responsibility of both parties to the general public, as enforced in elections. Party responsibility to the public, enforced in elections, implies that there be more than one party, for the public can hold a party responsible only if it has a choice. As a means of achieving responsibility, the clarification of party policy also tends to keep public debate on a more realistic level, restraining the inclinations of party spokesmen to make unsubstantiated statements and charges.[121]

Responsible parties would provide citizens with clear choices. In turn, adults could vote certain party platforms and candidates up or down as they deemed appropriate. Yet this is not what is happening in the era of weakened parties in the United States. This is clearly demonstrated in terms of how elections are conducted in the United States. In 2016, Democratic Party leaders were overwhelmingly in favor of Hillary Clinton winning the nomination for their party, which is precisely what transpired. Yet she just barely won the nomination over a candidate who is not even a Democrat (Bernie Sanders). Sanders is an Independent who happens to caucus with the Democrats in the Senate. Republican Party leaders, on the contrary, clearly did not want Donald Trump as their nominee, a person who has considered himself a Republican, Democrat, Independent, and Reform Party member in the course of his adult partisan evolution. Yet the voters across the states in the primaries, which have abysmally low voter turnout, gave him the nomination regardless.

One of the unfortunate realities of federal campaigns in the United States is that they are short on substance and a great deal of attention is afforded to style. This is undoubtedly not surprising, since Americans know very little about politics and public affairs. As a result, there are costs associated with having a deficient public affairs debate in this country. Candidate-centered campaigns supplanted party-centered campaigns in the 20th century. An unfortunate consequence is that the full range of options designed to address policy challenges in the United States is typically not debated. We tend to focus on the Republican and Democratic views on a given issue, understanding that in a complicated, diverse world, there are typically more than two perspectives about everything.

One way to have stronger parties in the United States is to require closed primaries in all states. A closed primary limits participation in the primaries to people who have made a commitment to a specific political party. In some states, citizens are required to register in either the Democratic or Republican parties; registered Independents waive their right to vote in the primary phase. Only nine states have this version exclusively (Delaware, Florida, Kentucky, Maryland, Nevada, New Mexico, New York, Oregon, and Pennsylvania). But more than half the states have some version of an open primary, where participants can wreak havoc on a rival party as party leaders can request that their fellow partisans vote in the opposing party's primary.[122] The strategy would be to help nominate the weakest rival to compete in the election against their nominee. While arguably well intended in that open primaries encourage citizens to participate even if they do not have mainstream Republican or Democratic values, it has the net result of making the major parties less cohesive and unified around a set of core values, beliefs, and policies. Recall Schattschneider's prophesy of 75 years ago on the subject.

Professor Morris Fiorina contended years ago that the decline of the parties in the modern era has made it easier for national politicians to blame other politicians for policy failures. In turn, it makes it difficult for voters to determine who should be punished and who should be rewarded in elections. Fiorina offers the following counsel, if our leaders are ever going to engage in collective responsibility:

The only way collective responsibility has ever existed and can exist, given American institutional arrangements, is through the agency of the political party. According to the textbook argument, a strong party can generate collective responsibility by creating incentives for leaders, followers, and popular supporters to think and act in collective terms. First, by providing party leaders with the capability (for example, control of institutional patronage and nominations) to discipline party members, genuine leadership becomes possible. Second, the subordination of individual officeholders to the party lessens their ability to separate themselves from party actions. Like it or not, their performance becomes identified with the performance of the collectivity to which they belong. Third, with individual candidate variation greatly reduced, voters have less incentive to support individuals and more to support or oppose the party as a whole. And fourth, party line voting in the electorate provides party leaders with the incentive to propose policies that will earn the support of a national majority, and party back-benchers with the personal incentive to cooperate with leaders in the attempt to compile a good record for the party as a whole.[123]

How do stronger parties help in the cause of winning the War on Poverty? Stronger parties will make it easier for party leaders to share their visions for how public policy can make people's lives better, especially those who are struggling the most in this society. Having stronger parties would make them more responsible to the electorate; in turn, citizens would be better equipped to hold members of both major parties accountable for their actions or their unwillingness to act.

The decline in union membership in the United States is well documented by government officials themselves. According to evaluators at the U.S. Bureau of Labor Statistics, union membership has declined sharply since 1983, when comparable data were first compiled. In 1983, there were 88.3 million wage and salary workers; in 2015, that figure increased to 133.7 million. Yet the number of employed union members has declined by almost 3 million since 1983; the union membership rate was 20.1 percent in 1983 and by 2015 had declined to 11.1 percent.[124] As of 2015, union membership is about the same between the private sector (7.6 million) and the public sector (7.2 million).[125]

What is increasing, however, is the number of right-to-work states. Right-to-work laws give workers the choice when it comes to union membership. While labor unions operate in the states in question, workers cannot be required to be a member of the union as a condition of employment. Twenty-one states enacted right-to-work statutes in the 20th century; seven more states have replicated this action in this century. Most are in the southern and western United States, but several midwestern states are also in this category now.[126]

According to evaluators at the Economic Policy Institute, the decline of organized labor in this country has contributed significantly to both wage stagnation and growing inequality. A key conclusion offered by the researchers is: "Rebuilding our system of collective bargaining is an important tool available for fueling wage growth for both low- and middle-wage workers and ending the era of persistent wage stagnation."[127] A key reality that oftentimes is not understood is that the existence of unions actually is helpful to both unionized and nonunionized personnel. Many nonunion firms will implement a wage scale that has been established in a unionized outfit. The expansion of the right-to-work states will do nothing for the poor except make them fall further and further behind in terms of their real purchasing power over time. Part of the key to winning the War on Poverty is to cease the ongoing assault on unions in this country.

Point 16: Reject the Doctrine of States' Rights and Revitalize the Spirit of Cooperative Federalism

The framers of the Constitution did not divide political power evenly in this federal republic. Under the supremacy clause of Article VI:

> This Constitution, and the Laws of the United States which shall be made in Pursuance thereof; and all Treaties made, or which shall be made, under the Authority of the United States, shall be the supreme Law of the Land; and the Judges in every State shall be bound thereby, any Thing in the Constitution or Laws of any State to the Contrary notwithstanding.

The Constitution is the supreme law of the land, and federal law supersedes state law. Despite this constitutional reality, the doctrine of states' rights has existed throughout U.S. history, though its interpretation by advocates today would be markedly different than in earlier times. To states' rights advocates, the Constitution protected them from undue interference from the federal government. Throughout the existence of this republic, and even before, during the Articles of Confederation and Perpetual Union, there has always been conflict regarding the proper allocation of power between the national and subnational levels of government.

In the arena of civil rights, this conflict has been quite apparent during many periods in U.S. history. During the slavery era, leaders in Southern states claimed that the slavery question was a states' rights issue, not a federal one. During the Jim Crow era, some state leaders relied on an extreme interpretation of the 10th Amendment to defend apartheid. When the United States industrialized after the Civil War, many state officials overturned federal actions, particularly governing the workplace and child labor, because their laissez-faire philosophy led them to believe that members of Congress had exceeded their constitutional mandate. To states' rights adherents, Congress had a limited mandate under the commerce clause. This ultimately prompted Franklin Roosevelt to attempt to pack the court in 1937.[128]

During the civil rights era of the 1950s and 1960s, federal judges intervened on many issues, especially with regard to public school desegregation.[129] To states' rights advocates, the federal government was usurping states' rights again, and a great deal of conflict ensued. Some people believed that states had the right to deny voting privileges to certain groups and to require literacy tests and poll taxes and that the federal government should have no authority to overrule state sovereignty. Ronald Reagan and many conservatives in the 1980s accentuated the plausibility of devolution, especially with regard to social policy and welfare benefits.[130] What Reagan truly sought to accomplish was to reverse course with regard to the Great Society. He had a markedly different vision of federalism than Lyndon Johnson, and Reagan actively attempted to decrease the size and scope of the federal government during his tenure as president in the 1980s.[131]

The notion of cooperative federalism dates back to the New Deal and is based on an understanding that officials representing all levels of government (state, local, and federal) must work together to address the needs of the people of the United States. This paradigm of federalism replaced the doctrine of dual federalism, which was predicated on the rigid premise that all powers not explicitly granted to the national government were reserved for the states or the people.[132] As the reader can discern, the vision presented to win the War on Poverty relies on the use of federal power to create the conditions to address poverty across the country. There is not only a constitutional basis for this premise, as delineated earlier, but a pragmatic one as well. The resources to win the War on Poverty exist primarily, though not exclusively, at the national level. Officials working in state and local governments need sufficient resources to triumph in the campaign against poverty in the United States. They can obtain them by working in unison with federal officials. In the end, the concrete issue is not ideology or turf battles; it is all about addressing the needs of the poor in this country. In that regard, a spirit of cooperation, common purpose, and common mission will ultimately yield positive results in the War on Poverty.

Point 17: Use Science and Data Analysis to Make Informed Judgments about the Impoverished

Using science and data analysis to enhance our knowledge about the impoverished would be preferable to relying on uninformed judgments and stereotypes. As a practitioner and academician (Annie Duflo and Dean Karlan) recently put it: "If social scientists and policy makers have learned anything about how to help the world's poorest people, it's not to trust our intuitions or anecdotal evidence about what kinds of antipoverty programs are effective. Rigorous randomized evaluations of policies, however, can show us what works and what doesn't."[133]

Sometimes well-intended interventions do not work for various reasons. That does not mean we must abandon the cause of fighting poverty; it means we all—conservative, moderate, and liberal alike—have to be amenable to using concrete data that will not always support our preconceived notions about the poor, or anything else for that matter. As the aforementioned practitioner and academician further noted: "We have found that pairing experts in behavioral science with 'on the ground' teams of researchers and field workers has yielded many good ideas about how to address the problems of poverty. Hope and rhetoric are great for motivation, but not for figuring out what to do. There you need data."[134]

Part of the plan to win the War on Poverty necessitates the willingness to learn and to make adjustments where necessary. Having experts assist policy makers in this cause is therefore essential.

The idea of having a "thinking person's" government is nothing new. This is what Franklin Roosevelt sought in 1935 when he created the Resettlement Administration (RA) through an executive order.[135] The RA was led by Rexford Tugwell, the undersecretary of agriculture,[136] and was an independent executive agency with three policy goals: restore land ownership through low-interest loans to farmers who had poor land; restore the productivity of ruined land during the Great Depression through soil conservation and rebuilding projects; and resettle-relocate-rehabilitate-renew farm families whose agricultural livelihoods had been destroyed by the Depression.[137] The RA only lasted two years, not necessarily due to the vision of Tugwell and others but due to politics.

The RA provided emergency loans and debt reduction to farmers, as well as soil conservation through planting trees, improving several hundred miles of streams, purchasing 9 million acres of land, and educating farmers about best practices for land use.[138] To critics, however, the program was too socialistic in that there was heavy emphasis on cooperation and collectivism as opposed to policies that would be embraced by small, isolated farm families. Accordingly, Tugwell resigned in December 1936.[139]

The RA attracted a great deal of attention at the time because it was a high-profile attempt at translating theory into practice. There were also some very impressive social scientists, such as Edward Banfield, Robert Lynd, Gunnar Myrdal, Harold Lasswell, and Grant McConnell, involved in studying its effectiveness. Artists and writers, including John Steinbeck, were inspired by the notion of a thinking person's government.[140] With the abundance of talent that currently exists in this country in a number of disciplines, it seems to me that a collaborative effort between scholars and practitioners would be immensely helpful in the cause of winning the War on Poverty.

Point 18: Do Right by Children at All Times

Doing right by children means many different things. If a child needs medical care, basic nutrition, mental health assistance, protection against an abusive caregiver or from woeful neglect, she or he should always be able to count on the members of this society to address her or his needs. Depending on the venue, not only do children need the three levels of government to collaborate effectively, they also need the public and private sectors to work well together. Citizens must also realize that to do right by children at all times in the cause of winning the War on Poverty, we must also do right by the adults in their lives. If a child's caregiver has a dependency issue or a physical and/or mental challenge, those afflictions will likely also impact the child. In order to help the child, the needs of the adult caregiver will have to be addressed as well, for children are inextricably linked to their caregivers and entirely dependent on them. A one-stop community center that could address multiple needs for children and adults in the same venue, as delineated in the second point above, should assist in the goal of doing right by children in a convenient and facilitative manner.

Conclusion

Winning the War on Poverty will not mean that every single person in this country will live above the federal poverty line. The sad reality is that poverty will always exist, and it is not necessarily the fault of anyone or any singular entity in particular. We will know that the War on Poverty has been a successful campaign when the proportion of Americans living in poverty is much lower than is presently the case. For a country blessed with tremendous comparative wealth, too many people are struggling for the basic necessities of life. The impact of this type of life is devastating on children, who cannot be blamed for their plight as they are not responsible for it. My fundamental premise is that there are millions of Americans currently living in poverty who could escape it, hopefully on a permanent basis. In order to experience a vast decline in poverty, we need to make some policy changes that will orchestrate the conditions needed for reform. I have presented a vision of how to assist those living in poverty. It is a conditional plan; it will take political will to be sure, but it will also challenge all citizens to either accept the status quo or truly pursue, in all earnestness, a more perfect union. I remain hopeful that we will choose the latter course.

Notes

1. Michael Harrington, *The Other America: Poverty in the United States* (New York: Penguin Books, 1981), ix–x. Professor Harrington lived from 1928 to 1989.

2. Harrington, *The Other America: Poverty in the United States*, xxviii–xxix.

3. Harrington later wrote another book entitled *The New American Poverty: A Provocative, Incisive Exposé of the Social and Political Roots of Poverty* (New York: Penguin Books, 1985). In it he explained that "the poor are still there" (p. 1).

4. David Easton, *The Political System: An Inquiry into the State of Political Science* (New York: Alfred A. Knopf, 1953), 4; and Fife, *Old School Still Matters: Lessons from History to Reform Public Education in America*, 172.

5. Dave Leip, "1934 Gubernatorial General Election Results—California," http://uselectionatlas.org/RESULTS/state.php?fips=6&year=1934&f=0&off=5& elect=0 (accessed August 1, 2017).

6. Upton Sinclair, *We, People of America: And How We Ended Poverty* (Pasadena, CA: National EPIC League, 1936), 3.

7. George G. Rising, "An EPIC Endeavor: Upton Sinclair's 1934 California Gubernatorial Campaign," *Southern California Quarterly* 79, no. 1 (1997): 101.

8. Rising, "An EPIC Endeavor: Upton Sinclair's 1934 California Gubernatorial Campaign," 112.

9. Rising, "An EPIC Endeavor: Upton Sinclair's 1934 California Gubernatorial Campaign," 120.

10. John Lewis Gillin, *Poverty and Dependency: Their Relief and Prevention* (New York: The Century Co., 1921), v. Professor Gillin lived from 1871 to 1958 and was president of the American Sociological Association in 1926. See American Sociological Association, "John Lewis Gillin," http://www.asanet.org/about-asa/asa-story/asa-history/past-asa-officers/past-asa-presidents/john-l-gillin (accessed August 6, 2017).

11. James Ford and Katherine Morrow Ford, *The Abolition of Poverty* (New York: Macmillan Company, 1937), 290. For more information about James Ford, see Massachusetts Institute of Technology, "James Ford (1885–1944)," http://web.mit.edu/ebj/www/ww1/Biography-Ford.html (accessed August 6, 2017). Katherine Morrow Ford was born in 1905 and has published work as recently as 2014.

12. George L. Record, *How to Abolish Poverty* (Jersey City, NJ: The George L. Record Memorial Association, 1936).

13. Record, *How to Abolish Poverty*, 22–3.

14. Record, *How to Abolish Poverty*, 23.

15. Record, *How to Abolish Poverty*, 173.

16. Here are some examples: William P. Quigley, *Ending Poverty as We Know It: Guaranteeing a Right to a Job at a Living Wage* (Philadelphia, PA: Temple University Press, 2003); Frank Stricker, *Why America Lost the War on Poverty: And How to Win It* (Chapel Hill: University of North Carolina Press, 2007); Randy Albelda and Ann Withorn (eds.), *Lost Ground: Welfare Reform, Poverty and Beyond* (Cambridge, MA: South End Press, 2002); Matthew Clarke and Simon Feeny (eds.), *Education for the End of Poverty: Implementing All the Millennium Development Goals* (New York: Nova Science Publishers, 2007); Willie Baptist and Jan Rehmann, *Pedagogy of the Poor: Building the Movement to End Poverty* (New York: Teachers College Press, 2011); Paul Polak, *Out of Poverty: What Works When Traditional Approaches Fail* (San Francisco: Berrett-Koehler Publishers, 2008); Jeffrey D. Sachs, *The End of Poverty: Economic Possibilities for Our Time* (New York: Penguin Books, 2006); James T. Patterson, *America's Struggle against Poverty in the Twentieth Century* (Cambridge, MA: Harvard University Press, 2000); Theresa Funiciello, *Tyranny of Kindness: Dismantling the Welfare System to End Poverty in America* (New York: Atlantic Monthly Press, 1993); Joel F. Handler, *The Poverty of Welfare Reform* (New Haven, CT: Yale University Press, 1995); Barbara Ehrenreich, *Nickel*

and Dimed: On (Not) Getting By in America (New York: Henry Holt and Company, 2002); Craig C. White, *Toward the Resolution of Poverty in America,* 2nd ed. (Dubuque, IA: Kendall/Hunt Publishing Company, 1995); John B. Williamson, Jerry F. Boren, Frank J. Mifflen, Nancy A. Cooney, Linda Evans, Michael F. Foley, Richard Steinman, Jody Garber, Nancy Theberge, and Donna J. B. Turek, *Strategies Against Poverty in America* (New York: John Wiley & Sons, 1975); U.S. Department of Labor, Office of Policy Planning and Research, *The Negro Family: The Case for National Action* (Washington, DC: Government Printing Office, March 1965); W. E. B. Du Bois, *The Negro American Family* (Westport, CT: Negro Universities Press, 1969); and John Edwards, Marion Crain, and Arne L. Kalleberg (eds.), *Ending Poverty In America* (New York: The New Press, 2007).

17. David K. Shipler, "Connecting the Dots," in *Ending Poverty in America,* eds. Edwards, Crain, and Kalleberg, 13–22.

18. Shipler, "Connecting the Dots," 15. See also David K. Shipler, *The Working Poor: Invisible in America* (New York: Alfred A. Knopf, 2004).

19. Shipler, "Connecting the Dots," 20–1.

20. American Presidency Project, "Progressive Party Platform of 1912, November 5, 1912," http://www.presidency.ucsb.edu/ws/?pid=29617 (accessed August 7, 2017).

21. World Health Organization, "Health Financing for Universal Coverage: What Is Universal Coverage?" http://www.who.int/health_financing/universal _coverage_definition/en/ (accessed August 7, 2017).

22. David Stucker, Andrea B. Feigl, Sanjay Basu, and Martin McKee, "The Political Economy of Universal Health Coverage," http://www.pacifichealthsummit .org/downloads/UHC/the%20political%20economy%20of%20uhc.PDF (accessed August 8, 2017).

23. Stuckler, Feigl, Basu, and McKee, "The Political Economy of Universal Health Coverage."

24. Gallup Poll, "U.S. Uninsured Rate Edges Up Slightly," April 10, 2017, http://www.gallup.com/poll/208196/uninsured-rate-edges-slightly.aspx (accessed August 10, 2017).

25. Gallup Poll, "U.S. Uninsured Rate Rises to 11.7%," July 10, 2017, http://www .gallup.com/poll/213665/uninsured-rate-rises.aspx (accessed August 10, 2017).

26. Physicians for a National Health Program, "What Is Single Payer?" http://www.pnhp.org/facts/what-is-single-payer (accessed August 10, 2017).

27. Congress.Gov, "H.R. 676-Expanded and Improved Medicare for All Act," https://www.congress.gov/bill/115th-congress/house-bill/676/cosponsors?q=%7 B%22search%22%3A%5B%22congressId%3A115+AND+billStatus%3A%5C%22 Introduced%5C%22%22%5D%7D&r=26 (accessed August 10, 2017).

28. Bernie Sanders, "Issues: Medicare for All: Leaving No One Behind," https://berniesanders.com/issues/medicare-for-all/ (accessed August 10, 2017).

29. Kaiser Family Foundation, "Medicare and Medicaid at 50," July 17, 2015, http://www.kff.org/medicaid/poll-finding/medicare-and-medicaid-at-50/ (accessed August 10, 2017).

30. Fife, *Old School Still Matters: Lessons from History to Reform Public Education in America*, 203–30.

31. Physicians for a National Health Program, "Beyond the Affordable Care Act: A Physicians' Proposal for Single-Payer Health Care Reform," http://www.pnhp.org/beyond_aca/Physicians_Proposal.pdf (accessed August 11, 2017).

32. Gallup Poll, "Most Americans in 15 Years Say Their Tax Bill Is Too High," April 14, 2016, http://www.gallup.com/poll/190778/americans-years-say-tax-bill-high.aspx (accessed August 13, 2017).

33. Center on Budget and Policy Priorities, "Top 10 Federal Tax Charts," April 15, 2016, https://www.cbpp.org/blog/top-10-federal-tax-charts-1 (accessed August 13, 2017). In a comparison of 31 nations in terms of total government receipts as a percentage of gross domestic product in 2015, the United States ranked 30 out of 31 in terms of having the lowest level of taxes. Finland had the highest tax rate in this comparison, and South Korea had the lowest, just below the United States.

34. Internal Revenue Service, "Worksheet Solutions: Comparing Regressive, Progressive, and Proportional Taxes," https://apps.irs.gov/app/understanding Taxes/whys/thm03/les05/media/ws_ans_thm03_les05.pdf (accessed August 13, 2017).

35. AmericanRhetoric.com, "Theodore: 'Teddy' Roosevelt: The Man with the Muck-rake," April 14, 1906, http://www.americanrhetoric.com/speeches /teddyrooseveltmuckrake.htm (accessed August 15, 2017).

36. American Presidency Project, "Franklin D. Roosevelt: Message to Congress on Tax Revision," June 19, 1935, http://www.presidency.ucsb.edu/ws /?pid=15088 (accessed August 15, 2017).

37. Center on Budget and Policy Priorities, "Policy Basics: Federal Payroll Taxes," March 23, 2016, https://www.cbpp.org/research/federal-tax/policy-basics -federal-payroll-taxes (accessed August 16, 2017).

38. Social Security Administration, "OASDI and SSI Program Rates & Limits, 2017," https://www.ssa.gov/policy/docs/quickfacts/prog_highlights/RatesLimits2017 .html (accessed August 16, 2017).

39. Center on Budget and Policy Priorities, "Policy Basics: Federal Payroll Taxes," March 23, 2016.

40. Pew Research Center, "Estimates of the Biggest Federal Tax Breaks (Fiscal Year 2016)," April 6, 2016, http://www.pewresearch.org/fact-tank/2016/04/06 /the-biggest-u-s-tax-breaks/ (accessed August 17, 2017).

41. Center on Budget and Policy Priorities, "Mortgage Interest Deduction Is Ripe for Reform: Conversion to Tax Credit Could Raise Revenue and Make Subsidy More Effective and Fairer," June 25, 2013, https://www.cbpp.org/research /mortgage-interest-deduction-is-ripe-for-reform (accessed August 17, 2017).

42. U.S. Treasury Direct, "The Debt to the Penny and Who Holds It," https:// www.treasurydirect.gov/NP/debt/current/ (accessed August 17, 2017).

43. Fife, *Old School Still Matters: Lessons from History to Reform Public Education in America*, 231–56.

44. Fife, *Old School Still Matters: Lessons from History to Reform Public Education in America*, 2–8.

45. Library of Congress, "Jefferson's Letter to the Danbury Baptists, January 1, 1802," http://www.loc.gov/loc/lcib/9806/danpost.html (accessed August 17, 2017).

46. Fife, *Old School Still Matters: Lessons from History to Reform Public Education in America*, 1–41.

47. Jonathan Kozol, *Savage Inequalities: Children in America's Schools* (New York: Crown Publishers, 1991).

48. WhiteHouse.gov, "The President Proposes to Make Community College Free for Responsible Students for 2 Years," January 8, 2015, https://obamawhite house.archives.gov/blog/2015/01/08/president-proposes-make-community -college-free-responsible-students-2-years (accessed August 18, 2017).

49. CNBC, "This Is the Age Most Americans Pay Off Their Student Loans," July 3, 2017,
https://www.cnbc.com/2017/07/03/this-is-the-age-most-americans-pay-off -their-student-loans.html (accessed July 3, 2017).

50. WhiteHouse.gov, "Fact Sheet: White House Unveils America's College Promise Proposal: Tuition-Free Community College for Responsible Students," January 9, 2015, https://obamawhitehouse.archives.gov/the-press-office/2015/01 /09/fact-sheet-white-house-unveils-america-s-college-promise-proposal-tuitio (accessed August 18, 2017).

51. American Presidency Project, "William J. Clinton: Address Before a Joint Session of Congress on the State of the Union," January 19, 1999, http://www .presidency.ucsb.edu/ws/index.php?pid=57577 (accessed August 18, 2017).

52. American Presidency Project, "Franklin D. Roosevelt: Campaign Address on Progressive Government at the Commonwealth Club in San Francisco, California," September 23, 1932, http://www.presidency.ucsb.edu/ws/?pid=88391 (accessed August 20, 2017).

53. American Presidency Project, "Franklin D. Roosevelt: Campaign Address on Progressive Government at the Commonwealth Club in San Francisco, California," September 23, 1932.

54. American Presidency Project, "Franklin D. Roosevelt: Campaign Address on Progressive Government at the Commonwealth Club in San Francisco, California," September 23, 1932.

55. University of Pennsylvania, "Can Trump—or Anyone—Bring Back American Manufacturing?" http://knowledge.wharton.upenn.edu/article/can-trump -anyone-bring-back-american-manufacturing/ (accessed August 21, 2017).

56. University of Pennsylvania, "Can Trump—or Anyone—Bring Back American Manufacturing?"

57. History.com, "Civilian Conservation Corps," http://www.history.com /topics/civilian-conservation-corps (accessed August 21, 2017).

58. American Society of Civil Engineers, "2017 Infrastructure Report Card," https://www.infrastructurereportcard.org/americas-grades (accessed August 21, 2017).

59. American Society of Civil Engineers, "2017 Infrastructure Report Card."

60. American Society of Civil Engineers, "2017 Infrastructure Report Card."

61. American Society of Civil Engineers, "2017 Infrastructure Report Card."

62. CQ Press, "High-Speed Rail: Does the High Cost Outweigh the Anticipated Benefits?" April 16, 1993, http://library.cqpress.com/cqresearcher/document.php?id=cqresrre1993041600 (accessed August 25, 2017).

63. The Transport Politic, "A Generational Failure: As the U.S. Fantasizes, the Rest of the World Builds a New Transport System," July 1, 2017, http://www.thetransportpolitic.com (accessed August 25, 2017).

64. *Los Angeles Times*, "Gov. Brown Asks President Trump for Help on the California Bullet Train," May 12, 2017, http://www.latimes.com/local/california/la-me-bullet-train-brown-20170512-story.html (accessed August 25, 2017); and *Charlotte Observer*, "Dallas to Houston in 90 Minutes? Texas Bullet Train Makes That a Reality," February 10, 2017, http://www.charlotteobserver.com/news/politics-government/article132038179.html (accessed August 25, 2017).

65. NBC News, "Ben Carson Says 'Poverty Is a State of Mind,'" May 24, 2017, http://www.nbcnews.com/news/nbcblk/ben-carson-says-poverty-state-mind-n764376 (accessed May 25, 2017).

66. Slate.com, "The Welfare Queen," December 19, 2013, http://www.slate.com/articles/news_and_politics/history/2013/12/linda_taylor_welfare_queen_ronald_reagan_made_her_a_notorious_american_villain.html (accessed June 7, 2017); *The New York Times*, "'Welfare Queen' Becomes Issue in Reagan Campaign," February 15, 1976, http://www.nytimes.com/1976/02/15/archives/welfare-queen-becomes-issue-in-reagan-campaign-hitting-a-nerve-now.html?mcubz=3 (accessed June 7, 2017); CNN, "Return of the 'Welfare Queen,'" January 23, 2012, http://www.cnn.com/2012/01/23/politics/weflare-queen/index.html (accessed June 7, 2017); and National Public Radio, "The Truth Behind the Lies of the Original 'Welfare Queen,'" December 20, 2013, http://www.npr.org/sections/codeswitch/2013/12/20/255819681/the-truth-behind-the-lies-of-the-original-welfare-queen (accessed June 7, 2017).

67. *The New York Times*, "'Welfare Queen' Becomes Issue in Reagan Campaign," February 15, 1976.

68. History.com, "June 20, 1782: Congress Adopts the Great Seal of the United States," http://www.history.com/this-day-in-history/congress-adopts-the-great-seal-of-the-united-states (accessed August 22, 2017).

69. History.com, "July 30, 1956: President Eisenhower Signs 'In God We Trust' into Law," http://www.history.com/this-day-in-history/president-eisenhower-signs-in-god-we-trust-into-law (accessed August 22, 2017).

70. Jane A. Grant, *The New American Social Compact: Rights and Responsibilities in the 21st Century* (Lanham, MD: Lexington Books, 2008).

71. U.S. Department of Homeland Security, U.S. Citizenship and Immigration Services, "Citizenship Rights and Responsibilities," https://www.uscis.gov/citizenship/learners/citizenship-rights-and-responsibilities (accessed August 23, 2017).

72. Public Law 81-171, July 15, 1949, "Housing Act of 1949," http://legisworks.org/congress/81/publaw-171.pdf (accessed August 23, 2017).

73. American Presidency Project, "Harry S. Truman: Statement by the President upon Signing the Housing Act of 1949, July 15, 1949," http://www.presidency.ucsb.edu/ws/?pid=13246 (accessed August 23, 2017).

74. National Alliance to End Homelessness, *State of the Homeless 2016*, http://endhomelessness.org/wp-content/uploads/2016/10/2016-soh.pdf (accessed August 24, 2017).

75. Coalition for the Homeless, *State of the Homeless 2017: Rejecting Low Expectations: Housing Is the Answer*, March 2017, https://www.coalitionforthehomeless.org/wp-content/uploads/2017/03/State-of-the-Homeless-2017.pdf (accessed August 24, 2017).

76. National Coalition for the Homeless, "How Many People Experience Homelessness?" July 2009, http://www.nationalhomeless.org/factsheets/How_Many.html (accessed August 24, 2017).

77. Center for American Progress, "Creating Safe and Healthy Living Environments for Low-Income Families," July 20, 2016, https://www.americanprogress.org/issues/poverty/reports/2016/07/20/141324/creating-safe-and-healthy-living-environments-for-low-income-families/ (accessed August 24, 2017).

78. Center for American Progress, "Creating Safe and Healthy Living Environments for Low-Income Families," July 20, 2016.

79. Alexia Fernández Campbell, "Gas Leaks, Mold, and Rats: Millions of Americans Live in Hazardous Homes," July 25, 2016, https://www.theatlantic.com/business/archive/2016/07/gas-leaks-mold-and-rats-millions-of-americans-live-in-hazardous-homes/492689/ (accessed August 24, 2017).

80. Harvard University, Joint Center for Housing Studies, *The State of the Nation's Housing 2017*, June 16, 2017, http://www.jchs.harvard.edu/research/publications/state-nations-housing-2017 (accessed August 24, 2017).

81. Harvard University, Joint Center for Housing Studies, *America's Rental Housing: Expanding Options for Diverse and Growing Demand*, http://jchs.harvard.edu/sites/jchs.harvard.edu/files/americas_rental_housing_2015_web.pdf (accessed August 24, 2017).

82. Center on Budget and Policy Priorities, "Chart Book: Federal Housing Spending Is Poorly Matched to Need," March 8, 2017, https://www.cbpp.org/research/housing/chart-book-federal-housing-spending-is-poorly-matched-to-need (accessed August 24, 2017).

83. Harvard University, Joint Center for Housing Studies, *America's Rental Housing: Expanding Options for Diverse and Growing Demand.*

84. U.S. Department of Labor, Wage and Hour Division, "Fair Labor Standards Act of 1938: Maximum Struggle for a Minimum Wage," https://www.dol.gov/general/aboutdol/history/flsa1938 (accessed August 24, 2017).

85. American Presidency Project, "Franklin D. Roosevelt: Message to Congress on Establishing Minimum Wages and Maximum Hours," May 24, 1937, http://www.presidency.ucsb.edu/ws/?pid=15405 (accessed August 24, 2017).

86. U.S. Department of Labor, Wage and Hour Division, "Fact Sheet: Final Rule to Implement Executive Order 13658, Establishing a Minimum Wage for

Contractors," February 12, 2014, https://www.dol.gov/whd/flsa/eo13658/fr-factsheet.htm (accessed August 24, 2017); and American Presidency Project, "Barack Obama: Executive Order 13658—Establishing a Minimum Wage for Contractors," February 12, 2014, http://www.presidency.ucsb.edu/ws/?pid=104737 (accessed August 24, 2017).

87. Economic Policy Institute, "Over 600 Economists Sign Letter in Support of $10.10 Minimum Wage," January 14, 2014, http://www.epi.org/minimum-wage-statement/ (accessed August 24, 2017).

88. Economic Policy Institute, "Over 600 Economists Sign Letter in Support of $10.10 Minimum Wage," January 14, 2014.

89. Congress.gov, "S.1832-Pay Workers a Living Wage Act," July 22, 2015, https://www.congress.gov/bill/114th-congress/senate-bill/1832 (accessed August 25, 2017).

90. Congress.gov, "S.1242-Raise the Wage Act," May 25, 2017, https://www.congress.gov/bill/115th-congress/senate-bill/1242 (accessed August 25, 2017).

91. Economic Policy Institute, "Over 600 Economists Sign Letter in Support of $10.10 Minimum Wage," January 14, 2014.

92. Union of Concerned Scientists, "Confronting the Realities of Climate Change: The Consequences of Global Warming Are Already Here," http://www.ucsusa.org/global_warming/ (accessed August 27, 2017).

93. Union of Concerned Scientists, "Confronting the Realities of Climate Change: The Consequences of Global Warming Are Already Here"; and Climate Reality Project, "Climate Crisis 101: Learn the Basics of Climate Change Science and How You Can Take Action," https://www.climaterealityproject.org/sites/climaterealityproject.org/files/Climate%20101_FINAL.pdf (accessed August 27, 2017).

94. Solomon Hsiang, Robert Kopp, Amir Jina, James Rising, Michael Delgado, Shashank Mohan, and D. J. Rasmussen, "Estimating Economic Damage from Climate Change in the United States," *Science* 356, no. 6345 (2017): 1362–69.

95. Hsiang et al. "Estimating Economic Damage from Climate Change in the United States."

96. Hsiang et al. "Estimating Economic Damage from Climate Change in the United States."

97. Hsiang et al. "Estimating Economic Damage from Climate Change in the United States."

98. United Nations, "Chapter XXVII: 7.d. Paris Agreement," December 12, 2015, https://treaties.un.org/doc/Publication/MTDSG/Volume%20II/Chapter%20XXVII/XXVII-7-d.en.pdf (accessed August 27, 2017).

99. United Nations, "Chapter XXVII: 7.d. Paris Agreement," December 12, 2015.

100. National Public Radio, "Trump Announces U.S. Withdrawal from Paris Climate Accord," June 1, 2017, http://www.npr.org/sections/thetwo-way/2017/06/01/530748899/watch-live-trump-announces-decision-on-paris-climate-agreement (accessed August 27, 2017).

101. Union of Concerned Scientists, "Each Country's Share of CO_2 Emissions," November 18, 2014, http://www.ucsusa.org/global_warming/science _and_impacts/science/each-countrys-share-of-co2.html (accessed August 27, 2017).

102. National Public Radio, "Trump Announces U.S. Withdrawal from Paris Climate Accord," June 1, 2017.

103. United Nations Framework Convention on Climate Change, "Paris Agreement," 2015, https://unfccc.int/files/essential_background/convention/application /pdf/english_paris_agreement.pdf (accessed August 29, 2017).

104. Fife, *Reforming the Electoral Process in America: Toward More Democracy in the 21st Century*.

105. David W. Abbott and James P. Levine, *Wrong Winner: The Coming Debacle in the Electoral College* (Westport, CT: Praeger, 1991).

106. FactCheck.org, "Presidents Winning Without Popular Vote," December 23, 2016, http://factcheck.org/2008/03/presidents-winning-without-popular-vote/ (accessed August 28, 2017).

107. Robert A. Dahl, *How Democratic Is the American Constitution?*, 2nd ed. (New Haven, CT: Yale University Press, 2003), 74.

108. Fife, *Reforming the Electoral Process in America: Toward More Democracy in the 21st Century*, 133–37.

109. New York University School of Law, Brennan Center for Justice, "Debunking the Voter Fraud Myth," January 31, 2017, https://www.brennancenter .org/analysis/debunking-voter-fraud-myth (accessed August 28, 2017).

110. *Dunn v. Blumstein*, 405 U.S. 330 (1972).

111. *The Washington Post*, "Is It Too Late to Register to Vote in Your State? Check Here," October 12, 2016, https://www.washingtonpost.com/news/the-fix /wp/2016/10/06/when-is-it-too-late-to-register-to-vote-in-your-state/?utm _term=.6235195321e0/ (accessed August 28, 2017).

112. National Conference of State Legislatures, "Same Day Voter Registration," July 27, 2017, http://www.ncsl.org/research/elections-and-campaigns/same -day-registration.aspx (accessed August 28, 2017).

113. *The New York Times*, "Five Ways Republicans Are Threatening Voting Rights," November 7, 2016, https://www.nytimes.com/2016/11/07/opinion/five -ways-republicans-are-threatening-voting-rights.html (accessed August 29, 2017).

114. American Presidency Project, "Theodore Roosevelt: Seventh Annual Message," December 3, 1907, http://www.presidency.ucsb.edu/ws/?pid=29548 (accessed August 29, 2017).

115. National Conference of State Legislatures, "Overview of State Laws on Public Financing," http://www.ncsl.org/research/elections-and-campaigns/public -financing-of-campaigns-overview.aspx (accessed August 30, 2017).

116. *The New York Times*, "Americans' Views on Money in Politics," June 2, 2015, https://www.nytimes.com/interactive/2015/06/02/us/politics/money-in-politics -poll.html?mcubz=1 (accessed August 30, 2017).

117. OpenSecrets.org, "Top Individual Contributors: All Federal Contributions," 2016 election cycle, https://www.opensecrets.org/overview/topindivs.php (accessed August 30, 2017).

118. Brian L. Fife, "Congress and Electoral Reform in the Early Twenty-First Century," in *Working Congress: A Guide for Senators, Representatives, and Citizens*, ed. Robert Mann (Baton Rouge: Louisiana State University Press, 2014), 69–71.

119. Gallup Poll, "Congress and the Public," http://www.gallup.com /poll/1600/congress-public.aspx (accessed August 30, 2017).

120. E. E. Schattschneider, *Party Government* (New York: Rinehart & Company, 1942), 1.

121. American Political Science Association, Committee on Political Parties, *Toward a More Responsible Two-Party System* (New York: Rinehart, 1950), 2; and Fife, "Congress and Electoral Reform in the Early Twenty-First Century."

122. National Conference of State Legislatures, "State Primary Election Types," July 21, 2016, http://www.ncsl.org/research/elections-and-campaigns /primary-types.aspx (accessed August 31, 2017).

123. Morris Fiorina, "The Decline of Collective Responsibility in American Politics," *Engineering and Science* 44, no. 2 (1980): 13.

124. U.S. Bureau of Labor Statistics, "Union Membership in the United States," September 2016, https://www.bls.gov/spotlight/2016/union-membership -in-the-united-states/pdf/union-membership-in-the-united-states.pdf (accessed August 30, 2017).

125. U.S. Bureau of Labor Statistics, "Union Membership in the United States," September 2016.

126. National Conference of State Legislatures, "Right-to-Work States," http:// www.ncsl.org/research/labor-and-employment/right-to-work-laws-and-bills .aspx (accessed August 30, 2017). The right-to-work states include Alabama (1953), Arizona (1947), Arkansas (1947), Florida (1943), Georgia (1947), Idaho (1985), Indiana (2012), Iowa (1947), Kansas (1958), Kentucky (2017), Louisiana (1976), Michigan (2012), Mississippi (1954), Missouri (2017), Nebraska (1947), Nevada (1952), North Carolina (1947), North Dakota (1947), Oklahoma (2001), South Carolina (1954), South Dakota (1947), Tennessee (1947), Texas (1993), Utah (1955), Virginia (1947), Wisconsin (2015), West Virginia (2016), and Wyoming (1963).

127. Economic Policy Institute, "Union Decline Lowers Wages of Nonunion Workers: The Overlooked Reason Why Wages Are Stuck and Inequality Is Growing," August 30, 2016, http://www.epi.org/publication/union-decline-lowers -wages-of-nonunion-workers-the-overlooked-reason-why-wages-are-stuck-and -inequality-is-growing/ (accessed September 1, 2017).

128. History.com, "This Day in History: Roosevelt Announces 'Court-Packing' Plan," February 5, 1937, http://www.history.com/this-day-in-history /roosevelt-announces-court-packing-plan (accessed September 1, 2017).

129. Brian L. Fife, "The Supreme Court and School Desegregation Since 1896," *Equity and Excellence in Education* 29, (1996): 46–55.

130. *The New York Times*, "Reagan and States' Rights; News Analysis," March 4, 1981, http://www.nytimes.com/1981/03/04/us/reagan-and-states-rights-news -analysis.html?pagewanted=all&mcubz=1 (accessed September 2, 2017).

131. Bill of Rights Institute, "Lyndon B. Johnson and Ronald Reagan and Federal Power," https://www.billofrightsinstitute.org/educate/educator-resources

/lessons-plans/presidents-constitution/johnson-and-reagan/ (accessed September 2, 2017).

132. David B. Walker, *The Rebirth of Federalism: Slouching toward Washington,* 2nd ed. (Chappaqua, NY: Chatham House Publishers, 2000); and Fife, *Reforming the Electoral Process in America: Toward More Democracy in the 21st Century,* 126–28.

133. *The New York Times,* "What Data Can Do to Fight Poverty," January 29, 2016, https://www.nytimes.com/2016/01/31/opinion/sunday/what-data-can-do-to-fight-poverty.html (accessed September 2, 2017).

134. *The New York Times,* "What Data Can Do to Fight Poverty."

135. American Presidency Project, "Franklin D. Roosevelt: Executive Order 7027 Establishing the Resettlement Administration," May 1, 1935, http://www.presidency.ucsb.edu/ws/?pid=15048 (accessed September 2, 1935).

136. American Presidency Project, "Franklin D. Roosevelt: Executive Order 7027 Establishing the Resettlement Administration."

137. Gawthrop, *Public Service and Democracy: Ethical Imperatives for the 21st Century,* 107.

138. LivingNewDeal.org, "Resettlement Administration (1935)," https://livingnewdeal.org/glossary/resettlement-administration-ra-1935/ (accessed September 2, 2017).

139. LivingNewDeal.org, "Resettlement Administration (1935)."

140. Gawthrop, *Public Service and Democracy: Ethical Imperatives for the 21st Century,* 102.

Bibliography

Abbott, David W. and James P. Levine. 1991. *Wrong Winner: The Coming Debacle in the Electoral College*. Westport, CT: Praeger.

Adams, Paul. 1985. Social Policy and the Working Class. *Social Service Review* 59, no. 3:387–402.

Albelda, Randy and Ann Withorn (eds.). 2002. *Lost Ground: Welfare Reform, Poverty, and Beyond*. Cambridge, MA: South End Press.

Almshouse Association. 2017. Historical Summary. Accessed January 16, 2017, from http://www.almshouses.org/history/historical-summary/.

American Historical Association. 2017. Perspectives on History: Oscar Handlin (1915–2011). Accessed January 13, 2017, from https://www.historians .org/publications-and-directories/perspectives-on-history/january-2012/in -memoriam-oscar-handlin.

American Political Science Association. 2004. American Democracy in an Age of Rising Inequality. Accessed March 3, 2016, from http://www.apsanet.org /portals/54/files/Task%20Force%20Reports/taskforcereport.pdf.

American Political Science Association, Committee on Political Parties. 1950. *Toward a More Responsible Two-Party System*. New York: Rinehart.

American Presidency Project. 2015. Lyndon B. Johnson: Annual Message to the Congress on the State of the Union, January 8, 1964. Accessed January 18, 2015, from http://www.presidency.ucsb.edu/ws/?pid=26787/.

American Presidency Project. 2017. Barack Obama: Executive Order 13658—Establishing a Minimum Wage for Contractors, February 12, 2014. Accessed August 24, 2017, from http://www.presidency.ucsb.edu/ws/?pid=104737.

American Presidency Project. 2017. Barack Obama: Remarks on Signing the Patient Protection and Affordable Care Act, March 23, 2010. Accessed March 31, 2017, from http://www.presidency.ucsb.edu/ws/?pid=87660.

American Presidency Project. 2017. Election of 1912. Accessed January 29, 2017, from http://www.presidency.ucsb.edu/showelection.php?year=1912.

American Presidency Project. 2017. Election of 1916. Accessed January 30, 2017, from http://www.presidency.ucsb.edu/showelection.php?year=1916.

American Presidency Project. 2017. Election of 1920. Accessed February 24, 2017, from http://www.presidency.ucsb.edu/showelection.php?year=19120.

American Presidency Project. 2017. Election of 1924. Accessed February 24, 2017, from http://www.presidency.ucsb.edu/showelection.php?year=1924.

American Presidency Project. 2017. Election of 1928. Accessed February 24, 2017, from http://www.presidency.ucsb.edu/showelection.php?year=1928.

American Presidency Project. 2017. Election of 1932. Accessed February 24, 2017, from http://www.presidency.ucsb.edu/showelection.php?year=1932.

American Presidency Project. 2017. Election of 1936. Accessed February 24, 2017, from http://www.presidency.ucsb.edu/showelection.php?year=1936.

American Presidency Project. 2017. Election of 1940. Accessed February 24, 2017, from http://www.presidency.ucsb.edu/showelection.php?year=1940.

American Presidency Project. 2017. Election of 1944. Accessed February 24, 2017, from http://www.presidency.ucsb.edu/showelection.php?year=1944.

American Presidency Project. 2017. Franklin D. Roosevelt: Campaign Address on Progressive Government at the Commonwealth Club in San Francisco, California, September 23, 1932. Accessed August 20, 2017, from http://www.presidency.ucsb.edu/ws/?pid=88391.

American Presidency Project. 2017. Franklin D. Roosevelt: Executive Order 7027 Establishing the Resettlement Administration, May 1, 1935. Accessed September 2, 2017, from http://www.presidency.ucsb.edu/ws/?pid=15048.

American Presidency Project. 2017. Franklin D. Roosevelt: Message to Congress Establishing Minimum Wages and Maximum Hours, May 24, 1937. Accessed August 24, 2017, from http://www.presidency.ucsb.edu/ws/?pid=15405.

American Presidency Project. 2017. Franklin D. Roosevelt: Message to Congress on Tax Revision, June 19, 1935. Accessed August 15, 2017, from http://www.presidency.ucsb.edu/ws/?pid=15088.

American Presidency Project. 2017. Franklin Roosevelt: Executive Order 6757: Initiating Studies on Social and Economic Security, June 29, 1934. Accessed March 14, 2017, from http://www.presidency.ucsb.edu/ws/index.php?pid=14707.

American Presidency Project. 2017. Harry S. Truman: Statement by the President upon Signing the Housing Act of 1949, July 15, 1949. Accessed August 23, 2017, from http://www.presidency.ucsb.edu/ws/?pid=13246.

American Presidency Project. 2017. John F. Kennedy: Inaugural Address, January 20, 1961. Accessed June 20, 2017, from http://www.presidency.ucsb.edu/ws/index.php?pid=8032&.

American Presidency Project. 2017. Lyndon B. Johnson, Remarks upon Signing the Economic Opportunity Act, August 20, 1964. Accessed March 21, 2017, from http://www.presidency.ucsb.edu/ws/?pid=26452.

American Presidency Project. 2017. Lyndon B. Johnson, Remarks upon Signing the Food Stamp Act, August 31, 1964. Accessed March 18, 2017, from http://www.presidency.ucsb.edu/ws/?pid=26472.

American Presidency Project. 2017. President Lyndon B. Johnson's Remarks at the University of Michigan, May 22, 1964. Accessed April 8, 2017, from http://www.presidency.ucsb.edu/ws/?pid=26262%20.

American Presidency Project. 2017. Progressive Party Platform of 1912, November 5, 1912. Accessed August 7, 2017, from http://www.presidency.ucsb.edu/ws/?pid=29617.

American Presidency Project. 2017. Theodore Roosevelt: Seventh Annual Message, December 3, 1907. Accessed August 29, 2017, from http://www.presidency.ucsb.edu/ws/?pid=29548.

American Presidency Project. 2017. William J. Clinton: Address Before a Joint Session of Congress on the State of the Union, January 19, 1999. Accessed August 18, 2017, from http://www.presidency.ucsb.edu/ws/index.php?pid=57577.

AmericanRhetoric.com. 2017. Theodore: "Teddy" Roosevelt: The Man with the Muck-rake, April 14, 1906. Accessed August 15, 2017, from http://www.americanrhetoric.com/speeches/teddyrooseveltmuckrake.htm.

American Society of Civil Engineers. 2017. 2017 Infrastructure Report Card. Accessed August 21, 2017, from https://www.infrastructurereportcard.org/americas-grades.

American Sociological Association. 2017. John Lewis Gillin. Accessed August 6, 2017, from http://asanet.org/about-asa/asa-story/asa-history/past-asa-officers/past-asa-presidents/john-l-gillin.

Bailey, Martha J. and Nicolas J. Duquette. 2014. How Johnson Fought the War on Poverty: The Economics and Politics of Funding at the Office of Economic Opportunity. *Journal of Economic History* 74, no. 2:351–88.

Baptist, Willie and Jan Rehmann. 2011. *Pedagogy of the Poor: Building the Movement to End Poverty.* New York: Teachers College Press.

Bellah, Robert N., Richard Madsen, William M. Sullivan, Ann Swidler, and Steven M. Tipton. *Habits of the Heart: Individualism and Commitment in American Life.* Berkeley: University of California Press.

BernieSanders.com. 2017. Issues: Medicare for All: Leaving No One Behind. Accessed August 10, 2017, from https://berniesanders.com/issues/medicare-for-all/.

Bill of Rights Institute. 2017. Lyndon B. Johnson and Ronald Reagan and Federal Power. Accessed September 2, 2017, from https://www.billofrightsinstitute.org/educate/educator-resources/lessons-plans/presidents-constitution/johnson-and-reagan/.

Bitler, Marianne P. and Lynn A. Karoly. 2015. Intended and Unintended Effects of the War on Poverty: What Research Tells Us and Implications for Policy. *Journal of Policy Analysis and Management* 34, no. 3:639–96.

Blank, Rebecca. 2015. The Measurement of Poverty: An Evolving Story. *LaFollette Policy Report* 25, no. 1:8–10.

Boaz, David (ed.). 1997. *The Libertarian Reader: Classic and Contemporary Writings from Lao-tzu to Milton Friedman.* New York: The Free Press.

Braun, Denny. 1997. *The Rich Get Richer: The Rise of Income Inequality in the United States and The World*. Chicago: Nelson-Hall.

Burnham, Walter Dean. 1986. Those High Nineteenth-Century American Voting Turnouts: Fact or Fiction? *Journal of Interdisciplinary History* 16, no. 4:613–44.

Callen, Tim. 2008. Back to Basics: What Is Gross Domestic Product? *Finance & Development* (December) 45, no. 4:48–9.

Campbell, Alexia Fernández. July 25, 2016. Gas Leaks, Mold, and Rats: Millions of Americans Live in Hazardous Homes. Accessed August 24, 2017, from https://www.theatlantic.com/business/archive/2016/07/gas-leaks-mold -and-rats-millions-of-americans-live-in-hazardous-homes/492689/.

Cappon, Lester J (ed.). 1959. *The Adams-Jefferson Letters: The Complete Correspondence Between Thomas Jefferson and Abigail and John Adams*. Chapel Hill: University of North Carolina Press.

Cassidy, John. April 3, 2006. Relatively Deprived: How Poor Is Poor? *The New Yorker*. Accessed April 13, 2016, from http://www.newyorker.com/magazine /2006/04/03/relatively-deprived.

Cato Institute. 2017. Key Concepts of Libertarianism. Accessed July 3, 2017, from https://www.cato.org/publications/commentary/key-concepts-liber tarianism.

Cato Institute. 2017. Milton Friedman: Biography. Accessed July 9, 2017, from https://www.cato.org/special/friedman/friedman/index.html.

Center for American Progress. July 20, 2016. Creating Safe and Healthy Living Environments for Low-Income Families. Accessed August 24, 2017, from https://www.americanprogress.org/issues/poverty/reports/2016/07/20 /141324/creating-safe-and-healthy-living-environments-for-low-income -families/.

Center on Budget and Policy Priorities. June 25, 2013. Mortgage Interest Deduction Is Ripe for Reform: Conversion to Tax Credit Could Raise Revenue and Make Subsidy More Effective and Fairer. Accessed August 17, 2017, from https://www.cbpp.org/research/mortgage-interest-deduction-is-ripe -for-reform.

Center on Budget and Policy Priorities. March 23, 2016. Policy Basics: Federal Payroll Taxes. Accessed August 16, 2017, from https://www.cbpp.org /research/federal-tax/policy-basics-federal-payroll-taxes.

Center on Budget and Policy Priorities. April 15, 2016. Top 10 Federal Tax Charts. Accessed August 13, 2017, from https://www.cbpp.org/blog/top -10-federal-tax-charts-1.

Center on Budget and Policy Priorities. March 8, 2017. Chart Book: Federal Housing Spending Is Poorly Matched to Need. Accessed August 24, 2017, from https://www.cbpp.org/research/housing/chart-book-federal-housing -spending-is-poorly-matched-to-need.

Central Intelligence Agency. 2017. The World Factbook. Accessed April 8, 2017, from https://www.cia.gov/library/publications/the-world-factbook/rank order/2119rank.html.

Ceriani, Lidia and Paolo Verme. 2012. The Origins of the Gini Index: Extracts from Variabilitá e Mutabilitá (1912) by Corrado Gini. *Journal of Economic Inequality* 10:421–43.

Ceriani, Lidia and Paolo Verme. January 2014. Individual Diversity and the Gini Decomposition. Accessed April 8, 2017, from https://openknowledge .worldbank.org/handle/10986/17315.

Charlotte Observer. February 10, 2017. Dallas to Houston in 90 Minutes? Texas Bullet Train Makes That a Reality. Accessed August 25, 2017, from http:// www.charlotteobserver.com/news/politics-government/article1320381 79.html.

Chernow, Ron. 1998. *Titan: The Life of John D. Rockefeller, Sr.* New York: Random House.

Citizens United v. Federal Election Committee, 558 U.S. 310 (2010).

Citro, Constance F. and Robert T. Michael (eds.). 1995. *Measuring Poverty: A New Approach*. Washington, DC: National Academy Press.

Clarke, Matthew and Simon Feeny (eds.). 2007. *Education for the End of Poverty: Implementing All the Millennium Development Goals*. New York: Nova Science Publishers.

Climate Reality Project. 2017. Climate Crisis 101: Learn the Basics of Climate Change Science and How You Can Take Action. Accessed August 27, 2017, from https://www.climaterealityproject.org/sites/climaterealityproject .org/files/Climate%20101_FINAL.pdf.

CNBC. July 3, 2017. This Is the Age Most Americans Pay Off Their Student Loans. Accessed July 3, 2017, from https://www.cnbc.com/2017/07/03/this -is-the-age-most-americans-pay-off-their-student-loans.html.

CNN. January 23, 2012. Return of the "Welfare Queen." Accessed June 7, 2017, from http://www.cnn.com/2012/01/23/politics/weflare-queen/index.html.

Coalition for the Homeless. March 2017. State of the Homeless 2017: Rejecting Low Expectations: Housing Is the Answer. Accessed August 24, 2017, from https://coalitionforthehomeless.org/wp-content/uploads/2017/03/State -of-the-Homeless-2017.pdf.

Cohen, Wilbur J. and Robert M. Ball. 1965. Social Security Amendments of 1965: Summary and Legislative History. *Social Security Bulletin* 28, no. 9:3–21.

Coll, Blanche D. 1969. *Perspectives in Public Welfare: A History*. Washington, DC: Government Printing Office.

Congress.gov. 2017. H.R. 676-Expanded and Improved Medicare for All Act. Accessed August 10, 2017, from https://www.congress.gov/bill/115th -congress/house-bill/676/cosponsors?q=%7B%22search%22%3A%5B%2 2congressId%3A115+AND+billStatus%3A%5C%22Introduced%5C%22 %22%5D%7D&r=26.

Congress.gov. 2017. S. 1242-Raise the Wage Act, May 25, 2017. Accessed August 25, 2017, from https://www.congress.gov/bill/115th-congress/senate-bill/1242.

Congress.gov. 2017. S. 1832-Pay Workers a Living Wage Act, July 22, 2015. Accessed August 25, 2017, from https://www.congress.gov/bill/114th-con gress/senate-bill/1832.

Connecticut Association for Community Action. 2017. History. Accessed March 21, 2017, from http://www.cafca.org/history.

Corak, Miles. 2013. Income Inequality, Equality of Opportunity, and Intergenerational Mobility. *Journal of Economic Perspectives* 27, no. 3:79–102.

Corbett, Thomas. June 2, 2013. The Rise and Fall of Poverty as a Policy Issue. Accessed March 5, 2017, from http://www.irp.wisc.edu/publications /focus/pdfs/foc302b.pdf.

Council on Foreign Relations. 2017. The U.S. Immigration Debate. Accessed January 13, 2017, from http://www.cfr.org/immigration/us-immigration -debate/p11149.

CQ Almanac. 1964. Permanent Food Stamp Program Set Up. Accessed March 18, 2017, from https://library.cqpress.com/cqalmanac/document.php?id=cqal64 -1303932.

CQPress. April 16, 1993. High-Speed Rail: Does the High Cost Outweigh the Anticipated Benefits? Accessed August 25, 2017, from http://library.cqpress .com/cqresearcher/document.php?id=cqresrre1993041600.

Dadush, Uri, Kemal Derviş, Sarah Puritz Milsom, and Bennett Stancil. 2012. *Inequality in America: Facts, Trends, and International Perspectives*. Washington, DC: Brookings Institution Press.

Dahl, Robert A. 2003. *How Democratic Is the American Constitution?* 2nd ed. New Haven, CT: Yale University Press.

DeWitt, Larry. 2010. The Development of Social Security in America. *Social Security Bulletin* 70, no. 3:1–26.

Drury, Shadia B. 1997. *Leo Strauss and the American Right*. New York: St. Martin's Press.

Du Bois, W. E. B. 1969. *The Negro American Family*. Westport, CT: Negro Universities Press.

Dunn v. Blumstein, 405 U.S. 330 (1972).

Easton, David. 1953. *The Political System: An Inquiry into the State of Political Science*. New York: Alfred A. Knopf.

Economic Policy Institute. January 14, 2014. Over 600 Economists Sign Letter in Support of $10.10 Minimum Wage. Accessed August 24, 2017, from http://www.epi.org/minimum-wage-statement/.

Economic Policy Institute. August 30, 2016. Union Decline Lowers Wages of Nonunion Workers: The Overlooked Reason Why Wages Are Stuck and Inequality Is Growing. Accessed September 1, 2017, from http://www .epi.org/publication/union-decline-lowers-wages-of-nonunion-workers -the-overlooked-reason-why-wages-are-stuck-and-inequality-is-growing/.

Edelman, Peter. 2012. *So Rich, So Poor: Why It's So Hard to End Poverty in America*. New York: The New Press.

Edwards, John, Marion Crain, and Arne L. Kalleberg (eds.). 2007. *Ending Poverty in America: How to Restore the American Dream*. New York: The New Press.

Ehrenreich, Barbara. 2002. *Nickel and Dimed: On (Not) Getting By in America*. New York: Henry Holt and Company.

Elazar, Daniel J. 1999. Tocqueville and the Cultural Basis of American Democracy. *PS: Political Science and Politics* 32, no. 2:207–10.

Etzioni, Amitai. 1993. *The Spirit of Community: Rights, Responsibilities, and the Communitarian Agenda.* New York: Crown Publishers.

Etzioni, Amitai. 1996. The Responsive Community: A Communitarian Perspective. *American Sociological Review* 61:1–11.

Etzioni, Amitai (ed.). 1998. *The Essential Communitarian Reader.* Lanham, MD: Rowman & Littlefield.

Etzioni, Amitai. 2015. Communitarianism. Accessed July 6, 2017, from https://icps.gwu.edu/sites/icps.gwu.edu/files/downloads/Communitarianism.Etzioni.pdf.

FactCheck.org. December 23, 2016. Presidents Winning Without Popular Vote. Accessed August 28, 2017, from http://factcheck.org/2008/03/presidents-winning-without-popular-vote.

Farber, David. 2010. *The Rise and Fall of Modern Conservatism: A Short History.* Princeton, NJ: Princeton University Press.

FederalReserveHistory.org. 2017. Stock Market Crash of 1929. Accessed February 25, 2017, from http://www.federalreservehistory.org/Events/DetailView/74.

Fife, Brian L. 1992. *Desegregation in American Schools: Comparative Intervention Strategies.* Westport, CT: Praeger.

Fife, Brian L. 1996. The Supreme Court and School Desegregation Since 1896. *Equity and Excellence in Education* 29:46–55.

Fife, Brian L. 2010. *Reforming the Electoral Process in America: Toward More Democracy in the 21st Century.* Santa Barbara, CA: Praeger.

Fife, Brian L. 2013. *Old School Still Matters: Lessons from History to Reform Public Education in America.* Santa Barbara, CA: Praeger.

Fife, Brian L. 2014. Congress and Electoral Reform in the Early Twenty-First Century. In Robert Mann (ed.), *Working Congress: A Guide for Senators, Representatives, and Citizens.* Baton Rouge: Louisiana State University Press, 62–78.

Fiorina, Morris. 1980. The Decline of Collective Responsibility in American Politics. *Engineering and Science* 44, no. 2:12–6, 30–2.

Fisher, Gordon M. 2008. Remembering Mollie Orshansky—The Developer of the Poverty Thresholds. *Social Security Bulletin* 68, no. 3:79–83.

Fitzgerald, F. Scott. 2004. *The Great Gatsby.* New York: Scribner.

Ford, James and Katherine Morrow Ford. 1937. *The Abolition of Poverty.* New York: Macmillan.

Fox, Liana, Christopher Wimer, Irwin Garfinkel, Neeraj Kaushal, and Jane Waldfogel. 2015. Waging War on Poverty: Poverty Trends Using a Historical Supplemental Poverty Measure. *Journal of Policy Analysis and Management* 34, no. 3:567–92.

Frances Perkins Center. 2017. Her Life: The Woman Behind the New Deal. Accessed March 14, 2017, from http://francesperkinscenter.org/life-new/.

Franklin D. Roosevelt Presidential Library and Museum. 2017. Action, and Action Now: FDR's First 100 Days. Accessed March 4, 2017, from https://

fdrlibrary.org/documents/356632/390886/actionguide.pdf/07370301
-a5c1-4a08-aa63-e611f9d12c34.

Freedom House. 2016. Freedom in the World 2015. Accessed March 1, 2016,
from https://freedomhouse.org/sites/default/files/01152015_FIW_2015
_final.pdf.

French, Michael T., Jenny Homer, Gulcin Gumus, and Lucas Hickling. 2016. Key
Provisions of the Patient Protection and Affordable Care Act (ACA): A
Systematic Review and Presentation of Early Research Findings. *Health
Services Research* 51, no. 5:1735–71.

Friedman, Milton. 1962. *Capitalism and Freedom.* Chicago: University of Chicago
Press.

Friedman, Milton and Rose Friedman. 1980. *Free to Choose: A Personal Statement.*
New York: Harcourt Brace Jovanovich.

Fuchs, Victor R. 1967. Redefining Poverty and Redistributing Income. *The Public
Interest* 8:88–95.

Funiciello, Theresa. 1993. *Tyranny of Kindness: Dismantling the Welfare System to
End Poverty in America.* New York: Atlantic Monthly Press.

Gallup Poll. June 13, 2016. Americans' Confidence in Institutions Stays Low.
Accessed June 13, 2017, from http://www.gallup.com/poll/192581/ameri
cans-confidence-institutions-stays-low.aspx.

Gallup Poll. January 5, 2017. Americans Still See Big Government as Top Threat.
Accessed February 12, 2017, from http://www.gallup.com/poll/201629
/americans-big-government-top-threat.aspx.

Gallup Poll. April 10, 2017. U.S. Uninsured Rate Edges Up Slightly. Accessed
August 10, 2017, from http://www.gallup.com/poll/208196/uninsured-rate
-edges-slightly.aspx.

Gallup Poll. July 10, 2017. U.S. Uninsured Rate Rises to 11.7%. Accessed August
10, 2017, from http://www.gallup.com/poll/213665/uninsured-rate-rises
.aspx.

Gallup Poll. August 13, 2017. Most Americans in 15 Years Say Their Tax Bill Is
Too High. Accessed August 13, 2017, from http://www.gallup.com/poll
/190778/americans-years-say-tax-bill-high.aspx.

Gallup Poll. 2017. Congress and the Public. Accessed August 30, 2017, from
http://www.gallup.com/poll/1600/congress-public.aspx.

Gallup Poll. 2017. Economy. Accessed May 24, 2017, from http://gallup.com/poll
/1609/consumer-views-economy.aspx.

Gawthrop, Louis C. 1998. *Public Service and Democracy: Ethical Imperatives for the
21st Century.* New York: Chatham House Publishers.

George Washington University. Amitai Etzioni. Accessed July 10, 2017, from
https://sociology.columbian.gwu.edu/amitai-etzioni.

George Washington University, Eleanor Roosevelt Papers Project. 2017. The Progressive Era (1890–1920). Accessed January 30, 2017, from https://www2
.gwu.edu/~erpapers/teachinger/glossary/progressive-era.cfm.

Gilbert, Geoffrey. 2008. *Rich and Poor in America: A Reference Handbook.* Santa
Barbara, CA: ABC-CLIO.

Gillin, John Lewis. 1921. *Poverty and Dependency: Their Relief and Prevention.* New York: The Century Company.

Gini, Corrado. 1912. Variabilitá e mutabilitá: Contributo allo studio delle distribuzioni e delle relazioni statistiche. *Studi Economico-giurdici della Regia Facoltà Giurisprudenza* 3, no. 2:3–159.

Gini, Corrado. 1921. Measurement of Inequality of Incomes. *The Economic Journal* 31, no. 121:124–26.

Global Policy Institute. 2017. Professor Stephen Haseler. Accessed May 24, 2017, from http://www.gpilondon.com/people/professor-stephen-haseler/.

Goldwater, Barry. 1960. *The Conscience of a Conservative.* New York: Hillman Books.

Gordon, Linda and Felice Batlan. 2017. The Legal History of the Aid to Dependent Children Program. Accessed March 16, 2017, from http://socialwelfare.library.vcu.edu/public-welfare/aid-to-dependent-children-the-legal-history/.

GovTrack.Us. 2017. H.R. 1 (108th): Medicare Prescription Drug, Improvement, and Modernization Act of 2003. Accessed March 30, 2017, from https://www.govtrack.us/congress/bills/108/hr1.

GovTrack.Us. 2017. H.R. 2015 (105th): Balanced Budget Act of 1997. Accessed March 27, 2017, from https://www.govtrack.us/congress/bills/105/hr2015.

GovTrack.Us. 2017. H.R. 3590 (111th): Patient Protection and Affordable Care Act. Accessed March 30, 2017, from https://www.govtrack.us/congress/bills/111/hr3590.

GovTrack.Us. 2017. H.R. 3734 (104th): Personal Responsibility and Work Opportunity Reconciliation Act of 1996. Accessed March 18, 2017, from https://govtrack.us/congress/bills/104/hr3734.

GovTrack.Us. 2017. H.R. 6124 (110th): Food, Conservation, and Energy Act of 2008. Accessed March 20, 2017, from https://www.govtrack.us/congress/bills/110/hr6124.

GovTrack.Us. 2017. H.R. 10222 Passage. Accessed March 18, 2017, from https://govtrack.us/congress/votes/88-1964/h149.

GovTrack.Us. 2017. S. 2642 Passage. Accessed March 21, 2017, from https://www.govtrack.us/congress/votes/88-1964/s452.

GovTrack.Us. 2017. S. 2642 Passage. Accessed March 21, 2017, from https://www.govtrack.us/congress/votes/88-1964/h201.

GovTrack.Us. 2017. To Pass H.R. 2362, the Elementary and Secondary Education Act of 1965. Accessed March 27, 2017, from https://www.govtrack.us/congress/votes/89-1965/h26.

GovTrack.Us. 2017. To Pass H.R. 2362, the Elementary and Secondary Education Act of 1965. Accessed March 27, 2017, from https://www.govtrack.us/congress/votes/89-1965/s48.

Grant, Jane A. 2008. *The New American Social Compact: Rights and Responsibilities in the 21st Century.* Lanham, MD: Lexington Books.

Gross, David C. 1987. *A Justice for All the People: Louis D. Brandeis.* New York: E. P. Dutton.

Handler, Joel F. 1995. *The Poverty of Welfare Reform*. New Haven, CT: Yale University Press.

Handlin, Oscar. 1948. *Race and Ethnicity in American Life*. Boston: Little, Brown and Company.

Handlin, Oscar. 1951. *The Uprooted: The Epic Story of the Great Migrations that Made the American People*. Boston: Little, Brown and Company.

Handlin, Oscar. 1954. *The American People in the Twentieth Century*. Cambridge, MA: Harvard University Press.

Handlin, Oscar. 1959. *Immigration as a Factor in American History*. Englewood Cliffs, NJ: Prentice-Hall.

Handlin, Oscar. 1969. *Boston's Immigrants: A Study in Acculturation*. New York: Atheneum.

Hansan, John E. 2017. Public Welfare: Aid for Dependent Children (ADC: 1935-61). Accessed March 16, 2017, from http://socialwelfare.library.vcu.edu/public-welfare/public-welfare-aid-for-dependent-children.

Harding, Warren. 1920. Back to Normal: Address Before Home Market Club. In Frederick E. Schortemeier (ed.), *Redirecting America: Life and Recent Speeches of Warren G. Harding*. Indianapolis: Bobbs-Merrill, 223–29.

Harrington, Michael. 1981. *The Other America: Poverty in the United States*. New York: Penguin Books.

Harrington, Michael. 1985. *The New American Poverty: A Provocative, Incisive Exposé of the Social and Political Roots of Poverty*. New York: Penguin Books.

Harvard University, Joint Center for Housing Studies. June 16, 2017. The State of the Nation's Housing 2017. Accessed August 24, 2017, from http://www.jchs.harvard.edu/research/publications/state-nations-housing-2017.

Harvard University, Joint Center for Housing Studies. 2017. America's Rental Housing: Expanding Options for Diverse and Growing Demand. Accessed August 24, 2017, from http://jchs.harvard.edu/sites/jchs.harvard.edu/files/americas_rental_housing_2015_web.pdf.

Haseler, Stephen. 2000. *The Super-Rich: The Unjust New World of Global Capitalism*. New York: St. Martin's Press.

Hatch, Megan E. and Elizabeth Rigby. 2015. Laboratories of (In)equality? Redistributive Policy and Income Inequality in the American States. *Policy Studies Journal* 43, no. 2:163–87.

Haveman, Robert, Rebecca Blank, Robert Moffitt, Timothy Smeeding, and Geoffrey Wallace. 2015. The War on Poverty: 50 Years Later. *Journal of Policy Analysis and Management* 34, no. 3:593–638.

Hayek, Friedrich. 1944. *The Road to Serfdom*. Chicago: University of Chicago Press.

Hayek, Friedrich. 1960. *The Constitution of Liberty*. Chicago: University of Chicago Press.

History Channel. 2017. January 8, 1815: Jackson Leads Troops to Victory at New Orleans. Accessed January 8, 2017, from http://www.history.com/this-day-in-history/jackson-leads-troops-to-victory-at-new-orleans.

History.com. 2017. Alexis de Tocqueville. Accessed June 11, 2017, from http://www.history.com/topics/alexis-de-tocqueville.

History.com. 2017. Civilian Conservation Corps. Accessed August 21, 2017, from http://www.history.com/topics/civilian-conservation-corps.

History.com. 2017. Franklin D. Roosevelt. Accessed February 25, 2017, from http://www.history.com/topics/us-presidents/franklin-d-roosevelt.

History.com. 2017. Hoovervilles. Accessed February 25, 2017, from http://www.history.com/topics/hoovervilles.

History.com. 2017. July 30, 1956: President Eisenhower Signs "In God We Trust" into Law. Accessed August 22, 2017, from http://www.history.com/this-day-in-history/president-eisenhower-signs-in-god-we-trust-into-law.

History.com. 2017. June 20, 1782: Congress Adopts the Great Seal of the United States. Accessed August 22, 2017, from http://www.history.com/this-day-in-history/congress-adopts-the-great-seal-of-the-united-states.

History.com. 2017. Stock Market Crash of 1929. Accessed February 24, 2017, from http://www.history.com/topics/1929-stock-market-crash.

History.com. 2017. The Roaring Twenties. Accessed February 24, 2017, from http://www.history.com/topics/roaring-twenties.

History.com. 2017. This Day in History: Roosevelt Announces "Court-Packing" Plan, February 5, 1937. Accessed September 1, 2017, from http://www.history.com/this-day-in-history/roosevelt-announces-court-packing-plan.

History.com. 2017. Warren G. Harding. Accessed February 24, 2017, from http://www.history.com/topics/us-presidents/warren-g-harding.

History.com. 2017. Why Does Inauguration Day Fall on January 20? Accessed February 28, 2017, from http://www.history.com/news/ask-history/why-does-inauguration-day-fall-on-january-20.

Holmes, Oliver Wendell. 1897. The Path of the Law. *Harvard Law Review* 10, no. 8:457–78.

Horton, Emily. March 31, 2017. The Legacy of the 2001 and 2003 "Bush" Tax Cuts. Accessed May 28, 2017, from http://www.cbpp.org/research/federal-tax/the-legacy-of-the-2001-and-2003-bush-tax-cuts.

Hsiang, Solomon, Robert Kopp, Amir Jina, James Rising, Michael Delgado, Shashank Mohan, and D. J. Rasmussen. 2017. Estimating Economic Damage from Climate Change in the United States. *Science* 356, no. 6345:1362–69.

Hudson, William E. 2008. *The Libertarian Illusion: Ideology, Public Policy, and the Assault on the Common Good.* Washington, DC: CQ Press.

Hudson, William E. 2017. *American Democracy in Peril: Eight Challenges to America's Future,* 8th ed. Thousand Oaks, CA: CQ Press.

Internal Revenue Service. 2017. Questions and Answers for the Additional Medicare Tax. Accessed March 30, 2017, from https://www.irs.gov/businesses/small-businesses-self-employed/questions-and-answers-for-the-additional-medicare-tax.

Internal Revenue Service. 2017. Worksheet Solutions: Comparing Regressive, Progressive, and Proportional Taxes. Accessed August 13, 2017, from https://apps.irs.gov/app/understandingTaxes/whys/thm03/les05/media/ws_ans_thm03_les05.pdf.

Isaak, Robert A. 2005. *The Globalization Gap: How the Rich Get Richer and the Poor Get Left Further Behind*. Upper Saddle River, NJ: Prentice Hall Financial Times.

James, David R. and Karl E. Taeuber. 1985. Measures of Segregation. *Sociological Methodology* 15:1–32.

Jansson, Bruce C. 1988. *The Reluctant Welfare State: A History of American Social Welfare Policies*. Belmont, CA: Wadsworth Publishing.

Kaiser Family Foundation. July 17, 2012. Summary of Coverage Provisions in the Patient Protection and Affordable Care Act. Accessed March 30, 2017, from http://kff.org/health-costs/issue-brief/summary-of-coverage-provisions-in-the-patient.

Kaiser Family Foundation. July 17, 2015. Medicare and Medicaid at 50. Accessed August 10, 2017, from http://www.kff.org/medicaid/poll-finding/medicare-and-medicaid-at-50/.

Kaiser Family Foundation. September 26, 2016. The Medicare Part D Prescription Drug Benefit. Accessed March 30, 2017, from http://kff.org/medicare/fact-sheet/the-medicare-prescription-drug-benefit-fact-sheet.

Kenworthy, Lane and Timothy Smeeding. January 2013. *Growing Inequalities and Their Impacts in the United States: Country Report for the United States*. Stockholm: GINI.

Kerwin, Cornelius M. and Scott R. Furlong. 2011. *Rulemaking: How Government Agencies Write Law and Make Policy,* 4th ed. Washington, DC: CQ Press.

Kolko, Gabriel. 1962. *Wealth and Power in America: An Analysis of Social Class and Income Distribution*. New York: Praeger.

Kozol, Jonathan. 1991. *Savage Inequalities: Children in America's Schools*. New York: Crown Publishers.

Krugman, Paul. 2006. "Economic Inequality Has Accelerated." In Robert Sims (ed.), *Is the Gap Between Rich and Poor Growing?* Detroit, MI: Greenhaven Press, 12–6.

Krugman, Paul. February 15, 2007. Who Was Milton Friedman? *New York Review of Books*. Accessed July 9, 2017, from http://www.nybooks.com/articles/archives/2007/feb/15/who-was-Milton-Friedman.

Lawrence, Charles. 1905. *History of the Philadelphia Almshouses and Hospitals from the Beginning of the Eighteenth Century to the Ending of the Nineteenth Centuries, Covering a Period of Nearly Two Hundred Years, Showing the Mode of Distributing Public Relief through the Management of the Boards of Overseers of the Poor, Guardians of the Poor and the Directors of the Department of Charities and Correction*. Philadelphia, PA: Published by the Author.

Leiby, James. 1978. *A History of Social Welfare and Social Work in the United States, 1815–1972*. New York: Columbia University Press.

Leip, Dave. 2017. 1934 Gubernatorial General Election Results—California. Accessed August 1, 2017, from http://uselectionatlas.org/RESULTS/state.php?fips=6&year=1934&f=0&off=5&elect=0.

Lerman, Robert I. and Shlomo Yitzhaki. 1984. A Note on the Calculation and Interpretation of the Gini Index. *Economics Letters* 15, no. 3-4:363–68.

Liao, Tim F. 2006. Measuring and Analyzing Class Inequality with the Gini Index Informed by Model-Based Clustering. *Sociological Methodology* 36:201–24.

Libertarian Party. 2017. 2016 Platform. Accessed July 3, 2017, from https://www.lp.org/platform.

Library of Congress. 2017. Jefferson's Letter to the Danbury Baptists, January 1, 1802. Accessed August 17, 2017, from https://www.loc.gov/loc/lcib/9806/danpre.html.

Library of Economics and Liberty. 2017. Milton Friedman (1912–2006). Accessed July 9, 2017, from http://www.econlib.org/library/Enc/bios/Friedman.html.

Lief, Alfred. 1930. *The Social and Economic Views of Mr. Justice Brandeis.* New York: Vanguard Press.

LivingNewDeal.org. 2017. Resettlement Administration (1935). Accessed September 2, 2017, from https://livingnewdeal.org/glossary/resettlement-administration-ra-1935/.

LivingNewDeal.org. 2017. The New Deal. Accessed February 25, 2017, from https://livingnewdeal.org/what-was-the-new-deal/.

Los Angeles Times. May 12, 2017. Gov. Brown Asks President Trump for Help on the California Bullet Train. Accessed August 25, 2017, from http://www.latimes.com/local/california/la-me-bullet-train-brown-20170512-story.html.

Lyndon Baines Johnson Presidential Library. 2017. Johnson's Remarks on Signing the Elementary and Secondary Education Act, Johnson City, Texas, April 11, 1965. Accessed March 27, 2017, from http://www.lbjlibrary.org/lyndon-baines-johnson/timeline/johnsons-remarks-on-signing-the-elementary-and-secondary-education-act.

Martin, Patricia P. and David A. Weaver. 2005. Social Security: A Program and Policy History. *Social Security Bulletin* 66, no. 1:1–15.

Massachusetts Institute of Technology. 2017. James Ford (1885–1944). Accessed August 6, 2017, from http://web.mit.edu/ebj/www/ww1/Biography-Ford.html.

Matthews, Dylan. January 8, 2014. Everything You Wanted to Know about the War on Poverty. *The Washington Post.* Accessed March 20, 2017, from https://www.washingtonpost.com/news/wonk/wp/2014/01/08/everything-you-need-to-know-about-the-war-on-poverty/?utm_term=.477a95b56a76.

McGerr, Michael. 2003. *A Fierce Discontent: The Rise and Fall of the Progressive Movement in America.* New York: Oxford University Press.

Medicare.gov. 2017. What's Medicare? Accessed March 30, 2017, from https://www.medicare.gov/sign-up-change-plans/decide-how-to-get-medicare/whats-medicare/what-is-medicare.html.

Milanovic, Branko and Shlomo Yitzhaki. 2002. Decomposing World Income Distribution: Does the World Have a Middle Class? *Review of Income and Wealth* 48, no. 2:155–75.

Mises Institute. 2017. Profiles: Friedrich Hayek. Accessed July 8, 2017, from https://mises.org/profile/friedrich-hayek.

Nasaw, David. 2006. *Andrew Carnegie*. New York: Penguin.

National Alliance to End Homelessness. 2016. *State of the Homeless 2016*. Accessed August 24, 2017, from http://endhomelessness.org/wp-content/uploads /2016/10/2016-soh.pdf.

National Coalition for the Homeless. July 2009. How Many People Experience Homelessness? Accessed August 24, 2017, from http://www.nationalhome less.org/factsheets/How_Many.html.

National Conference of State Legislatures. March 2011. The Affordable Care Act: A Brief Summary, March 2011. Accessed March 31, 2017, from http:// www.ncsl.org/portals/1/documents/health/hraca.pdf.

National Conference of State Legislatures. July 21, 2016. State Primary Election Types. Accessed August 31, 2017, from http://www.ncsl.org/research /elections-and-campaigns/primary-types.aspx.

National Conference of State Legislatures. July 27, 2017. Same Day Voter Regis- tration. Accessed August 28, 2017, from http://www.ncsl.org/research /elections-and-campaigns/same-day-registration.aspx.

National Conference of State Legislatures. 2017. Overview of State Laws on Public Financing. Accessed August 30, 2017, from http://www.ncsl.org/research /elections-and-campaigns/public-financing-of-campaigns-overview .aspx.

National Conference of State Legislatures. 2017. Right-to-Work States. Accessed August 30, 2017, from http://www.ncsl.org/research/labor-and-employ ment/right-to-work-laws-and-bills.aspx.

National Poverty Center. March 2005. The GINI Coefficient and Segregation on a Continuous Variable. Accessed April 8, 2017, from http://www.npc.umich .edu/publications/workingpaper05/paper02/Kim_Jargowsky_Gini_Seg regation.pdf.

National Public Radio. December 20, 2013. The Truth Behind the Lies of the Original "Welfare Queen." Accessed June 7, 2017, from http://www.npr .org/sections/codeswitch/2013/12/20/255819681/the-truth-behind-the -lies-of-the-original-welfare-queen.

National Public Radio. June 1, 2017. Trump Announces U.S. Withdrawal from Paris Climate Accord. Accessed August 27, 2017, from http://www.npr .org/sections/thetwo-way/2017/06/01/530748899/watch-live-trump -announces-decision-on-paris-climate-agreement.

NBC News. May 24, 2017. Ben Carson Says "Poverty Is a State of Mind." Accessed May 25, 2017, from http://www.nbcnews.com/news/nbcblk/ben-carson -says-poverty-state-mind-n764376.

New York Times. May 15, 1863. The Doctrine of State Rights; Exploded Ideas Revived the True Power of the Rebellion False Political Doctrines Their Danger, and the Necessity of Their Destruction. Accessed July 14, 2017, from   http://www.nytimes.com/1863/05/15/news/doctrine-state-rights -exploded-ideas-revived-true-power-rebellion-false.html?pagewanted=all.

New York Times. February 15, 1976. "Welfare Queen" Becomes Issue in Reagan Campaign. Accessed June 7, 2017, from http://www.nytimes.com/1976/02

/15/archives/welfare-queen-becomes-issue-in-reagan-campaign-hitting -a-nerve-now.html?mcubz=3.

New York Times. March 4, 1981. Reagan and States' Rights; News Analysis. Accessed September 2, 2017, from http://nytimes.com/1981/03/04/us /reagan-and-states-rights-news-analysis.html?pagewanted=all&mcubz=1.

New York Times. September 12, 1996. Two Clinton Aides Resign to Protest New Welfare Law. Accessed May 26, 2017, from http://www.nytimes.com/1996 /09/12/us/two-clinton-aides-resign-to-protest-new-welfare-law.html.

New York Times. June 2, 2015. Americans' Views on Money in Politics. Accessed August 30, 2017, from https://www.nytimes.com/interactive/2015/06/02 /us/politics/money-in-politics-poll.html?mcubz=1.

New York Times. January 29, 2016. What Data Can Do to Fight Poverty. Accessed September 2, 2017, from https://nytimes.com/2016/01/31/opinion/sunday /what-data-can-do-to-fight-poverty.html.

New York Times. November 7, 2016. Five Ways Republicans Are Threatening Voting Rights. Accessed August 29, 2017, from https://www.nytimes.com/2016 /11/07/opinion/five-ways-republicans-are-threatening-voting-rights.html.

New York Times. December 18, 2016. Trump's Electoral College Victory Ranks 46th in 58 Elections. Accessed February 28, 2017, from https://www.nytimes.com/interactive/2016/12/18/us/elections/donald-trump -electoral-college-popular-vote.html?_r=0.

New York University School of Law, Brennan Center for Justice. January 31, 2017. Debunking the Voter Fraud Myth. Accessed August 28, 2017, from https://brennancenter.org/analysis/debunking-voter-fraud-myth.

Oliver, Thomas R., Philip R. Lee, and Helene L. Lipton. 2004. A Political History of Medicare and Prescription Drug Coverage. *The Milbank Quarterly* 82, no. 2:283–354.

OpenSecrets.org. 2017. Top Individual Contributors: All Federal Contributions (2016 Election Cycle). Accessed August 30, 2017, from https://www.opense crets.org/overview/topindivs.php.

Orshansky, Mollie. 1963. Children of the Poor. *Social Security Bulletin* 26, no. 7:3–13.

Orshansky, Mollie. 1965a. Counting the Poor: Another Look at the Poverty Profile. *Social Security Bulletin* 28, no. 1:3–29.

Orshansky, Mollie. 1965b. Who's Who Among the Poor: A Demographic View of Poverty. *Social Security Bulletin* 28, no. 7:3–32.

Orshansky, Mollie. 1969. Perspectives on Poverty: How Poverty Is Measured. *Monthly Labor Review* 92, no. 2:37–41.

Orshansky, Mollie. 1976. *The Measure of Poverty (Technical Paper 1: Documentation of Background Information and Rationale for Current Poverty Matrix.* Washington, DC: U.S. Department of Health, Education, and Welfare.

Orshansky, Mollie. 1988. Commentary: The Poverty Measure. *Social Security Bulletin* 51, no. 10:22–4.

Orshansky, Mollie, Harold Watts, Bradley R. Schiller, and John J. Korbel. 1978. Measuring Poverty: A Debate. *Public Welfare* 36, no. 2:46–55.

Page, Stephen B. and Mary B. Larner. 1997. Introduction to the AFDC Program. *The Future of Children: Welfare to Work* 7, no. 1:20–7.

Palmer, Guy. 2014. Relative Poverty, Absolute Poverty and Social Exclusion. Accessed October 3, 2014, from http://www.poverty.org.uk/summary /social%20exclusion.shtml.

Paper, Lewis J. 1983. *Brandeis: An Intimate Biography of One of America's Truly Great Supreme Court Justices.* Englewood Cliffs, NJ: Prentice-Hall.

Patterson, James T. 2000. *America's Struggle Against Poverty in the Twentieth Century.* Cambridge, MA: Harvard University Press.

Payne, George Henry. 1912. *The Birth of the New Party or Progressive Democracy.* Naperville, IL: J. L. Nichols & Company.

Pew Research Center. March 12, 2015. How Do Americans Stand Out from the Rest of the World? Accessed September 12, 2017, from http://www .pewresearch.org/fact-tank/2015/03/12/how-do-americans-stand-out-from -the-rest-of-the-world/.

Pew Research Center. April 6, 2016. The Biggest U.S. Tax Breaks. Accessed August 17, 2017, from http://www.pewresearch.org/fact-tank/2016/04/06 /the-biggest-u-s-tax-breaks/.

Pew Research Center. April 19, 2016. 5 Ways Americans and Europeans Are Different. Accessed September 12, 2017, from http://www.pewresearch.org /fact-tank/2016/04/19/5-ways-americans-and-europeans-are-different/.

Pew Research Center. May 2, 2017. Why People Are Rich and Poor: Republicans and Democrats Have Very Different Views. Accessed September 12, 2017, from http://www.pewresearch.org/fact-tank/2017/05/02/why-people-are -rich-and-poor-republicans-and-democrats-have-very-different-views/.

Physicians for a National Health Program. 2017. Beyond the Affordable Care Act: A Physicians' Proposal for Single-Payer Health Care Reform. Accessed August 11, 2017, from http://www.pnhp.org/beyond_aca/Physicians_Proposal.pdf.

Physicians for a National Health Program. 2017. What Is Single Payer? Accessed August 10, 2017, from http://www.pnhp.org/facts/what-is-single-payer.

Piketty, Thomas and Emmanuel Saez. 2003. Income Inequality in the United States, 1913–1998. *The Quarterly Journal of Economics* 117, no. 1:1–39.

Piven, Frances Fox and Richard A. Cloward. 1997. *The Breaking of the American Social Compact.* New York: The New York Press.

Polak, Paul. 2008. *Out of Poverty: What Works When Traditional Approaches Fail.* San Francisco, CA: Berrett-Koehler Publishers.

Proctor, Bernadette D., Jessica L. Semega, and Melissa Kollar. September 2016. Income and Poverty in the United States: 2015. Washington, DC: U.S. Census Bureau. Accessed May 2, 2017, from https://www.census.gov/con tent/dam/Census/library/publications/2016/demo/p60-256.pdf.

Public Law 59-242. June 30, 1906. Federal Meat Inspection Act. Accessed February 12, 2017, from https://www.loc.gov/law/help/statutes-at-large/59th -congress/session-1/c59s1ch3913.pdf.

Public Law 59-384. June 30, 1906. Pure Food and Drug Act. Accessed February 12, 2017, from https://www.loc.gov/law/help/statutes-at-large/59th-con gress/session-1/c59s1ch3915.pdf.

Public Law 63-212. September 26, 1914. Federal Trade Commission Act. Accessed February 12, 2017, from https://www.loc.gov/law/help/statutes-at-large/63rd -congress/session-2/c63s2ch311.pdf.

Public Law 63-212. October 15, 1914. Clayton Act. Accessed February 12, 2017, from https://www.loc.gov/law/help/statutes-at-large/63rd-congress/session -2/c63s2ch323.pdf.

Public Law 74-271. August 14, 1935. The Social Security Act of 1935. Accessed March 5, 2017, from http://www.legisworks.org/congress/74/publaw-271.pdf.

Public Law 81-171. July 15, 1949. Housing Act of 1949. Accessed August 23, 2017, from http://legisworks.org/congress/81/publaw-171.pdf.

Public Law 88-452. August 20, 1964. Economic Opportunity Act of 1964. Accessed March 21, 2017, from https://www.gpo.gov/fdsys/pkg/STATUTE -78/pdf/STATUTE-78-Pg508.pdf.

Public Law 88-525. August 31, 1964. The Food Stamp Act of 1964. Accessed March 18, 2017, from https://fns-prod.azureedge.net/sites/default/files/PL _88-525.pdf.

Public Law 89-10. April 11, 1965. Elementary and Secondary Education Act of 1965. Accessed March 27, 2017, from http://files.eric.ed.gov/fulltext /ED017539.pdf.

Public Law 89-97. July 30, 1965. Social Security Amendments of 1965. Accessed March 27, 2017, from https://www.gpo.gov/fdsys/pkg/STATUTE-79/pdf /STATUTE-79-Pg286.pdf.

Public Law 104-193. August 22, 1996. Personal Responsibility and Work Opportunity Reconciliation Act. Accessed March 10, 2016, from https://www .gpo.gov/fdsys/pkg/PLAW-104publ193/pdf/PLAW-104publ193.pdf.

Public Law 105-33. January 7, 1997. Balanced Budget Act of 1997. Accessed March 27, 2017, from https://www.gpo.gov/fdsys/pkg/PLAW-105publ33 /pdf/PLAW-105publ33.pdf.

Public Law 108-173. December 8, 2003. Medicare Prescription Drug, Improvement, and Modernization Act of 2003. Accessed March 30, 2017, from https://www.gpo.gov/fdsys/pkg/PLAW-108publ173/pdf/PLAW-108pub l173.pdf.

Public Law 110-246. June 18, 2008. Food, Conservation, and Energy Act of 2008. Accessed March 19, 2017, from https://www.gpo.gov/fdsys/pkg /PLAW-110publ246/pdf/PLAW-110publ246.pdf.

Public Law 111-148. March 23, 2010. Patient Protection and Affordable Care Act of 2010. Accessed March 30, 2017, from https://www.ssa.gov/OP_Home /comp2/F111-148.html.

Putnam, Robert D. 1995. Bowling Alone: America's Declining Social Capital. *Journal of Democracy* 6, no. 1:65–78.

Putnam, Robert D. 2000. *Bowling Alone: The Collapse and Revival of American Community.* New York: Simon & Schuster.

Quigley, William P. 2003. *Ending Poverty as We Know It: Guaranteeing a Right to a Job at a Living Wage.* Philadelphia, PA: Temple University Press.

Rainwater, Lee. 1974. *What Money Buys: Inequality and the Social Meanings of Income.* New York: Basic Books.

Record, George L. 1936. *How to Abolish Poverty.* Jersey City, NJ: The George L. Record Memorial Association.

Reich, Robert. 1992. *The Work of Nations: Preparing Ourselves for 21st-Century Capitalism.* New York: Vintage Books.

Reich, Robert. 2007. *Supercapitalism: The Transformation of Business, Democracy, and Everyday Life.* New York: Alfred A. Knopf.

Rising, George G. 1997. An EPIC Endeavor: Upton Sinclair's 1934 California Gubernatorial Campaign. *Southern California Quarterly* 79, no. 1:101–24.

Roosevelt, Theodore. 1914. *Theodore Roosevelt: An Autobiography.* New York: Macmillan.

Rosen, Jeffrey. 2016. *Louis D. Brandeis: American Prophet.* New Haven, CT: Yale University Press.

Ruggles, Patricia. 1990. *Drawing the Line: Alternative Poverty Measures and Their Implications for Public Policy.* Washington, DC: Urban Institute Press.

Sachs, Jeffrey D. 2006. *The End of Poverty: Economic Possibilities for Our Time.* New York: Penguin Books.

Salvation Army. 2017. History of the Salvation Army. Accessed January 14, 2017, from http://www.salvationarmyusa.org/usn/history-of-the-salvation-army.

Schattschneider, E. E. 1942. *Party Government.* New York: Rinehart & Company.

Schudson, Michael. 1998. *The Good Citizen: A History of American Civic Life.* New York: The Free Press.

Schwarz, John E. 2013. Recalibrating the Poverty Line. *Los Angeles Times*, October 24, 2013. Accessed March 7, 2016, from http://articles.latimes.com/2013/oct/24/opinion/la-oe-schwarz-poverty-line-income-gap-20131024.

Semuels, Alana. April 1, 2016. The End of Welfare as We Know It: America's Once-Robust Safety Net Is No More. Accessed March 18, 2017, from https://www.theatlantic.com/business/archive/2016/04/the-end-of-welfare-as-we-know-it/476322.

Shipler, David K. 2004. *The Working Poor: Invisible in America.* New York: Alfred A. Knopf.

Shipler, David K. 2007. Connecting the Dots. In John Edwards, Marion Crain, and Arne L. Kalleberg (eds.), *Ending Poverty in America.* New York: The New Press, 13–22.

Sinclair, Upton. 1935. *We, People of America, and How We Ended Poverty: A True Story of the Future.* Pasadena, CA: National EPIC League.

Sinclair, Upton. 1965. *The Jungle.* New York: The Heritage Press.

Slate.com. December 19, 2013. The Welfare Queen. Accessed June 7, 2017, from http://www.slate.com/articles/news_and_politics/history/2013/12/linda_taylor_welfare_queen_ronald_reagan_made_her_a_notorious_american_villain.html.

Smith, Adam. 1910. *The Wealth of Nations*, 2 vols. New York: E. P. Dutton.

Smith, David G. and Judith D. Moore. 2008. *Medicaid Politics and Policy: 1965–2007.* New Brunswick, NJ: Transaction Publishers.

SNAP to Health Organization. 2017. The History of SNAP. Accessed March 18, 2017, from https://www.snaptohealth.org/snap/the-history-of-snap.

Social Security Administration. 2017. Brief History: The Committee on Economic Security. Accessed March 14, 2017, from https://www.ssa.gov/history/ces.html.

Social Security Administration. 2017. Edwin E. Witte: The Beginnings of Social Security. Accessed March 14, 2017, from https://www.ssa.gov/history/cohenwitte.html.

Social Security Administration. 2017. Fact Sheet: 2017 Social Security Changes. Accessed March 15, 2017, from https://www.ssa.gov/news/press/factsheets/colafacts2017.pdf.

Social Security Administration. 2017. Medicaid Information. Accessed March 30, 2017, from https://ssa.gov/disabilityresearch/wi/medicaid.htm.

Social Security Administration. 2017. OASDI and SSI Program Rates & Limits, 2017. Accessed August 16, 2017, from https://www.ssa.gov/policy/docs/quickfacts/prog_highlights/RatesLimits2017.html.

Social Security Administration. 2017. Social Security and Medicare Tax Rates. Accessed March 30, 2017, from https://ssa.gov/oact/progdata/taxRates.html.

Social Security Administration. 2017. Social Security: Historical Background and Development of Social Security. Accessed March 14, 2017, from https://www.ssa.gov/history/briefhistory3.html.

Social Security Administration. 2017. Social Security History: President Lyndon B. Johnson. Accessed March 30, 2017, from https://www.ssa.gov/history/lbjstmts.html.

Social Security Administration. 2017. The Roots of Social Security, by Frances Perkins, Delivered at Social Security Administration Headquarters—Baltimore, Maryland, October 23, 1962. Accessed March 14, 2017, from https://www.ssa.gov/history/perkins5.html.

Social Security Administration. 2017. The Social Security Act of 1935. Accessed March 5, 2017, from https://www.ssa.gov/history/35act.html.

Social Security Administration. 2017. 1935 Congressional Debates on Social Security. Accessed March 15, 2017, from https://www.ssa.gov/history/tally.html.

Sommeiller, Estelle, Mark Price, and Ellis Wazeter. June 16, 2016. *Income Inequality in the U.S. by State, Metropolitan Area, and County.* Washington, DC: Economic Policy Institute. Accessed May 15, 2017, from http://www.epi.org/files/pdf/107100.pdf.

Stockholm International Peace Research Institute. 2016. Trends in World Military Expenditure, 2014. Accessed February 25, 2016, from http://books.sipri.org/files/FS/SIPRIFS1504.pdf.

Stone, Chad, Danilo Trisi, Arloc Sherman, and Emily Horton. October 11, 2017. *A Guide to Statistics on Historical Trends in Income Inequality.* Washington, DC: Center on Budget and Policy Priorities. Accessed January 7, 2018, from https://www.cbpp.org/research/poverty-and-inequality/a-guide-to-statistics-on-historical-trends-in-income-inequality.

Strauss, Leo. 1950. Natural Right and the Historical Approach. *The Review of Politics* 12, no. 4:422–42.

Strauss, Leo. 1953. *Natural Right and History.* Chicago: University of Chicago Press.

Strauss, Leo. 1963. *On Tyranny.* New York: Free Press of Glencoe.

Stricker, Frank. 2007. *Why America Lost the War on Poverty—And How to Win It.* Chapel Hill: The University of North Carolina Press.

Stockholm International Peace Research Institute. 2016. Trends in World Military Expenditure, 2014. Accessed February 25, 2016, from http://books.sipri.org/files/FS/SIPRIFS1504.pdf.

Strum, Philippa. 1993. *Brandeis: Beyond Progressivism.* Lawrence: University Press of Kansas.

Strum, Philippa (ed.). 1995. *Brandeis on Democracy.* Lawrence: University Press of Kansas.

Stucker, David, Andrea B. Feigl, Sanjay Basu, and Martin McKee. 2017. The Political Economy of Universal Health Coverage. Accessed August 8, 2017, from http://www.pacifichealthsummit.org/downloads/UHC/the%20political%20economy%20of%20uhc.PDF.

Tax Foundation. 2017. 2017 Tax Brackets. Accessed August 16, 2017, from https://taxfoundation.org/2017-tax-brackets/.

The Transport Politic. July 1, 2017. A Generational Failure: As the U.S. Fantasizes, the Rest of the World Builds a New Transport System. Accessed August 25, 2017, from http://www.thetransportpolitic.com.

Tocqueville, Alexis de. 2000. *Democracy in America.* Chicago: University of Chicago Press.

Twain, Mark and Charles Dudley Warner. 1968. *The Gilded Age: A Tale of Today.* Seattle: University of Washington Press.

Union of Concerned Scientists. November 18, 2014. Each Country's Share of CO_2 Emissions. Accessed August 27, 2017, from http://www.ucsusa.org/global_warming/science_and_impacts/science/each-countrys-share-of-co2.html.

Union of Concerned Scientists. 2017. Confronting the Realities of Climate Change: The Consequences of Global Warming Are Already Here. Accessed August 27, 2017, from http://www.ucsusa.org/global_warming/.

United Nations. December 12, 2015. Chapter XXVII: 7.d. Paris Agreement. Accessed August 27, 2017, from https://treaties.un.org/doc/Publication/MTDSG/Volume%20II/Chapter%20XXVII/XXVII-7-d.en.pdf.

United Nations Children's Fund. May 2012. Measuring Child Poverty: New League Tables of Child Poverty in the World's Rich Countries. Accessed April 8, 2017, from https://www.unicef-irc.org/publications/660/.

United Nations Educational, Scientific and Cultural Organization. 2014. Poverty. Accessed October 3, 2014, from http://www.unesco.org/new/en/social-and-human-sciences/themes/international-migration/glossary/poverty.

United Nations Framework Convention on Climate Change. 2015. Paris Agreement. Accessed August 29, 2017, from https://www.unfccc.int/files/essential_background/convention/application/pdf/english_paris_agreement.pdf.

University of California, Berkeley, Goldman School of Public Policy. 2017. Robert Reich. Accessed May 24, 2017, from https://gspp.berkeley.edu/directories/faculty/robert-reich.

University of Chicago. 2017. The Leo Strauss Center. Accessed July 8, 2017, from https://leostrausscenter.uchicago.edu/.

University of Pennsylvania. 2017. Can Trump—or Anyone—Bring Back American Manufacturing? Accessed August 21, 2017, from http://knowledge.wharton.upenn.edu/article/can-trump-anyone-bring-back-american-manufacturing/.

University of Virginia, Miller Center of Public Affairs. 2017. Woodrow Wilson: Campaigns and Elections. Accessed January 29, 2017, from http://miller center.org/president/biography/wilson-campaigns-and-elections.

Urofsky, Melvin I. 2009. *Louis D. Brandeis: A Life.* New York: Pantheon Books.

U.S. Bureau of Labor Statistics. September 2016. Union Membership in the United States. Accessed August 30, 2017, from https://www.bls.gov/spot light/2016/union-membership-in-the-united-states/pdf/union-membership -in-the-united-states.pdf.

U.S. Bureau of Labor Statistics, Office of Occupational Statistics and Employment Projections. 2017. Employment Projections: Unemployment Rates and Earnings by Educational Attainment. Accessed May 22, 2017, from https://www.bls.gov/emp/ep_chart_001.htm.

U.S. Census Bureau. 2017. Historical Poverty Tables—People. Accessed April 8, 2017, from https://www.census.gov/data/tables/time-series/demo/income -poverty/historical-poverty-people.html.

U.S. Census Bureau. 2017. Median Annual Household Income (1967–2015). Accessed April 8, 2017, from https://www.census.gov/data/tables/time -series/demo/income-poverty/historical-income-households.html.

U.S. Census Bureau. 2017. Poverty Thresholds. Accessed April 8, 2017, from https://www.census.gov/data/tables/time-series/demo/income-poverty /historical-poverty-thresholds.html.

U.S. Census Bureau. 2017. Statistical Abstract of the United States: 2012. Section 7: Elections. Accessed June 22, 2017, from https://www.census.gov/prod /2011pubs/12statab/election.pdf.

U.S. Census Bureau. 2017. U.S. Cities Are Home to 62.7 Percent of the U.S. Population, but Comprise Just 3.5 Percent of Land Area: March 4, 2015. Accessed June 19, 2017, from https://www.census.gov/newsroom/press-releases/2015 /cb15-33.html.

U.S. Department of Agriculture. 2017. Supplemental Nutrition Assistance Program Participation and Costs. Accessed March 18, 2017, from https:// www.fns.usda.gov/sites/default/files/pd/SNAPsummary.pdf.

U.S. Department of Agriculture. 2017. Supplemental Nutrition Assistance Program (SNAP). Accessed March 18, 2017, from https://www.fns.usda.gov /snap/short-history-snap.

U.S. Department of Health and Human Services. 2017. Poverty Guidelines. Accessed April 8, 2017, from https://aspe.hhs.gov/poverty-guidelines.

U.S. Department of Health and Human Services. 2017. What Is the Difference between Medicare and Medicaid? Accessed March 30, 2017, from https:// www.hhs.gov/answers/medicare-and-medicaid/what-is-the-difference -between-medicare-medicaid/index.html.

U.S. Department of Health and Human Services, Office of the Assistant Secretary for Planning and Evaluation. 2015. Frequently Asked Questions Related to the Poverty Guidelines and Poverty. Accessed February 16, 2015, from http://aspe.hhs.gov/poverty/faq.cfm.

U.S. Department of Homeland Security, U.S. Citizenship and Immigration Services. 2017. Citizenship Rights and Responsibilities. Accessed August 23, 2017, from https://www.uscis.gov/citizenship/learners/citizenship-rights-and-responsibilities.

U.S. Department of Labor, Office of Policy Planning and Research. March 1965. *The Negro Family: The Case for National Action*. Washington, DC: Government Printing Office.

U.S. Department of Labor, Wage and Hour Division. 2017. Fact Sheet: Final Rule to Implement Executive Order 13658, Establishing a Minimum Wage for Contractors, February 12, 2014. Accessed August 24, 2017, from https://www.dol.gov/whd/flsa/eo13658/fr-factsheet.htm.

U.S. Department of Labor, Wage and Hour Division. 2017. Fair Labor Standards Act of 1938: Maximum Struggle for a Minimum Wage. Accessed August 24, 2017, from https://www.dol.gov/general/aboutdol/history/flsa1938.

U.S. Department of Labor, Wage and Hour Division. 2017. History of Federal Minimum Wage Rates Under the Fair Labor Standards Act, 1938–2009. Accessed on August 24, 2017, from https://www.dol.gov/whd/minwage/chart.htm.

U.S. Elections Project. 2017. Voter Turnout. Accessed June 22, 2017, from http://www.electproject.org/home/voter-turnout/voter-turnout-data.

U.S. Treasury Direct. 2017. The Debt to the Penny and Who Holds It. Accessed August 17, 2017, from https://www.treasurydirect.gov/NP/debt/current/.

Virginia Commonwealth University, Social Welfare History Project. 2017. Poor Relief and the Almshouse. Accessed January 16, 2017, from http://socialwelfare.library.vcu.edu/issues/poor-relief-almshouse/.

Wagner, David. 2005. *The Poorhouse: America's Forgotten Institution*. Lanham, MD: Rowman & Littlefield.

Walker, David B. 2000. *The Rebirth of Federalism: Slouching Toward Washington*, 2nd ed. Chappaqua, NY: Chatham House Publishers.

Warren, Kenneth F. 2011. *Administrative Law in the Political System*, 5th ed. Boulder, CO: Westview Press.

Washington Post. March 21, 2014. The House Has Voted 54 Times in Four Years on Obamacare. Here's the Full List. Accessed March 31, 2017, from https://washingtonpost.com/news/the-fix/wp/2014/03/21/the-house-has-voted-54-times-in-four-years-on-obamacare-heres-the-full-list/?utm_term=.f15371c83a0b.

Washington Post. October 12, 2016. Is It Too Late to Register to Vote in Your State? Check Here. Accessed August 28, 2017, from https://www.washingtonpost.com/news/the-fix/wp/2016/10/06/when-is-it-too-late-to-register-to-vote-in-your-state/?utm_term=.6235195321e0/.

Watts, Steven. 2005. *The People's Tycoon: Henry Ford and the American Century.* New York: Alfred A. Knopf.

White, Craig C. 1995. *Toward the Resolution of Poverty in America,* 2nd ed. Dubuque, IA: Kendall/Hunt Publishing Company.

Whitehouse.gov. January 8, 2015. The President Proposes to Make Community College Free for Responsible Students for 2 Years. Accessed August 18, 2017, from https://obamawhitehouse.archives.gov/blog/2015/01/08 /president-proposes-make-community-college-free-responsible-students -2-years.

Whitehouse.gov. January 9, 2015. Fact Sheet: White House Unveils America's College Promise Proposal: Tuition-Free Community College for Responsible Students. Accessed August 18, 2017, from https://obamawhitehouse .archives.gov/the-press-office/2015/01/09/fact-sheet-white-house-unveils -america-s-college-promise-proposal-tuitio.

Williamson, John B., Jerry F. Boren, Frank J. Mifflen, Nancy A. Cooney, Linda Evans, Michael F. Foley, Richard Steinman, Jody Garber, Nancy Theberge, and Donna J. B. Turek. 1975. *Strategies Against Poverty in America.* New York: John Wiley & Sons.

Wilson, James Q. 1978. The Rise of the Bureaucratic State. In Francis E. Rourke (ed.), *Bureaucratic Power in National Politics,* 3rd ed. Boston: Little, Brown and Company, 54–78.

World Bank. 2016. World Development Indicators: Distribution of Income or Consumption. Accessed March 1, 2016, from http://wdi.worldbank.org /table/2.9?tableNo=2.9.

World Bank. 2017. World Development Indicators Database. Accessed April 8, 2017, from http://databank.worldbank.org/data/download/GDP.pdf.

World Health Organization. 2017. Health Financing for Universal Coverage: What Is Universal Coverage? Accessed August 7, 2017, from http://www .who.int/health_financing/universal_coverage_definition/en/.

Young Men's Christian Association. 2017. The Story of Our Founding. Accessed January 14, 2017, from http://www.ymca.net/history/founding.html.

Index

About the Author

Brian L. Fife is professor and chair of the Department of Public Policy at Indiana University–Purdue University Fort Wayne, which will transition to Purdue University Fort Wayne in 2018. His published works include *Old School Still Matters: Lessons from History to Reform Public Education in America*, *Reforming the Electoral Process in America: Toward More Democracy in the 21st Century*, *Political Culture and Voting Systems in the United States: An Examination of the 2000 Presidential Election*, *Higher Education in Transition: The Challenges of the New Millennium*, *School Desegregation in the Twenty-First Century: The Focus Must Change*, and *Desegregation in American Schools: Comparative Intervention Strategies*.